NO MORE

THE BATTLE AGAINST HUMAN RIGHTS VIOLATIONS

NO MORE

THE BATTLE AGAINST
HUMAN RIGHTS
VIOLATIONS

DAVID MATAS

DUNDURN PRESS
TORONTO • OXFORD

Edited by Dennis Mills
Printed and bound in Canada by Webcom

The publisher wishes to acknowledge the generous assistance and ongoing support of the **Canada Council**, the **Book Publishing Industry Development Program** of the **Department of Canadian Heritage**, the **Ontario Arts Council**, the **Ontario Publishing Centre** of the **Ministry of Culture, Tourism and Recreation**, and the **Ontario Heritage Foundation**.

   Care has been taken to trace the ownership of copyright material used in the text. The author and publisher welcome any information enabling them to rectify any reference or credit in subsequent editions.

J. Kirk Howard, Publisher

Canadian Cataloguing in Publication Data

Matas, David
      No more : the battle against human rights violations

(Towards the new millennium)
Includes bibliographical references.
ISBN 1-55002-221-0

1. Crimes against humanity. 2. International offenses.
3. Human rights. I. Title. II. Series.

JX5418.M37 1994   341.4'81   C94-932663-1

Dundurn Press Limited	Dundurn Distribution	Dundurn Press Limited
2181 Queen Street East	73 Lime Walk	1823 Maryland Avenue
Suite 301	Headington, Oxford	P.O. Box 1000
Toronto, Canada	England	Niagara Falls, N.Y.
M4E 1E5	0X3 7AD	U.S.A. 14302-1000

Contents

FOREWORD

by Laurie Wiseberg

This book is a major and original contribution to international human rights literature. Much of its originality derives from the fact that David Matas draws extensively on his two and a half decades of experience as a human rights advocate and as a refugee lawyer.

Thus, for example, the chapters on Amnesty International offer a perspective – and information – that could only be provided by someone who has followed the movement closely, from the inside. Similarly, much of the material on the Helsinki process and Eastern Europe has clearly been shaped by David Matas's leadership in the Canadian Helsinki Committee.

Another dimension of the originality of the book is the Canadian perspective that David Matas brings to bear on the norms and processes of international human rights protection. To date, few Canadian writers have addressed this question. The Canadian dimension emerges not only in Part V, entitled "Canada," but throughout the volume, for example, under "State Remedies" – where David Matas looks at the question of Canada's policy on compensation to victims for human rights violations.

David Matas's approach is extremely refreshing. He draws on his personal experience, including his extensive experience as a practising attorney. He often argues as if he were before the bench – building his case step by step, using logic and empirical evidence.

The book is written well and clearly. It will be a welcome addition to the currently sparse literature on the role of nongovernmental organizations in the protection of human rights, and on the Canadian dimension of international human rights protection.

Laurie Wiseberg is executive director of Human Rights Internet, Ottawa.

INTRODUCTION

What leads to human rights violations? What can be done to stop them? What remedies are available for victims? *No More* attempts to answer these questions.

Human rights has become the secular religion of our time. Its vocabulary is universally accepted. Its standards are in constitutions, in treaties, and international declarations.

Yet human rights violations continue to occur around the world, in a gross and flagrant manner. One day it is the Iraqi gassing of the Kurds. The next day it is death squads assassinating church workers in El Salvador. Tamil youths are tortured in Sri Lanka. Demonstrators for democracy are crushed by tanks in Beijing's Tiananmen Square.

No More is both an attempt at explaining why human rights violations occur and a guide as to what nongovernmental organizations, governments, and the United Nations can do to counter violations.

One focus of the book is how regimes move from pervasive human rights violations to democracy and respect for human rights. Because the problems of transition are embedded in time and place, a number of chapters look at countries in the recent past, during a moment of human rights change.

Part I, "Root Causes," looks at ideological sources of human rights violations. Torture, disappearance, death-squad killings, and unfair trials are often manifestations of political ideas.

The book examines four ideologies as examples of root causes of human rights violations: the national security state, religion, communism, and apartheid.

The doctrine of national security is a theory that has developed in Latin America to combat communism. It contains such concepts as total war, dirty war, the primacy of security, and the leading role of the military. Each concept is examined to show how it involves a rejection of human rights values. The return to democracy in Latin America can be traced to a revulsion against the violations to which the national security doctrine has led.

The notion of communism as a root cause of human rights violations is approached both from a theoretical and a practical perspective. Theoretically, the beliefs in violent revolution, historical necessity, and the new socialist personality contain within themselves rejections of human rights values.

Practically, Part II on Eastern Europe looks at Yugoslavia, Poland, and the USSR, in particular, as they moved from communism to democracy.

The chapters on Yugoslavia, Poland, and the Soviet Union are general, surveying the human rights situation in these countries. They are snapshots of Eastern Europe: Yugoslavia in 1988, Poland in 1989, the Soviet Union in 1990. Together they demonstrate how the human rights picture has developed in Eastern Europe. The link is made between the more theoretical discussion and the evolving day-to-day reality.

Part II closes with a chapter on the Helsinki process, the process of intergovernmental meetings generated by the Final Act of the Conference on Security and Cooperation in Europe, signed in Helsinki in 1975. The process is described and its impact on respect for human rights in Eastern Europe is assessed.

Of all the contemporary ideological root causes of human rights violations, apartheid has been the most blatant, since it rejects human rights values the most explicitly. The first chapter in Part III, "Apartheid in South Africa," looks at that system as a concept, as a legal structure, and as a practical reality.

A second chapter looks at black-on-black violence in South Africa and past state complicity in the violence. The chapter attempts to explain why the state was involved on the side of Inkatha and why the state used Inkatha to do its dirty work.

A third chapter addresses the issue of crimes against humanity in South Africa. What should be done in a new democratic South Africa to those who have committed international crimes under apartheid? The chapter balances the cost of doing nothing against the cost of disrupting a peaceful transition to democracy.

What are the appropriate state remedies for violations of international crimes? Prosecution and reparations are obvious steps to take. Yet, where the state is the perpetrator, each of these remedies presents problems.

The first chapter in Part IV, "State Remedies," looks at sovereignty as a limit on the promotion of human rights. When state sovereignty and the rights of the individual are in conflict, which is to prevail? How can human rights be asserted internationally in the face of assertions of sovereignty?

After World War II, the Federal Republic of Germany established an elaborate scheme to compensate victims of the Nazi Holocaust. A chapter describes the scheme. The chapter also looks at other compensation schemes for violation of international standards, including the compensation of Japanese Americans and Canadians for mass deportation during and after World War II. The contribution of nongovernmental organizations to this effort of compensation is described.

How well does Canada conform to international human rights standards?

In Part V, one chapter assesses how well Canada has done to meet international standards. A second chapter argues for the insertion of economic, social, and cultural rights in the Canadian Charter of Rights and Freedoms. Economic, social, and cultural rights are as much human rights as civil and political rights. Canadian law treats the two sets of rights differently, but should not.

The first chapter in Part VI, "The United Nations," asks the question: should the UN be in the business of promoting human rights? The problems the United Nations has faced in coming to grips with human rights violations are presented.

Given the limitations of the United Nations, should nongovernmental organizations even attempt to promote human rights through that body? The plethora of United Nations' human rights mechanisms is described in greater detail in a second chapter, and suggestions are made for improvement.

Why has Amnesty International developed in the manner it has? The first chapter in Part VII, "Nongovernmental Organizations," looks at the growth of the Amnesty mandate as a strategy for combatting human rights violations.

When neither prosecution nor reparations are available as remedies, there is still much that can be done. The final chapter argues that nongovernmental organizations are inherently better equipped to provide a remedy for human rights violations than either governments or intergovernmental organizations.

Nongovernmental organizations provide the remedy for the violations of international human rights standards. The last chapter also argues that governments and the United Nations should continue to develop standards, even if the UN implementation system is weak.

A number of organizations have given me the opportunity to be involved in international human rights work, in a variety of capacities. I want, in particular, to thank B'nai B'rith, the International Helsinki Human Rights Federation, Amnesty International, the International Defence and Aid Fund for South Africa (Canada), Canada South Africa Cooperation, the South Africa Education Trust Fund, the Canadian Council for Refugees, and the International Commission of Jurists. The opinions in this book are, of course, my own, and do not necessarily represent the official positions of any of these organizations.

Above all, it is individuals around the world I have to thank, for their inspiration, their example, and also, for many of them, for their comments on earlier drafts of parts of this work.

The human rights movement around the world is filled with perceptive, gracious, giving, informed people. To all of those who have provided me with their comments on any part of this work, I offer my thanks.

PART I

ROOT CAUSES

CHAPTER ONE

IDEOLOGY AS A ROOT CAUSE OF HUMAN RIGHTS VIOLATIONS

Human rights violations reports are body counts, torture practices, an endless list of horrors. The violations seem beyond comprehension, madmen acting without reason. And the reports seem to be written by someone with the stomach of a physician and the mind of a statistician.

These violations are commonly done for a purpose, in pursuit of a cause. Madmen may perpetrate them, but the reason for the madness is often the frenzy of an idea. Violations are frequently the consequences of the idea. John Maynard Keynes wrote in 1936: "Madmen in authority, who hear voices in the air, are distilling their frenzy from some academic scribbler, of a few years back."[1] While Keynes was referring to economic ideas, what he said remains equally true of political ideas.

Torture, disappearances, extra-judicial executions, unfair trials, do not exist in an ideological vacuum. In many places, they are manifestations of an ideology.

Human rights standards now are universally accepted. Every country's government endorses the Universal Declaration of Human Rights. This acceptance in principle allows international human rights instruments to proliferate at the same time as human rights violations continue.

There is an obvious hypocrisy in accepting human rights in principle and violating human rights in practice. Yet, the hypocrisy is not always the result of a conflict between principle and practice. The hypocrisy can be a result of a conflict of principles. Ideologists may not advocate human rights violations, but some ideologies have human rights violations as their inevitable consequence. The madman may not have sought authority to kill and torture, but the idea that has seized him may lead inexorably to that end.

Implementing an ideology means applying an idea logically. There are ideologies for which a logical result is human rights violations.

The ideology of racism took a totalitarian form in Hitler's Germany. The ideology of communism took a totalitarian form in Stalin's Soviet Union.

Hannah Arendt argues that the ideologies of racism and communism are no more totalitarian than any other.[2] She asserts that we saw totalitarian governments in this century based on communism and racism only because these ideologies were more popular than others, politically more important. If ideology is an idea carried out logically, totalitarianism is an ideology applied unrelentingly, (i.e. to a logical extreme). For Arendt, any ideology carried out unrelentingly leads to totalitarianism.

I disagree with that proposition. The trouble with Hitler's racism was not just that it was too logically applied. Even applied in a mild form it violates human rights. While there is something to be said against the consistent application of any idea to the political realm, not all ideologies applied logically lead to disastrous results.

The faults of racism and communism are faults of the ideologies, not faults of logic. The faults are inherent in the ideas manifest. Totalitarianism is not just the logic of an idea made unrelenting; it is the logic of a faulty idea made unrelenting. The human rights violations that come from the applications of the ideology demonstrate that the ideology is faulty.

Even if it is true that there are root causes of human rights violations and these root causes are ideological, should we be looking at root causes of human rights violations at all? If we do, does it make sense to talk of any ideology as a root cause of human rights violations?

There is a sentiment sometimes expressed that looking at root causes of human rights violations is an unproductive, and even counterproductive effort. An examination of immediate causes (for instance the fact that incommunicado detention leads to torture) is obviously useful in promoting respect for human rights. An examination of root causes, on the other hand, it is said, is potentially troublesome.

A discussion of root causes, so this objection goes, pushes people back into history and politics. While there may be general agreement about ending human rights violations, there will be no general agreement about the root causes. Amnesty International, for instance, makes a point of staying away from root-cause discussions.

One might even say that discussions of root causes of human rights violations may themselves be a cause of human rights violations. If human rights violations come from exaggerated and uncontrolled political debate, then anything that exacerbates or envenoms political debate is problematic.

To put the matter in another way, what is the point of looking at root causes? International standards require freedom of expression, except for hate propaganda and war propaganda. Prohibition of the expression of an ideology that may be a root cause of human rights violations would be a violation of those standards. If we are not to prohibit the expression of these root-cause ideologies, and it is certainly not my intent to suggest that we do, where is a discussion of root causes leading us?

My own answer to these objections is that it leads us to understanding. I believe we have to be alert to the dangers that certain ideologies pose. Those of us who are concerned about human rights must warn against those dangers and defend against them as best we can.

There is, no doubt, disagreement, and legitimate disagreement about what the root causes are. But not every disagreement represents a threat to peace. On the contrary, it is only through discussion and disagreement that we will arrive at the truth. So long as the goal is worth reaching, and I believe the goal of determining the root causes of human rights violations is worth reaching, then it is also worthwhile to try to reach the goal.

At the end of the day, the battle for respect for human rights is not so much a legal battle as a battle for hearts and minds. Winning this battle means exposing the fault lines in ideologies that generate human rights violations.

Do human rights violations have any ideological foundations at all? One can find gross abuses of human rights which do not proceed from an ideological base.

The notion of ideology as a root cause of human rights violations assumes people move from thought to action. Yet some people act unthinkingly or out of base motives alone. Others move from action to thought. They violate human rights first, and then use an ideology to rationalize what they have done.

Certainly that was the experience of Nazi Germany, where anti-Semitism was widespread during the Third Reich. Yet, it diminished sharply once the Allies liberated Germany. Part of the reason was simply the discrediting of Nazism because Germany lost the war. But part also was the removal of the compulsion to be involved passively or actively in atrocities against Jews. When the need for the ideology disappeared as a rationalization for unjustifiable behaviour, so did the ideology itself.

Even for human rights violations there is learning through doing. Violations may be committed for the basest and most unideological of motives. Perpetrators commit violations and then seize on an ideology that appears to give their acts some higher purpose.

But whether an ideology generates human rights violations or rationalizes them after they are committed, the ideology is equally dangerous. An unjustified violation is much less likely to be replicated than a justified one. A self-justifying violator is going to be more difficult to stop, to bring to justice, than a violator who claims no justification at all. An ideology is as much a root cause for the continuation of violations as it is a root cause for the initiation of violations.

Some people say that the root cause of human rights violations is, despite appearances, never ideological. The suggestion is that the root cause is the uneven distribution of power, and the attempt to maintain power by denying human rights to others.

I disagree. I start from the premise that those who talk of murder, preach it, promote it, justify it, advocate it, end up committing murder. At the very least, when people talk of murder, it should be seen as a threat or warning. But more than that, there is a linkage between what people say and what they do.

It is of course true that some people murder without warning, saying nothing about their plans before, and not pretending to justify their deeds afterwards. There are others who are actively hypocritical, proclaiming against murder before, and claiming total innocence afterwards. These phenomena, however, do not diminish the reality of those who talk about murder first, and then do it afterwards.

In some ways, those who preach murder are a good deal more dangerous than those who do not. Those who preach murder win converts. Their philosophy and their murders spread. Those who kill silently or hypocritically are more self-contained in their behaviour. They do not end up leading movements of murder.

A second premise I have is that murder is unjustifiable. There is no such thing as a just murder in a good cause, or an unjust murder in a bad cause. No matter what the cause, murder, the killing of an innocent person in a premeditated fashion, is inexcusable.

These premises can also be stated in terms of armed aggression of one state against another. Those who talk of aggression or invasion, and preach it, promote it, justify it, advocate it, end up doing it. Military invasion, aggression by one state against another innocent victim state, is unjustifiable.

These propositions may seem obvious, even banal. Yet, once we put the same propositions in the context of human rights discourse, they become controversial.

The discourse of human rights violations has become politicized. Political opponents are criticized as human rights violators. Violations by allies are met with silence.

When people with a political agenda criticize a human rights violation, one has to look beyond the criticism itself. Is the human rights violation criticism only a facade that hides political disagreement?

The suggestion that social injustice is an underlying problem leading to human rights violations falls prey to the very problem of politicization of criticism of human rights violations.

The logic of that suggestion appears to be that human rights violations are committed by people in pursuit of an unjust cause, the establishment and maintenance of their own privileged position. The suggestion is that the root cause is uneven distribution of power.

Uneven distribution of power is unjust, and even distribution of power is just. These statements are tautologies. However, human rights violations can be committed in a just cause, as well as in an unjust one. Marxism was an attempt, although an abysmally unsuccessful one, to redistribute power more evenly.

To suggest that maldistribution of power leads to human rights violations manifests a political penchant. It falls into the trap of using human rights violations to discredit a disfavoured political option.

Probably the greatest political debate of our time is how political and economic power should be distributed. Right-wing capitalism preaches laissez-faire enterprise, which can lead to extreme inequalities. Left-wing socialism preaches active government intervention to promote total equality. This book takes no sides in this debate, advocating neither capitalism nor socialism, neither free enterprise nor government intervention.

People in advantageous positions may try to maintain their positions by means of human rights violations. It is also true that people who are committed to removing inequalities may try to achieve the removal of inequalities through human rights violations. But to state that inequalities are the root cause of the violations is incorrect. Explaining the content of a disagreement does not explain the means used to resolve it. Major disagreements may be resolved in peaceful ways; minor disagreements may be resolved in violent ways. The primary explanation for resort to violence is often the willingness to resort to violence, and not the subject matter of the dispute. And willingness to resort to violence is explained, in a political context, by an ideology.

One logical fallacy is the fallacy encapsulated by the Latin phrase *post hoc, ergo propter hoc:* after that, therefore because of that. Because a person preaches human rights violations, and then commits them, does not mean that the ideology is the cause of the violation. The cause may lie elsewhere. The ideology may be a rationalization.

Human rights violations, as with most human behaviour, have a confluence of causes. It is unlikely any violation would occur, if the perpetrator did not see the violations to be in his/her own self-interest, however misguided that perception of self-interest might be. That is one reason why, in the analysis of communism, this book focuses in on the egocentricity of its believers. Ideologies do not lead everyone to violations. Nor is everyone, in pursuit of their self-interest, prone to violations. Ideologies reinforce pursuit of perceived self-interest. In that sense, the powerful use ideologies to justify and maintain their positions.

People end up believing ideologies that reinforce their self-interest. They do not just use the ideologies; ideologies become grafted on to the souls of those who use them. Perpetrators develop a world view in which they believe what they are doing is right. That is what makes these ideologies so damaging, and so frightening. That is why it is worthwhile focusing in on them as separate, root causes of human rights violations, independently of the pursuit of the self-interest which they serve.

How does the United Nations deal with ideological causes of human rights violations? The ideological foundations of human rights violations are dealt with at the Commission on Human Rights of the United Nations in the way that all human rights issues are dealt with, politically. Politically unpopular ideologies are roundly denounced. Politically popular ideologies escape uncriticized.

No other ideology has incurred the criticism that apartheid has. The universal condemnation of apartheid has only partially been tied to its abhorrent nature. It was also, in some measure, because South Africa, when it was the sole proponent and practitioner of apartheid, was politically isolated, without friends.

Religious intolerance and fascism are both on the agenda of the Commission on Human Rights. One agenda item is Implementation of the Declaration on the Elimination of All Forms of Intolerance and of Discrimination based on Religion or Belief. Another agenda item is Measures to be taken against all totalitarian or other ideologies and practices, including Nazi, fascist and neo-fascist, which are based on racial or ethnic exclusiveness or intolerance, hatred, terror, systematic denial of human rights and fundamental freedoms, or which have such consequences.

In 1981 the United Nations General Assembly proclaimed the Declaration on the Elimination of All Forms of Intolerance and of Discrimination Based on Religion or Belief.[3] The Subcommission on Prevention of Discrimination and Protection of Minorities appointed a special rapporteur, Mrs. Elizabeth Odio Benito, to prepare a study on the current dimensions of the problems of intolerance and of discrimination on the grounds of religion or belief. The special rapporteur made a report in 1987, on the basis of a questionnaire sent out to governments and organizations.[4] The Commission on Human Rights in 1986 decided to appoint its own special rapporteur to examine incidents of religious intolerance and to recommend remedial measures.[5] This rapporteur prepares annual reports.

The United Nations efforts to combat religious intolerance manifest another hallmark of the United Nations when dealing with human rights issues, superficiality. Though human rights intolerance is condemned, it is all in generalities. No attempt is made to identify the violators or the causes of the violations. In answer to the queries by the subcommission's and commission's special rapporteurs, state after state replied that religious intolerance does not exist in their country. The rapporteurs make no attempt to go beyond those bald assertions.

It may seem paradoxical to suggest that religion is a root cause of human right violations. Religion, after all, is a force for good, the source of the world's moral codes and human rights standards themselves. Yet religion and power, like drinking and driving, are a potent and dangerous combination.

Power corrupts all who hold it, including the religious – especially the religious. Indeed, Lord Acton, who made the statement "Power tends to corrupt and absolute power corrupts absolutely" made it in a religious context. Acton wrote these words to Mandel Creighton, who was discussing Acton's review of Creighton's work "History of the Papacy during the Reformation."[6] Acton viewed Creighton's treatment of the Inquisition as altogether too kind to the papacy.

The certainties of religion fit uneasily with the certainties of power. Politics is the art of compromise: religion is dogma. Political power that does not come from repression rests on popularity; religious rectitude comes from conformity to religious texts. Politics is temporal and ever changing; religion is spiritual and constant. Politics tends to cynicism because of its deference to others; religion rests on belief. Politics is realistic; religion is idealistic.

When religion is separate from power, religion can be and has been a moral force. Religion in power means corrupting religion or using power for religious oppression. Usually it means both. Instead of the good of religion transforming power, the corrupting influence of power transforms religion. Indeed, of all the sources of human rights violations, religion is the most enduring. Before this century, the main causes of human rights violations were religious, and the main victims were religious. Today, we still see victims of human rights violations caused by religion.

There is a spectrum of associations between religion and power. In some states, like the United Kingdom, the association is tenuous: the head of the Church of England is also the head of state. Yet the Queen, in reality, has power over neither; she governs neither the Church nor the state.

In other states, like Iran, the association has been close. The former spiritual leader of Iran, the Ayatollah Khomeini, was also the secular leader, in fact as well as in law. It is no coincidence that fundamentalist religious Iran was

engaged both in a bloody uncompromising war with Iraq and gross and flagrant violations of human rights directed at, amongst others, the Bahai. The
Bahai are a religious group with which the Shiite Muslims of Iran are in dog-
matic disagreement.

These violations continue to exist; however, the full force of the fury of
religion has passed. To return to Keynes, although the madmen in authority
are distilling their frenzy from some academic scribbler of a few years back,
the sane in authority distil their sanity from some academic scribbler of a few
years back. Though people in power today may not read writers like Jean
Jacques Rousseau or Immanuel Kant, these philosophers have had a profound
effect on contemporary secularism.

In 1781 Rousseau, in his *Social Contract*, wrote what he saw as the true
principle of political rights[7] – that tolerance should be given to all religions
that tolerate others. He asserted that it is impossible to distinguish between
civil and theological tolerance. It is impossible to live in peace with those we
regard as damned.

In 1781 Kant, in his *Critique of Pure Reason*, wrote that it is impossible
either to prove or disprove the existence of God. The proposition that God
exists is one that can neither hope for confirmation nor need fear a refutation
from experience. Reason can achieve nothing: it stretches its wings in vain, if
it tries to show that God exists, or does not exist.[8]

Religious intolerance today is anachronistic and atavistic. The intellectual
underpinnings of religious intolerance have disappeared.

That does not mean that the danger from religious intolerance has gone.
The intellectual development of humanity does not have an inevitable
progress. We can regress as well as progress. Each generation, each culture,
must discover for itself the fundamental truths that have been unearthed earlier. Because of the experience through which humanity has lived, because of
the efforts of thinkers who have gone before, the rediscovery should, in principle, be an easy task. If the task is ignored, and on different occasions in different places it is ignored, we bring calamity upon ourselves.

Condemnation of fascism is a regular routine at the United Nations. The
Commission on Human Rights, as well as its parent bodies, the Economic
and Social Council and the General Assembly, unfailingly pass resolutions
denouncing fascism. The General Assembly has called upon all states to provide the secretary-general with their comments on the question. It has asked
the secretary-general to provide a report on the basis of the comments provided by states and international organizations.

Comments by states on this issue, as on the religious intolerance issue,
and indeed on every issue, have been all self-serving. Each replying state lists

its efforts to combat Nazism and fascism.[9] The secretary-general's report makes no attempt to question these efforts. Questioning has occurred, at the Commission on Human Rights, but in a highly political way. The 1986 discussion on this agenda item degenerated into name calling and led to a motion for closure of debate.[10]

The resolution against fascism at the 1986 Commission on Human Rights was adopted without a vote.[11] No state wished to record an opposing vote, or even an abstention. The unanimity over the resolution and the name calling in the debate stem from the same basic cause – the rejection of fascism and Nazism as labels. Indeed, a representative from the U.K. viewed the whole exercise as anachronistic since no one today defends Nazism or fascism as such. It was said that the United Nations was concentrating on defunct, historical examples of totalitarianism.[12]

Communism, on the other hand, has been nowhere on the United Nations agenda. It was never part of the resolutions on totalitarian ideologies. Nor, given the nature of the United Nations, could one reasonably expect it to be there. Communism remains contemporary ideology. A number of the United Nations members claim to be communist or Marxist-Leninist. It would be impossible, at the United Nations, to get the unanimity or near unanimity necessary to mobilize the institution to look at the elements of intolerance within communist regimes.

Anti-Semitism is present at the United Nations, but rather than being condemned, in the way religious intolerance or fascism are, anti-Semitism is actually practised. Statements are made, from time to time, in the context of the Middle East debate, alleging the same world Jewish conspiracy that the Nazis alleged. Until 1994 the United Nations resolutions that condemned racism and religious intolerance left anti-Semitism unmentioned. The reason, again, is politics. Because Israel is a Jewish state, the only Jewish state, and because Israel has been politically unpopular at the United Nations, for decades the United Nations could do nothing to organize itself to deal with anti-Semitism.

It was not always so. The UN General Assembly in 1947 voted for the partition of Palestine that led to the creation of the state of Israel. However, as the UN membership expanded in the post-colonial era, the political composition of the UN changed, and an anti-Israeli majority developed.

At its best, the United Nations can offer leadership to the world. At its worst, it exacerbates disputes by bringing states into disputes in which they otherwise would not be involved, and by providing a platform for intemperate vilification. However, on an day-to-day basis, the United Nations is neither at its best nor at its worst, but simply a reflection of the world as it is. If the United Nations is a political place, the reason is that our world is political. The United Nations is a place where we can see our problems more than a place where we can solve them.

Nongovernmental organizations, human rights organizations, however, do not suffer, need not suffer, from the handicaps that prevent governments from dealing effectively with human rights violations.

Human rights organizations can offer balance and political impartiality. They can do the research, the fact finding, the investigations, to go beyond the self-serving exculpatory statements emanating from violators. These organizations can make judgements and come to conclusions about whether violations have taken place or not. They can publicize their findings. The United Nations, with few exceptions, has been able to do none of these things.

Though governments purport to speak for the people within their territories, the true spokesmen for human rights violations are the nongovernmental organizations. When governments are silent about tortures and executions, the voluntary organizations speak out.

Human rights organizations have done a good deal to combat human rights violations. They have done very little to combat the ideological foundations of these violations.

Let us look at what happened at the 1986 Commission on Human Rights. As I just wrote, the commission had agenda items on fascism and religious intolerance. The commission also had agenda items on torture and on disappearances. For each of these items, the commission heard statements from nongovernmental organizations. What was striking was that the organizations that made statements on religious intolerance and on fascism were mostly religious and ethnic.[13] The human rights organizations restricted themselves to statements on torture and disappearances.[14] The one exception was the International Commission of Jurists, which made a statement on fascism, but not on religious intolerance.

For human rights organizations, it was as if these two sets of agenda items were two separate sets of issues. It is as if torture and disappearances exist in one world and religious intolerance and fascism in another. Yet the two are inextricably linked. It is blindness to ignore the linkage.

Human rights organizations have not failed because they have ignored the ideological foundations of human rights violations. What they have set out to do, they have done well. They have just done their task incompletely.

These organizations must go beyond the chamber of horrors and into the arena of ideas. Instead of dealing only with violations, the organizations must also deal with their causes. In addressing those causes, the organizations must rely on the same techniques they have used to such effect in dealing with violations. There must be research.

And there must be impartiality and political balance. It is not enough to look at one or a few ideologies. The full range of problematic ideologies must be examined.

The organizations must look not only to what perpetrators do but to what perpetrators say. Human rights organizations must deal with ideology by observing, recording, analysing, and publicizing. The problems inherent in the ideologies of intolerance must be made evident.

Should we tolerate those who do not tolerate others? The answer is both yes and no. Yes, we should tolerate them, by not prohibiting the advocacy of their ideas, except for hate propaganda. No, we should not tolerate them, in the sense that we should just ignore them and let them be.

The Genocide Convention commits signatories to punish incitement to commit genocide.[15] The International Covenant on Civil and Political Rights commits its state parties to prohibit war propaganda, as well as advocacy of national, racial, or religious hatred that constitutes incitement to discrimination, hostility or violence.[16] The Convention on the Elimination of all Forms of Racial Discrimination commits its state parties to punish the dissemination of ideas based on racial superiority or hatred, incitement to racial discrimination, and incitement to racial violence.[17]

These instruments do not specify the punishments that must be imposed. That is left to each signatory state to decide. The international obligation is to take the necessary steps to implement the commitment to punish.

These international instruments can and should be used to combat ideological causes of human rights violations. I do not suggest new instruments with new prohibitions against advocacy of intolerance. Hate propaganda is a form of incitement to violence that requires a criminal prohibition. Beyond that, prohibiting advocacy of intolerance is a form of intolerance itself.

The answer to the question should we tolerate the behaviour of those who do not tolerate the behaviour of others is no. But we should not ignore the intolerant. Ideologies that generate intolerance represent a danger. Human rights organizations have a duty to warn of that danger.

People's actions are related to what they think. Thought accompanies action. A complete human rights strategy means dealing with the thought as well as the action. If the goal of universal respect for human rights is to be achieved, both have to be addressed.

Not every human rights violation has an ideological cause. But many do. For those that do, it is folly to ignore the cause. The remedy is exposure. Speaking against human rights violations means speaking out against the causes, as well as the manifestations.

Combatting the ideological causes of human rights violations is only a part of the solution. Human rights violations will not go away merely because the anti human rights tendencies of ideologies that generate violations are exposed. However, the exposure will weaken and discourage adherence to these ideologies. Exposing and opposing ideologies or those facets of ideologies that lead to human rights violations should be one tool amongst many used to combat the violations.

CHAPTER TWO

FASCISM AND THE NATIONAL SECURITY STATE

Fascism is an ideological root cause of human rights violations. Fascist ideologies are ideologies that are nationalistic, militaristic, undemocratic, that give primacy to law and order, that glorify the leader. Fascist governments can range from the simply authoritarian military dictatorships to the totalitarian governments of the Nazis. Fascist oppression can even exist in a democratic context, where the democratic institutions do not control the military or the police, and the military act on their own, without constraint to combat what they see as threats to national security.

Though rightist dictatorships are quite common, and though fascism as an ideology is of relatively recent vintage, fascism has little contemporary intellectual appeal. The philosophers of fascism, such as Giovanni Gentile or Georges Sorel, are rarely read, and nowhere believed.

Jeane Kirkpatrick wrote that the rightist dictatorships are far more likely to progress towards liberalization and democratization than Marxist regimes.[1] Rightist dictatorships permit limited contestation and participation. This contestation and participation can be encouraged. Marxist regimes rarely permit even limited dissent.

While this distinction may well explain the instability of fascist regimes, equally important, I suggest, is the rejection of fascism as an ideology. Rightist dictatorships represent no persuasive idea. There is little that can be said to justify their continuation. Their absence of accepted philosophical foundation makes them inherently unstable.

Because rightist dictatorships justify themselves on the basis of a need for law and order, they have no reason for existence unless there is disorder, real or imagined. The main culprits to the fascists are the communists. The threat of subversive communism becomes the ground for existence of these fascist dictatorships.

While the existence of communist guerillas is real enough, rightist dictatorships manufacture a communist threat, even where it does not exist, and exaggerate it where it does. Every communist thinker, every reformer, every

villager living in a communist guerilla area, every human rights worker reporting human rights violations becomes part of the threat. This exaggerated anti-
communism is not just paranoia. It is an attempt to manufacture a justification for rightist regimes. If a communist threat does not exist, it has to be
invented.

For the Nazis, this hostility to disorder took the form of anti-Semitism. Nazis
fabricated a Jewish conspiracy of world domination, which they used to justify
their own attempts at domination. Today it is hard to realize the prevalence
and penetration that anti-Semitism had fifty years ago.

The disappearance of anti-Semitism, as an ideological foundation for
rightist regimes is, in part, due to the collapse of Nazism, its main proponent.
It is, in part, due to the revulsion against atrocities the Nazis committed in the
name of anti-Semitism. No less important, I suggest, is the collapse of the
belief in anti-Semitism as an ideology. The philosophers of racism and anti-
Semitism like Joseph Arthur Comte de Gobineau or Houston Stewart
Chamberlain are virtually unknown in our day, advocates without followers.

Anthropologists today reject the concept of race as a way of demarcating
people. One anthropologist, Clyde Kluckholm, writes: "If all living people
were ranged in a single sequence according to degree of resemblance, there
would be no sharp breaks in the line, but rather a continuum where each
specimen differed from the next by almost imperceptible variation."[2]

Anti-Semitism has been analyzed for what it really is, not a philosophy,
but a passion, the passion of hatred. Jean-Paul Sartre has written: "The anti-
Semite has chosen hate because hate is a faith; at the outset he has chosen to
devaluate words and reasons."[3]

Anti-Semitism still exists, and even has modern mutants like Holocaust
denial. The Holocaust was the Nazi-organized murder of six million Jews and
the attempt to exterminate the Jewish people. Holocaust denial is an attempt
to assert that the Holocaust is a fabrication of the world Jewish conspiracy to
win sympathy for the Jews.

It is wrong to blame anti-Semitism on Jews. Blaming anti-Semitism on
Jews is blaming victims for their own victimization. There are places in
Europe where the Jewish population has virtually disappeared and yet anti-
Semitism still continues.

While military repression may be spurred by communist guerilla or terrorist tactics, it is wrong to blame the excesses of repression on these tactics.
The excesses are just that, above and beyond what the situation requires. They
are motivated by a militaristic ideology. Indeed, like anti-Semitism without
Jews, we see anti-communist repression without communists.

Racism, too, can exist without races. Race may not exist as a scientific anthropological concept. But, it exists, nevertheless, in people's minds. Racial tolerance, like political tolerance, ethnic tolerance, and political tolerance, remains to be learned.

We have had our intellectual work done for us by people like Clyde Kluckholm and Jean-Paul Sartre. The lessons of tolerance are easy enough to learn if we set about trying to learn them. Yet, unless we make the effort, we shall fall prey to the very atrocities mankind has already suffered.

The ideology of the national security state is a form of fascism. In the face of a supposed threat of subversive aggression, and if the democratic system of government is considered inadequate, then the military sets up an authoritarian and repressive framework.[4] However, fascism as a label has gone out of fashion. Today it is only a derogatory epithet. Calling someone a fascist now is more an insult than a description. It may be clearer simply to treat the ideology of the national security state as a case apart.

The doctrine of national security was developed in the National War College of Brazil between 1949 and 1964, most notably by Golbery de Couto e Silva. Its theorists have included Augusto Pinochet, a former president of Chile, who set out his views of the doctrine in a 1974 work titled *Geopolitics*.

The literature on the national security doctrine, by proponents, commentators, and critics is huge.[5] Much of the doctrine of the national security state is either platitudinous or common sense. There are, however, five interlinked elements of the doctrine which are central to its core and which have a direct impact on respect for human rights. They are the concept of total war, the related notion of dirty war, the equation of the state with the nation, the primacy of security, and the leading role of the military in promoting security.

Golbery refers to total war as economic, financial, political, and scientific. It involves the whole economic, political, cultural, and military capacity of the nation. The participants in this war are not just soldiers. They include civilians as well as the military, women and children as well as men. War is total in time and space. It covers the entire territorial space of the state. It is continuous, permanent, without a pre-war or post-war period.

The threat to national security does not come solely from a strictly limited military war, what we have become used to thinking of as war. It comes, above all, from the danger of total war.

The concept of total war focuses on the threat of internal subversion. Castelo Branco, the first president of Brazil after the military coup of 1964, has written that with the impossibility of a direct nuclear confrontation, hostilities between the superpowers were channeled into peripheral wars, wars of liberation, revolutionary wars, or local wars.[6]

Chilean General Alejandro Medina has written that even apparently innocent organizations and activities may be fronts for those with Marxist ideological inclinations. The danger is not only Marxists and their fronts but those who are easy prey to the Marxists. In the case of Chile, this came to mean radical parties, Christian Democrats, union members, professionals, and the church.[7]

Total war, in isolation, is just a theoretical concept. What gave it reality to the theorists of the national security doctrine was the East-West conflict. Total war, to them, was not just a possibility; it was actually happening. Marxism was the enemy, engaged in this subversive, comprehensive, omnipresent war. And Latin America was the battlefield. Faced with an enemy fighting this total war, the state must respond, with all its resources, to defend itself.

The notion of a dirty war follows from the notion of a total war. Because the threat to security comes from civilians as well as armed combatants, the war must be fought against those enemy civilians. Since politics, economics, finance, and science are all part of the war, the world of ideas becomes a source of danger, a threat in itself. Since war is omnipresent and permanent, it must be fought everywhere, all the time.

National security theorists equate the state with the nation. That is to say, they equate the interests of the population with the interests of the government. President Pinochet, in his book *Geopolitics* refers to the state as a product of its citizenry. Citizens are united under the idea of the state. The state is the legal manifestation of the nation and is dedicated to the common good of all members of society.[8]

Security, under the national security doctrine, is an end in itself, rather than a means to an end. It is, as well, the primary goal of the state. National security has primacy over personal security. According to the Brazilian Amaral Gurgel, national security is the guarantee given by the state to achieve or defend national governments.[9] It is the ability of the state to maintain itself and survive. The Argentinian General Villegas wrote that there can be no development of the state without security.[10]

Advocating the leading role of the military in promoting security is something that comes naturally to the military people who elaborated the doctrine of national security. It was set out in unequivocal form in decrees of the military government of Chile following the coup. These decrees stated that the armed forces – the army, navy, air force, and police – have been organized by the state to safeguard and defend its moral and physical integrity. Their supreme mission was to ensure the survival of the permanent and superior realities and values of the Chilean nationality.

The military saw themselves as above political disputes. This view they had of themselves and their professionalization in security led them to believe they were the best interpreters of what national security required.

It may, perhaps, be obvious, just from stating these components of the national security doctrine, the problems they pose for respect for human rights. The notion of total war is a form of paranoia. When anybody doing almost anything is your enemy, when even the innocent may be fronts for subversives, or easy prey for subversives, no reaction is out of bounds.

The law of war assumes that there are combatants who are taking part in hostilities, and others who are not. The law sets a higher standard for treatment of noncombatants, for civilians, than for combatants. Combatants may, according to the laws of war, be killed. Wilful killing of noncombatants is a violation of the laws of war. In a situation of total war, however, everyone is a combatant. The protections of humanitarian law apply to no one. Women and children, the armed as well as the unarmed, become acceptable targets. The concept of total war is a recipe for genocide.

It is, as well, a form of totalitarianism – total control of all aspects of society in the interests of the state. Total war is an attack on all components of society which are or may be subversive or easy prey to subversives, because they represent a threat to the interests of the state.

The concept of a dirty war has the notion of human rights violations built right into it. War is, by nature, dirty.[11] All war inevitably generates excesses and extremes. The concept of a dirty war justifies and even glorifies these excesses.

A clean war is, for all practical purposes, an oxymoron. Insofar as it has any meaning at all, it means a war that is fought in conformity with the laws of war. The concept of a dirty war means that violations of the laws of war become an end in themselves. There is not even the pretense of attempting to comply with international humanitarian and human rights laws.

The equation of the state with the nation should send out warning signals to anyone involved with human rights. When it comes to respect for human rights, a government cannot be the only protector and guarantor. Human rights are rights of individuals against governments. Once the government becomes the sole interpreter of the need to protect human rights, compliance with human rights standards invariably disintegrates.

When the state is equated with the nation, those holding power confuse loyalty to the government with loyalty to the nation. Lack of support for the government becomes treason.

A pastoral communication from the Episcopal Conference of Brazil, in 1977, expressed the following: the nation is not synonymous with the state. It is not the state which grants liberties and human rights. Rights and liberties exist prior to the state.[12]

The dangers of the primacy of security is something human rights observers commonly see in a prison setting. Cruel, inhuman, or degrading treatment of prisoners is often the consequence of an exaggerated concern with security. When security is given primacy, the state becomes a prison and a prison of the worst sort.

Security has to be balanced with freedom. Outside of prisons, in a "civil" society, security considerations deserve a good deal less consideration than they do in prison. A country should not, after all, become a prison.

Civil society must be based on the free consent of the governed. It must not be based on force. Yet a national security state is a state that rules by force, rather than by consent. Placing national security above the human person generates a society that is inevitably inhumane.

The leading role of the military in protecting national security has an ironic parallel with the leading rule of the Communist Party in protecting the interests of the working class in a socialist state. And it has the same disastrous consequences.

Even in a democracy, national security bureaucracies have had difficulty distinguishing subversion from legitimate dissent. To be effective, any national security service needs close control and supervision by people who are not primarily security people themselves.

A national security state is a security apparatus run wild. The tendency of a national security state to view every disagreement with the government as subversive and treasonous is accentuated when the security people control the state. Any threat to the status quo is seen as potentially subversive. The national security state becomes a government devoted to the protection of vested interests.

The national security doctrine has had the military as its adherents throughout Latin America. It was the spur to the coups that brought military governments to power in the '70s and '80s. The doctrine helped to keep those governments in place. Above all, the doctrine was the motor and justification for the widespread human rights violations that occurred.

Latin America had a history of military intervention in civil politics even before the national security doctrine was articulated. But the doctrine brought the military into politics in countries, like Chile, where it had never been before. And in countries where the military had traditionally intervened, the doctrine kept the military in power for a good deal longer than was the tradition.

The traditional coup in Latin America moderated a crisis during times of extreme confrontation among different components of a civil society. Once the crisis subsided, the military withdrew. The national security doctrine gave the military an ideology, a mission for themselves that made it harder to withdraw once they were in power. They viewed the crisis that brought them to power no longer in terms of the moderation of battling civilian elements, but in terms of total war and the threat to the state by subversion.

The national security doctrine gave the military both a reason for perpetrating human rights violations and a legitimization for the human rights violations that did occur. These violations, rather than calling into question the value of the regimes, became, to the adherents of the national security doctrine, part of the reason why the regimes were there in the first place.

Adherence to the national security doctrine has now subsided throughout Latin America. As national security regimes viewed ever larger segments of society as threats to national security, the ideology of the regimes became harder to credit. No population will view significant components of its society, its professionals, its religious leaders, its union leaders, as threats to national security. The more threats to national security the military regimes saw the less credible they became.

The ebbing of the Cold War also undercut the paranoia of national security regimes at its base. The notion of a subversive internal war as a reflection of a superpower ideological geopolitical struggle has no foundation when that universal geopolitical struggle has ceased.

Above all, the human rights violations generated by the national security doctrine have discredited it. General Golbery of Brazil, the grandfather of the national security doctrine, became part of the Castello Branco government after the 1964 military coup, and he formed the National Intelligence Service, the Brazilian Secret police. He later wrote, in his papers, about this secret service, the SNI: "I have created a monster."[13] In a later (1974) military government of Ernesto Geisel, Golbery became a key figure in lessening repression. He became the subject of attack in right-wing newspapers as a traitor to the 1964 coup.

Just as, in turn, Nazism, fascism, and communism have lost their appeal because of the widespread havoc and misery they have caused, the national security doctrine has come to be known by its fruits. The general perception is that a national security doctrine means disappearances, torture, unlawful confinement, and extrajudicial executions. This is enough to dissuade most people from accepting the doctrine, no matter what its theoretical justifications.

PART II

COMMUNISM IN EASTERN EUROPE

CHAPTER THREE

COMMUNISM AS A ROOT CAUSE OF HUMAN RIGHTS VIOLATIONS

Communism was motivated, originally, by human rights concerns, by the poor working conditions of labour in nineteenth-century industrial society, by the exploitation of workers by employers. Yet it has led to some of the greatest human rights violations this century has seen. Karl Marx and Friedrich Engels wrote in the *Communist Manifesto*: "Workers have nothing to lose but their chains. They have a world to win. Workers of the World unite."

But when workers did unite to form communist governments, they lost a lot more than their chains imposed on them by capitalist employers. They acquired a new set of chains clamped on by the communist state. Millions lost their health and their lives.

The tyranny of communism emanated from three interrelated concepts: the dictatorship of the proletariat, the Communist Party as vanguard of the proletariat, and democratic centralism within the Communist Party. The dictatorship of the proletariat is also referred to as the state of the whole people, the state as collective individual, the state as the perfect embodiment of the will of the people.

The Communist Party as vanguard of the proletariat is also referred to as the leading role of the Communist Party. Leonid Brezhnev said that separating the Communist Party from the people was "tantamount to trying to separate, say, the heart from the whole of the body."[1]

Democratic centralism means that once a decision is made by the party leaders, it must be obeyed. That is a principle that is more applicable to a military chain of command than a political party.

In practice, the vanguard of the proletariat were all dictatorship, all vanguard, and no proletariat. Democratic centralism was all centralism and no democracy.

Mieczyslaw Rakowski, the last head of the Communist Party in Poland, said, in a speech at a Congress which decided, on June 27, 1990 to disband the party, that the dictatorship of the proletariat became the dictatorship of one party and degenerated into oligarchic or personal tyranny.[2]

The leading role of the Communist Party is, in effect, the belief in historical necessity, the historical inevitability of communism. The reason communists believed in democratic centralism, in the leading role of the Communist Party, is that they believed they were right. They believed they knew what was good for workers, without the approval of workers through elections.

The notion of historical necessity itself can be traced back to Hegel. But it is as unfair to blame Hegel for the Gulag Archipelago as it is to blame Albert Einstein for the nuclear bombing of Hiroshima and Nagasaki. Both were theorists motivated by intellectual curiosity to explain the world around them. They neither intended nor expected destruction from their efforts. The calamities that have followed show that even the most innocent intellectual pursuits can have the most devastating practical consequences.

There is a further irony in the influence of Hegel. Hegel set out to explain the development of thought or being as a conceptual or ontological hierarchy. He explained the development of political institutions as an historical hierarchy. Each level of the hierarchy is more sophisticated than the one before. Each level grows out of the one before. The motor or engine for the development of this hierarchy is the dialectic. The dialectic is a process of thesis, antithesis, synthesis.

The culmination of the ontological dialectic is the conception of a universe posited by a Spirit whose essence is rational necessity.[3] The culmination of the historical dialectic is a state to which the individual owes allegiance as an embodiment of universal subjectivity.[4]

For many, these assertions are quite meaningless. A.J. Ayer has written, when commenting on the writings of F.H. Bradley, a British Hegelian, that his metaphysical pseudo-propositions were not even in principle verifiable, that he fails to communicate anything to us, that he was making utterances which have no literal significance, even for himself.[5]

Of course it is unfair to Hegel, especially, to focus on his conclusions without looking at the process by which he arrived at them. He argued eloquently that it is inappropriate and misleading to divorce the conclusions of philosophy from the process by which the conclusions are reached. The real subject matter of philosophy is not exhausted in its conclusions, but in working the matter out.[6]

Nevertheless, if philosophy is not only conclusions, it is not only method either. For Hegel, in particular, the method is inextricably bound up with the conclusions. His conclusions contained and crowned his purpose.[7] If the conclusions are wrong, then the method is wrong.

A point of irony is that Marx, and communist theorists generally, have done just that. They have jettisoned the Hegelian conclusions but retained the Hegelian method. Marx argued for a historical dialectic in the economic sphere rather than in the political sphere as Hegel had done. The culmination of that dialectic was socialism. Socialism is the inevitable and necessary conclusion of history.

An even more important shift, important as a cause of intolerance, is the shift from an ex-post-facto to a forward-looking perspective. Hegel's conceptual structure was a rationalization after the fact. Marx's conceptual structure was a call to arms. His conclusions were not something that had happened. They were things that would be and should be made to happen.

Terrorist guerillas motivated by Marxist ideology claim they are making manifest the inherent contradictions in pre-communist societies. Communist revolutionaries are the vanguard of the proletariat leading humanity to a higher civilization. Communists in power actualize the iron laws of history. They make society conform to what they believe it will become. Their laws of history become self-fulfilling prophecies.

Bernard-Henri Levy writes that the Gulag was not a blunder or an accident. It was a necessary corollary of Marxism. The Soviet camps were as Marxist as Auschwitz was Nazi. The camps attempted to conceal one truth in the process of trying to form another.[8]

It is easy enough, intellectually, to sit back and note the inconsistency between claiming historical necessity and trying to impose it. If historical development really is inevitable, then nothing need be done to bring about the development. This criticism is not, by itself, an answer to Marxism. It overlooks the powerful motivating force: a feeling of being on the side of history.

While the shift to a forward-looking perspective and to an economic analysis are uniquely Marxist, the Hegelian source remains the basis of the problem. The problem is not so much that history has an end in the future rather than the past, but that history has an end at all.

An unending dialectic would not pose the problems that a terminating dialectic does. Yet an unending dialectic is a contradiction in terms. We can only grasp the rationality of history if we are at the end of history. If history continues, then it has some higher rationality, some higher synthesis of which we can not yet be aware. The dialectic would not explain history. There would be some further principle, not yet conceived, that would explain it.[9]

There is something fundamentally egocentric about the whole notion of the dialectic. Indeed, that is part of its appeal. A person who asserts the dialectic asserts that the development of history and of thought has ended with his understanding of it. A person who believes in the dialectic believes that he is the embodiment of the ultimate truth. It is not just that he has grasped the ultimate truth. His understanding means history has come to an end.

For someone whose view is retrospective, this conceit is harmless. A Marxist, whose view is prospective, who not only sees himself as embodying the ultimate truth, but as well, imposing that truth on others, wreaks catastrophe.

The whole notion of historical necessity violates a basic aspect of the human condition, freedom of will. Put retrospectively, the violation is of little importance, since we cannot change the past. While it may be true that history could have been different than it was, it is of little importance to say it. Put prospectively, the violation is egregious. It is crucial that we have an opportunity to choose between different courses of action. If a group with its own sense of history imposes a choice on us we do not want (in the name of historical inevitability) our humanity is denied.

The very application of the Hegelian dialectic to reality, and this is, no doubt, a point Hegel himself would have appreciated, has generated its own disproof, its own contradiction. The human rights violations the communist world saw showed that mankind has not been going through some sort of intellectual and historical ascendancy. We regress as well as progress, destroy as well as create. Human rights violations do not just come from old ideas. They come from new ideas, as well. We must be as wary of communist thought as of older ideologies.

Socialism in a communist state bears little resemblance to the platform of socialist parties in the West. We tend to think of socialist parties in the West as favouring public ownership of more activities or industries than the centre or right parties would favour.

The communist form of socialism has meant total control of all aspects of the economy. It gives priority to society over individual and private life. Every institution, every aspect of a person's life is regulated by the state.

Human rights are individualistic by nature; their focus is the individual human being, his/her dignity, his/her self-realization. Socialism, of the Marxist Leninist form, is antagonistic to the whole concept of human rights. Marx and Lenin viewed human rights as a disguise for class rule by the bourgeoisie over the worker – the privileges of the capitalist ruling class. Selected rights, they believed, are granted only to ensure the ruling class maintains its power.

Marxist-Leninist governments signed international human rights instruments and incorporated them into their constitutions. There was an obvious hypocrisy in this lip service to human rights while the rights themselves were being violated. But it was more than just hypocrisy. The very vocabulary of human rights meant something different to the socialist states than it did to the capitalist states.[10]

In theory, the vocabulary of human rights was a shared vocabulary, which allowed for a bridging of the gap between East and West. Peace could only come through shared understanding. And, it was thought, human rights was a domain in which all could agree.

At the verbal level, even before glasnost, there was agreement on human rights, but there was no agreement on the meaning of the human rights vocabulary. The use of human rights as a road to peace was itself an illusion, as long as the two sides differed about what human rights meant.

Marxism-Leninism has a collectivist rather than individualistic approach to self-realization. V. Chkhikvadze, a communist theorist, wrote: "Personality founded upon the individualism characteristic of bourgeois relationships is egotistical and places its own well being above that of society."[11] The self-realization that socialists sought was not of the individual, with all his/her idiosyncrasies, achieved through freedom, but of the socialist personality, achieved through ideological education and societal constraints.

Adam Smith saw the public interest being served through the working of an invisible hand. Each person pursuing his/her own interest benefitted the public as a whole. For Marx and Lenin, the hand was visible. Every individual was to be fashioned into a socialist personality who would act only in a way that was in the interests of society as a whole.

Communism is an attempt to change human nature. George Orwell considered this aspect "the terrifying thing" about communism. He wrote that in the past every tyranny was overthrown because human nature desired liberty. But, he said, "It may be just as possible to produce a band of men who do not wish for liberty as to produce a breed of hornless cows."[12]

Chkhikvadze makes the same point from another perspective. He writes: "Collectivism ... moulds a member of society, a citizen who cannot conceive of himself outside the social situation, who is aware not only of his rights, but also of his duties."[13]

According to Marxism, the person who is truly free is not the person who is free to act without constraints. It is, rather, the person who on his/her own initiative, acts in a selfless way, in the interests of the state.

In a logical sense, whenever there is a right that one person has, there is a correlative duty that others have to respect the right. With human rights, it is the individual who has the rights, and the state has the duty to respect those rights.

Marxism flips this relation between rights and duties. Because, in principle in a Marxist state, there is a unity of purpose between state and individual, the duties do not just rest on the state. They rest, as well, on the individual. Human rights, on the other hand, do not just belong to the individual, alone. They belong as well to the state.[14]

This socialist equation of rights and duties has three basic consequences.

It means everyone who has a right has a corresponding duty. The Soviet constitution used to say, "Citizens' exercise of their rights and freedoms is inseparable from the performance of their duties and obligations."[15] Another provision used to say that the exercise of rights and liberties is not to "be to the detriment of the interests of society or the state."[16] The right to freedom of speech, for instance, carries a corresponding duty to speak in such a way as to benefit the state. The Soviet constitution used to say that citizens may exercise this right to free speech only "in accordance with the interests of the people and in order to strengthen and develop the socialist system."[17]

Second, the equation of rights and duties means that while rights belong both to the state and the individual, the state has a prior claim, because the state is the source of rights of the individual. The state guarantees the rights the individual has. Without the state, human rights are, according to Marxist legal scholar Andrei Vyshinsky, "a mere abstraction, an empty illusion."[18] According to Vyshinsky, "The state is the primary condition essential for ... individual well being."[19] Because rights emanate from the state, it is for the state to determine the content and scope of rights, as well as how the rights are to be exercised.

Thirdly, because the individual has duties, as well as the state, the individual must fulfil his/her duties in order to be entitled to exercise his/her rights. It is not just the correlative duty associated with the right that must be fulfilled. It is all the duties that fall on an individual in a socialist state that must be fulfilled, before any rights can be exercised. The compliance with all duties is the pre-condition for the exercise of any right. The failure to comply with any duty justifies the loss of all rights.

The right to life is the most basic human right. The right to life must be respected for all other rights to be meaningful. The international instruments have accepted derogable rights, those which can be temporarily suspended in times of publicly declared emergency, which threaten the security of the state, and nonderogable rights, which must be respected even in times of emergency. Civil and political rights are to be respected immediately. States are expected, on the other hand, only to make their best efforts to work towards the realization of economic, social and cultural rights. There is no requirement that these rights be realized immediately. Beyond that there is no ranking. Human rights form an indivisible whole. They are different components of the overall goal of realizing the self-worth of the individual.

Marxism, on the other hand, produces an internal ranking within human rights. The highest-ranking rights are the rights associated with the state and the community. At a second level, only, are the rights associated with the individual. For instance, in the criminal codes of socialist states, theft from work carries a higher penalty than theft of the same goods from someone's home.

The socialist conception of human rights has repression built into it. For those who do not do their duty willingly, repression is available to promote responsibility.[20] Human rights violations perpetrated against the individual are the road to respect for the state as the giver of rights.

Yuri Andropov, Brezhnev's successor and a former head of the KGB, said both candidly and ominously, "Any citizen of the Soviet Union whose interests coincide with the interests of society feels the entire scope of our democratic freedoms. It is another matter if those interests [of the citizen] ... do not coincide [with the interests of society]."[21] Or, as the Hungarian writer Miklos Haraszti has put it: "Within the Revolution, complete freedom; against the Revolution, none."[22]

Zbigniew Brzezinski wrote:

Humanity's catastrophic encounter with Communism during the twentieth century has provided a painful but critically important lesson: Utopian social engineering is fundamentally in conflict with the complexity of the human condition, and social creativity blossoms best when political power is restricted.[23]

Mikhail Gorbachev said much the same thing from a different perspective. He wrote:

Experience has demonstrated that what one needs is not a total legislative regulation of diversified phenomenon of social life but sound rationality and constant support for the worker, work force and all forms of popular initiative. Let us strictly observe the principle: anything which is not prohibited by law is allowed.[24]

It became evident that the socialist conception of human rights is a perversion of the notion of human rights. It is easy to understand how human rights could be so easily violated, given the socialist interpretation of the concept of human rights.

CHAPTER FOUR

YUGOSLAVIA: MAY 1988

I was in Yugoslavia in May 1988, for the International Helsinki Human Rights Federation, as co-chair of the Canadian Helsinki Watch Group, the Canadian member of the Federation. This chapter was written on my return. At the time, Communist repression was lifting. There were signs of both hope and despair. The regional and ethnic disintegration was beginning.

The human rights situation in Yugoslavia was a study in contrasts. There was, first of all, the contrast between Yugoslavia and the other communist countries of Eastern Europe. Indeed, Yugoslavs did not refer to themselves as either communist or Eastern European. They called themselves socialist and Central European.

The contrast between Yugoslavia and the Soviet bloc can best be illustrated by an incident. The International Helsinki Federation, which scheduled its annual (1988) general meeting for Yugoslavia, is a nongovernmental organization that promotes the human rights component of the Helsinki Accord. The Helsinki Accord, the Final Act of the Conference on Security and Cooperation in Europe, signed in Helsinki in 1975 by thirty-five states of Europe and North America, links disarmament, human contacts, and respect for human rights. The Accord takes the place of a World-War-II peace treaty in Europe that was never signed.

The Helsinki Federation informed the Government of Yugoslavia that the Federation was planning to meet in Yugoslavia, but did not ask the government's permission. The Yugoslav authorities, when informed of our plans, wrote to the Helsinki Federation to inform it that, in the opinion of the Government of Yugoslavia, it would be "useful" to postpone the Federation's meeting. The government wanted the Helsinki Federation to come later to meet with a human rights forum the government was about to establish.

While expressing interest in meeting with the forum when it was established, the Helsinki Federation decided to go ahead with its planned meeting. The government then considered whether or not to prohibit the meeting the Federation had planned.

Gerald Nagler, the secretary-general of the Helsinki Federation, and I met with Mirko Ostojic, the chairman of the International Affairs Commission of the Socialist Alliance of the Working People of Yugoslavia and a member of its presidency. The Socialist Alliance was a front for the Communist Party of Yugoslavia. Indeed, it used to be called the Popular Front. Darko Mrvos, secretary of the International Affairs Commission of the Alliance, called it the transmission of the voice of the Communist Party. The alliance "recommended" candidates for the local, provincial, republic, and federal assemblies. The Alliance was going to "recommend" to the minister of the interior whether the Federation would be allowed to meet or not.

In the end, the Alliance made a favourable recommendation and the Helsinki Federation meeting took place. It was the first annual general meeting of the Federation in a communist country. Darko Mrvos of the Alliance even came to the meeting to address it about the government's proposed human rights forum.

That behaviour had to be contrasted with what had happened to the Federation in Hungary just two and a half years previously. Hungary was the most liberal of the Soviet bloc countries. The Helsinki Federation had organized, for Hungary, a nongovernmental cultural forum to coincide with the opening of the intergovernmental forum on culture that was part of the Helsinki Accord process. The Hungarian government forbade the Federation forum. The authorities told the hotel where the forum was planned to cancel the meeting rooms. The forum did take place, but in private apartments only.

The Czechs and Soviets, according to information the Federation received from friendly diplomatic sources, wanted Hungary to evict the Helsinki Federation people from the country. The Hungarian authorities moderated the hard line to this extent: the Federation-sponsored forum could take place, but in difficult conditions and under an aura of illegality designed to intimidate Hungarians who might want to attend.

The point of this comparison is to show that Yugoslavia was more liberal than Hungary, but it came nowhere near democratic standards. In a democracy, what is not forbidden is permitted. In Yugoslavia, what was not permitted was forbidden. The Helsinki Federation was able to meet in Yugoslavia only because, in the end, permission was given whether it was requested or not. The mere fact that meeting there was not forbidden was not enough.

This human rights contrast is not just a contrast between what happened in Yugoslavia and what happened in the rest of Eastern Europe. It is also a contrast between what was happening in different parts of Yugoslavia.

Yugoslavia was a federation with six component republics and two provinces. The Federal Criminal Code was administered by the republics and the provinces. The Criminal Code contained a number of verbal offences, crimes that could be committed just for saying the wrong thing. There was the offence of disseminating hostile propaganda, of malicious and false representation of conditions in Yugoslavia, of association for purposes of hostile activity, of participating in hostile activity, and of counter-revolutionary activity endangering of the social order. The crimes were punishable by up to fifteen years in prison.

These provisions had widely different applications in different parts of Yugoslavia. In the Republic of Slovenia, in the north, and in Belgrade, in the Republic of Serbia, prosecutions for verbal offences were rare. Sentences for convictions were light. In the Republic of Bosnia, in Central Yugoslavia, and in the Province of Kosovo, near Albania, in the south, prosecutions for verbal offences were common, and sentences severe. There was extortion of testimony through torture, and forged and falsified documents were submitted in support of the prosecution.

There were eight different ways, in the six republics and two provinces, of applying the same law. Milovan Djilas, a former vice-president of Yugoslavia and author of several communist critiques, referred in an interview to the situation in Yugoslavia as disintegration of communism from within. In his view, the Party was dividing along national lines into a series of national oligarchies. What Djilas saw as happening to communism may have been nothing other than balkanization, disintegration endemic to the region, rather than to communism.

Here is an example of the varying standards. A young female entertainer working at a restaurant in Kosovo was sentenced to thirty days in jail because she refused to sing a song, which a restaurant patron had requested of her, in praise of Tito. A prosecution for such an offence would have been unlikely in Slovenia or Belgrade.

There was a great deal of liberty of expression in Yugoslavia in 1968. That interval of freedom was followed by prosecutions and suppression. People, three, four, and five years later, were prosecuted for what they had said in 1968. Milan Nikolic, for instance, was put on trial in 1971 and 1972 because of his part in student protests in 1968.

One analysis I heard while I was in Yugoslavia was that the Communist Party more or less systematically alternated between liberalism and repression. At times the Party would lighten the burden of oppression in an attempt to curry popular support. The freedom soon got out of hand. People took advantage of it to criticize the Party. The Party felt threatened and decided the situation needed stabilization. Lists were made, in liberal times, when people spoke up. Repression returned and the trials began.

The Federation witnessed an aborted attempt at a return to repression while it was meeting in Yugoslavia. The Military Council of the Federation in

March, proposed a crackdown in Slovenia, a mass arrest of the leading intellectuals and journalists who had been critical of the Party. Because Slovenia has been the most liberal of the republics, a crackdown there would have had repercussions throughout Yugoslavia. The effect would have been equivalent to the effect of the Soviet invasion of Czechoslovakia in 1968 on the whole Soviet bloc.

The federal minister of defence, Mamula, asked the chief of the army in Slovenia, Visnjic, to inform the minister of the interior of Slovenia of this planned mass arrest. The minister of the interior insisted that the president of the Slovenian Communist Party, Kucan, be part of his briefing session. When Kucan found out about the plan for a crackdown, he opposed it. The dissent in Slovenia was, after all something that the local Communist Party itself had tolerated.

Kucan spoke in favour of the current liberalism in Slovenia at a Federal Communist Party Presidium Meeting in Belgrade in April. He argued that what was happening was not counter-revolutionary. Mamula was thwarted in his plans for repression and was forced to resign. He was replaced by Kadijevic, who became the minister of defence.

The speech of Kucan to the Presidium was leaked to the Slovenian periodical *Mladina*. The speech referred to the planned mass arrests. The issue of *Mladina* that was supposed to print the speech, the May 13 issue, was censored. Excerpts from the speech the journal planned to print were replaced by another unrelated article. The following issue, of May 20, argued against a coup d'état by the Federation against Slovenia.

The Party then came out with a statement on May 21, denying the rumours of mass arrests. However, the Party, in its statement confirmed all the other details from the meeting of the Military Council, the contact of the Slovenian army chief of staff with the minister of the interior – but claimed that they were just normal procedures. The confirmation of these details, the censorship of *Mladina*, as well as the text of the Kucan speech itself, left little doubt these rumours were true.

After the Helsinki Federation left Yugoslavia, two journalists and an army sergeant were arrested, because of the leak. Ivan Jansa, a regular contributor to *Mladina*, was arrested on May 31. Ivan Berstner, an army sergeant major, was arrested June 3. David Tasic, an editor of *Mladina*, was arrested June 5. They were all held in prison on suspicion of betraying military secrets.

Although the authorities did not divulge which military secrets those arrested were accused of betraying, it seemed apparent that the secret was the planned mass arrests in Slovenia. The three were denied access to relatives and family. A domestic and international campaign was launched for their release. On July 27, the four were convicted of leaking army secrets and sentenced to jail terms of up to four years. They were freed pending appeals.

The point of this story is that the liberalism in Slovenia was, by no means, irreversible. If the Party learned anything from the incident, it was not that repression in Slovenia was no longer possible. It was only that, the next time, the local Slovenian Communist Party would not be alerted in advance.

The most striking contrast, in Yugoslavia on first impression, was the contrast between the simultaneous liberalism and repression. The repression, though more dramatic in Bosnia and Kosovo, was, by no means restricted to these two areas. While people generally seemed free to say what they wanted, side by side with this freedom were political trials, political imprisonment, disbarment of lawyers for political reasons, political abuse of psychiatry, and torture and forgery in order to get political convictions.

Yugoslavia had more political prisoners than all of the rest of Eastern Europe combined, outside the Soviet Union. Yugoslavia had more known political prisoners than the Soviet Union. The Helsinki Federation knew of some 360 political prisoners within the Soviet Union, although the possibility of many more, who were not identified, existed. Within Yugoslavia, there were over 1,100 political prisoners.

The explanation for this discrepancy, to a certain extent, was the liberalism itself. In a liberal period, people are more brash. They speak up more boldly. They test the outer limits of the freedom given to them. In a repressive period, there is a good deal more self-censorship. During liberal times, the number of political prisoners remains high.

The same point can be made about political censorship or banning. Banning of books and articles continued in Yugoslavia at about the same rate, year in year out, at about twenty items a year. Yet these numbers did not indicate a constant level of repression. At some times, the range of permitted expression was wide. At other times, it was narrow. At all times, there were authors, either by accident or design, who bumped up against the barriers and who suffered the consequences.

The high level of repression, even in "liberal" times, highlighted an external contrast. Abuses of human rights in the Soviet Union and in Soviet bloc countries were relatively well known, world-wide. About the violations that occurred in Yugoslavia, there was relative ignorance outside of Yugoslavia. It was not just that the repression, by comparison with the Soviet bloc, was less. Nor was the ignorance from a lack of available information. The ignorance was rather a studied, ideological one.

Tito broke with Stalin in 1948. During the Cold War and the battle of the superpowers for world hegemony, Yugoslavia was neutral. Criticism of the human rights record of any regime can easily be turned into a weapon of delegitimization. The West was eager to point to the human rights abuses of the

Soviet bloc, in an attempt to discredit Soviet communism. The West had no comparable interest in discrediting Tito. On the contrary, since his regime was outside the Soviet bloc, the Western attitude was rather one of support than of destabilization. Human rights violations were observed in silence.

For those concerned with the promotion of human rights for its own sake, this silence has been harmful. It made the work of the Helsinki Federation and other human rights activists concerned with Yugoslavia all that more important.

As a lawyer, I could not help but notice the contrast, in Yugoslavia, between law and lawlessness. It was not only that the wide list of verbal crimes flouted international human rights law and the international obligations Yugoslavia had undertaken. Yugoslavia, a signatory to the International Covenant on Civil and Political Rights, paid scant regard to some of its provisions. The Human Rights Committee established under the Covenant wondered, when Yugoslavia presented its report of compliance with the Covenant to the Committee in 1983, whether Yugoslavia would allow an organization advocating abolition of the death penalty to exist. The Yugoslav answer, internally, if not to the Committee, was that the death penalty was in the Constitution. Therefore advocating abolition of the death penalty was unconstitutional. An organization advocating abolition of the death penalty would not be allowed.

The courts were clearly not independent from government. Not every person accused of a political crime was convicted. But where a person was not convicted, the reason was that the prosecution dropped the case. It was unheard of for a judge to rule, on a charge of hostile propaganda, that the propaganda was published, but that it was not hostile. Indeed, the courts were not even prepared to hear defence witnesses who wished to establish the truth of the statements for which prosecutions had been launched. The theory seemed to be that a judgment favourable to the defendants would have opened the floodgates. Critics of the Party or the government would have been emboldened, if they had felt they could turn to the courts for recourse. It had to be made clear that recourse was not available.

The legal system had job ghettoes which demonstrated sexually the powerlessness of the judiciary. The prosecution, which in effect decided who would be convicted and punished and who could go free, was overwhelmingly male. The judiciary, which went along with whatever the prosecution decided, had a high proportion of women.

Lawlessness was an attribute shared both by the bench and the bar. Vladimir Seks, for instance, the spokesperson for the Osijek and Zagreb branch of the Yugoslav Helsinki Committee, whom I met, was sentenced to jail for hostile propaganda. He was a lawyer and his "offence" was defending someone else who was accused of hostile propaganda. The charges were eventually dropped against his client, Vladimir Mijanovic, but Seks himself was convicted. He served a seven-month sentence and was disbarred. The bar refused to admit him to practice, because they considered him morally and socially unfit.

Yet, side by side with this lawlessness was an extreme focus on legal technicalities. As an example of this contrast, Dobroslav Paraga spent four years in prison for circulating a petition calling for an amnesty for all political prisoners. After his release he wrote of his ill treatment in prison, and the harsh prison conditions generally. He was prosecuted and convicted for these writings, and sentenced to six months imprisonment, suspended for three years, and to a three year ban on public expression. During these three years, Paraga wrote an article calling for the human rights of prisoners in the jails of Yugoslavia. The prosecution began proceedings to enforce the suspended sentence on the ground that the ban on public expression had been defied.

Paraga, at his second trial, which led to his three-year sentence, was charged with spreading false information under the Croatian Criminal Code. His lawyer, Srdja Popovic, attempted to call evidence to establish the truth of what Paraga had written, that he was ill treated in prison, that prison conditions were indeed harsh. Paraga had 108 witnesses ready to testify. The court refused to recognize any of them. Only the prosecution witnesses could attest to prison conditions.

The Paraga litigation seemed to be proceeding, from start to finish, without any regard for legal principle, international standards, domestic law, or justice. Yet, when the case of Paraga was supposed to come up, for revocation of his suspended sentence, on May 13, 1988, it was not heard. Popovic had objected that notice of the three-year suspended sentence had not been properly served on Paraga. The notice of sentence had been served on the address of the parents of Paraga in Croatia. But Paraga had changed his address to Slovenia. The notice of sentence had not been served on the Slovenian address and, because of that, Popovic argued, the three years had not yet begun to run. The prosecution was sufficiently concerned with this objection not to proceed on May 13.

Another difference I wish to mention was the contrast between the extreme deference given to some nationalist and ethnic groups, and the severe repression of others. The whole federal system was based on respect for nationality. Serbs, Croats, Slovenes, Macedonians, Bosnians, Montenegrans were each given their own republic. Yugoslav law guaranteed nationalities use of their language in exercise of their rights, including education in their own language. Yet, for Gypsies, and ethnic Albanians, assertion of ethnic identity was severely circumscribed.

Ethnic Albanians are concentrated in the Serbian province of Kosovo. They represent 80 percent of the population of that province. An Albanian nationalist movement has been brutally repressed. Albanian dress, language, books, and songs were outlawed as nationalist provocation. Albanians who joined in their nationalist song in public were sentenced to jail. I mentioned earlier an incident of a singer jailed for refusing to sing a song in praise of Tito. So, in Yugoslavia, you could go to jail for singing – as well as for not singing.

If there was one reason for the high level of political imprisonment in Yugoslavia, it was the Albanian national question. Almost half of the political prisoners in Yugoslavia were ethnic Albanians jailed for asserting their identification with the Albanian nationalist cause.

Albanian nationalism takes the form not so much as a desire to join neighbouring Albania, whose desperate economic and political situation is obvious, nor as a desire for an independent state, but rather as a desire for an autonomous republic within the federal state. Albanian nationalists wanted Kosovo to secede from Serbia, but not from Yugoslavia. However, that desire was something that Serbians would not tolerate. Kosovo, although predominantly Albanian, has important historical associations for Serbia. Many Serbian monuments and churches are in Kosovo. The mere suggestion that Serbia should part with them became a crime of hostile propaganda.

At the time the Helsinki Federation was meeting in Belgrade, an appeal was pending from the convictions of eight young ethnic Albanians convicted in Skopje, Macedonia, of having founded a hostile organization. The "hostile organization" had the aim of obtaining republic status for Kosovo. Sentences handed down in late 1987 ranged from two years to seven years in prison.

The Gypsies in Yugoslavia are a good deal more passive than the ethnic Albanians, but their situation was, if anything, worse. The Gypsies had varying legal status throughout the country. In Bosnia they were recognized as a nationality. In other republics they had the status of an ethnic group. In some republics, they had no status at all.

There were approximately one million Gypsies in Yugoslavia. Yet they had no cultural institutions, no schools, no journals. Their living conditions were deplorable. They had no political representatives. There was a trade in Gypsy children to Italy for prostitution, without the Yugoslav authorities intervening. There was, generally, no organized effort to help the community.

The last contrast I will draw is between word and deed. Hypocrisy is a world-wide vice. Politicians everywhere find it easy to promise and hard to deliver; however, there are three reasons why hypocrisy is a particular problem for a communist state.

One is the pervasiveness of government. The more government does, the more scope there is for government hypocrisy, and in communist states, government does virtually everything.

The second is the existence of the one party state. A multiparty system institutionalizes criticism. An active opposition makes it hard for the government to stray from the truth too far, or for too long. In a one-party state, this institutionalized criticism is missing: hypocrisy can be more bold, and it can go on for longer.

The third is parallelism. One strategy or tactic communists have developed is the establishment of institutions that are parallel to nongovernmental organizations. These institutions purport to serve the same purposes as the nongovernmental organizations, but, in fact, serve primarily the interests of the Communist Party. These institutions are, in reality, Communist Party fronts. So, for instance, in a communist state, there are trade unions, professional associations, cultural groupings, and so on, which, while purporting to be nongovernmental, reflect the voice of the Communist Party and the state.

Until recently, human rights organizations had escaped this communist technique. Historically, the typical response of communist states to the activities of international human rights organizations has been that there are no violations, or the matters are of internal domestic concern only. The communist states by 1987 had begun to apply parallelism to the human rights arena. In 1987 the Soviets created a commission on human rights headed by Fyodor Bourlatsky. And the Yugoslavs were planning to create a human rights forum.

Both the Soviets and the Yugoslavs wanted their quasi-governmental human rights institutions to represent their countries in the Helsinki Human Rights Federation. Mirko Ostojic of the Socialist Alliance of Yugoslavia wrote to the Helsinki Federation that the Yugoslav Human Rights Forum would be "an adequate and representative interlocutor" of the Helsinki Federation in Yugoslavia.

The Helsinki Federation insisted that its representatives in the Soviet Union, and in Yugoslavia, be strictly nongovernmental. The Federation designated as its representative, in the Soviet Union, the Press Club Glasnost, and in Yugoslavia, the Yugoslav Helsinki Committee, a group of human rights activists, who had been promoting, on their own, the cause of human rights. The Yugoslav Committee includes Seks, Paraga, and Nikolic, people I had all mentioned earlier.

Darko Mrvos of the Socialist Alliance of Yugoslavia met with the Federation at their Annual General Meeting in Belgrade, to provide information about the human rights forum. The Helsinki Federation urged on him that the Forum be more than a state public-relations exercise for human rights, that the forum get involved in assisting individuals who had been victims of human rights violations.

The chiaroscuro of Yugoslav life had its individual as well as structural aspect. Economic historians say that it takes bad economies to produce good economists. One can say the same of political history. The hardships of Yugoslavia have produced many good people, people dedicated to the exposure and removal of human rights violations.

In democratic countries, intellectuals are people who pursue knowledge and think through ideas for their own sake. In a country like Yugoslavia, the word "intellectual" had a broader meaning. Intellectuals were the people who saw through party propaganda to the reality of the Yugoslav situation. When I was in Yugoslavia I met people with a sophisticated and an acute understanding of the dynamics of repression.

Milovan Djilas wrote a book, *The New Class*, 1957, in which he described the nomenklatura, the bureaucracy that holds power in socialist states. In Yugoslavia, there were two new classes, the nomenklatura and the intellectuals. And it was the intellectuals who held the best hope for the future of the country.

In 1940 Arthur Koestler wrote a book describing Stalinist oppression, which he titled *Darkness at Noon*. In Yugoslavia, in the late 1980s, there existed, side by side, both darkness and brightness at noon.

The feelings of hope and despair I picked up in what was Yugoslavia in 1988 both turned out to be justified. In Slovenia, since that time, respect for human rights has improved dramatically. Bosnia, by contrast, has become the scene of some of the worst contemporary human rights atrocities. What was then a jumble of possibilities has now sorted itself into extremes. Now, there is shading from light to pitch black as we move across the terrain of former Yugoslavia from Slovenia to Bosnia.

CHAPTER FIVE

POLAND: MAY 1989

The International Helsinki Federation continued to use its annual general meetings as a device to assist in pushing aside the rusting Iron Curtain. After Yugoslavia in 1988, the Federation next targetted Poland, in May 1989.

When a regime moves from repression to democracy, the transition can happen in one of two ways – instantaneously or gradually.

An abrupt transition is the easiest and least painful. International human rights standards which were being violated one day can be respected the next. One example is the defeat of Nazi Germany, and the occupation by the Allied forces of the Federal Republic of Germany. Another example is the negotiated withdrawal of South Africa from what was called South West Africa and the establishment of Namibia.

Gradual transitions are more common. The violators hang on to vestiges of power, maintain privileges, legislate immunities. They hamstring their successors to prevent much undoing of what the violators have done. This has been the pattern in Latin America, as various countries have moved away from the doctrine of the national security state to democracy.

Transitional regimes are subject to the same standards as established regimes. Moving in the direction of realization of human rights, for transitional regimes, is not good enough. There is no indulgence or dispensation, just because they are transitional regimes.

Indeed, if anything, the obligations on a new regime, whether transitional or totally reformed, are greater than on established democratic regimes. There is a duty to compensate victims of human rights violations. Perpetrators of gross and flagrant violations of human rights must be brought to justice. The truth of what happened in the past must be disclosed. These obligations are imposed on both established and new regimes. But established democratic regimes should have no need to fulfil them, except to prosecute perpetrators who attempt to seek haven in their territory. In addition to the difficulties of establishing new institutions, new regimes must also come to grips with the crimes of the past.

That is the legal reality. But it is not the practical reality. Inevitably, once a regime shifts course, once it accepts in principle that human rights should be realized, and moves to implement at least some of these rights, the vigil of the international community relaxes. Remedies cease to be invoked. Judgment is suspended. Condemnations cease. The intent is taken for the achievement.

Six very specific problems arise from this relaxation. One is that halfway measures may be accepted as satisfactory. If international attention slackens before respect for human rights is complete, then the victory for human rights may be partial only. Just because the situation has improved, it does not necessarily mean it will continue to improve. The improvement in human rights in any country is almost invariably linked to international pressure. When that pressure ceases, the momentum for change may also cease.

Second, progress in human rights realization may not just slow down or stop. It may actually reverse. The struggle for human rights in the country of violations ends up being a political struggle. Human rights advocates may win the day because of the balance of forces in their favour, but if international attention slackens, the power equation changes. The forces of repression may do more than just stop progress. They may be able to undermine the achievements that have been made.

Once a problem is seen as having been solved, or on the way to being resolved, it is hard to refocus the world community on the problem. International human rights pressure has its own inertia: it is hard to stop once started, and hard to start once stopped.

A certain amount of wishful thinking goes into the solution of any human rights problem, a temptation to believe a problem is solved once it is on the way to being solved. Dealing with a half-solved problem is more time consuming, more messy, more intricate than just pretending it is solved.

The third specific problem that comes with the relaxation of vigilance is the transformation of the form of oppression. In a transition regime, repression often continues, but in a less visible, less blatant way. In Latin America, for instance, we see democratically elected regimes and government-sponsored death squads at one and the same time. The military dictatorships have, by and large, gone. But violations continue in a way that is more difficult to attribute to the regimes.

Fourthly, attitudes of repression continue even when the forms of repression have gone. Democracy is more than just a structure: it is a culture, a set of attitudes, a way of life. And so is repression. The mere existence of a transition regime does not change a culture of repression into a human rights culture. People still relate to each other in the old ways. Intolerance persists, even though its weapons are fewer.

Totalitarianism is habit forming. Totalitarianism is more than politics: it is a way of life, a pattern of relationships between government and citizens. Cruelty is corrupting. It is character destroying, both for the perpetrators and the victims. Totalitarianism may be politically motivated and ideologically founded but, over time, the political reasons fade, the ideology becomes a memory. All that remains is the behaviour.

Ideological revision may justify a totally different political system, but old habits cannot be switched off because political expediency or philosophical shifts dictate it. The patterns continue after their political justifications and ideological foundations have gone.

The cruel remain cruel: they continue to harass, to beat, to intimidate, to humiliate. The victims continue to behave as victims: they remain passive, cynical, pessimistic. The state is frozen in a configuration. Its leaders attempt a thaw, and the more disciplined will follow. But for many the attempt is irrelevant.

The past has a momentum that keeps it moving into the present, which is as hard to stop as a rapidly moving train. A totalitarian past takes a long time to stop.

How do people come to believe what they do believe? For some, beliefs are matters of thought, of logic, of analysis. For these people, different thought, different logic, a different analysis, will lead to different beliefs.

For others, belief comes through action. Belief serves as a rationalization for past behaviour. State terrorists may terrorize out of conviction, out of convenience, or cowardice. Joining or condoning state violence may help a career or help avoid a sanction.

When people act out of convenience or cowardice, a justifying ideology helps ennoble their actions. The morally wrong becomes morally right. A totalitarian ideology is a fig leaf to cover the naked brutality of the thugs of the state. When the thinkers have long abandoned the ideology, the thugs continue to hold on to the fig leaf.

The apologists of totalitarianism continue to advocate its ideology long after the political realities that put it in place have disappeared. Totalitarianism has compromised its practitioners. The compromise becomes an indenture from which they cannot escape. Escape is a form of self-denunciation, of self-condemnation. Those who are prepared to engage in this self-condemnation are few.

The fifth and related problem in a transitional regime is a continuation of personnel. West Germany after World War II went through a process of denazification. Although the program was not completely successful, the intent was to remove all the perpetrators and their supporters from power. In a transition regime, there is no similar cleansing. Perpetrators remain in power. The names at the top may change, but the rank and file of the military, the police, and the administration remain by and large the same. When these people remain, and their attitudes don't change, the potential for trouble is obvious.

The sixth problem is the crystallization of pre-existing patterns. Repression exists to take power away from people who would have it in a democracy and give it to those who would not have it otherwise. If democracy returns, the majority may be enfranchised. But in a transitional regime, they are not necessarily in a position to reacquire all that was taken away from them, to reverse the expropriations, the divestitures, the ill gotten gains of repression. Transitional regimes protect what have become the vested interests. The majority may be able to prevail at the ballot box, but may remain power- less in other ways.

Disadvantage is not first and foremost political. And it takes more than political change to overcome disadvantage once it has been inflicted. The cure to a long period of inflicted disadvantage may be as lengthy as the disease. Transitional regimes, habitually, do not even address themselves to this sort of problem.

Poland, during the late 1980s, was living this transition dynamic. It went through a period of liberalization. And there were strong political reasons for its doing so. The Gorbachev era of glasnost and perestroika in the Soviet Union made a Soviet invasion of Poland less likely. The Polish declaration of martial law in December 1981 and the criminalization of Solidarity were "jus- tified" at the time by fear of Soviet invasion, but that justification no longer seemed credible.

The economy was going through progressive impoverishment. Inflation in 1988 was 70 percent. The black-market rate in that year for U.S. dollars quadrupled. Consumer goods disappeared from the stores. There was a two- decade waiting period for an apartment, and Poland had an estimated 300,000 homeless people. Increasing pollution was making the water undrinkable and the air unbreathable. The economic policies of the regime were clearly not working. Economic liberalization is an attempt to shift the economy into a growth pattern. Political liberalization is a necessary partner. It is also an appeasement to those discontented with the regime for both eco- nomic and political reasons.

Poland had a strong, committed, organized and disciplined opposition – Solidarity. Solidarity was more than just a trade union. In an economy where small, private-enterprise businesses were uncommon, most of the population were employees. The self-employed were the exceptions. Solidarity had, as part of its purpose, a whole list of political and human rights platforms. The demands of Solidarity were not just demands for higher wages or better work-ing conditions. There were equal demands for political and legal reform.

The weakness of the economy and the strength of Solidarity interconnect-ed. Despite its illegality during martial law, Solidarity remained the effective voice, the leadership of the workers. A wave of strikes in the spring and in August 1988 sparked by the poor conditions of the economy were Solidarity-led strikes. Or, rather, the workers on strike accepted the Solidarity leadership and Solidarity demands as their own. Settling the strikes meant more than negotiating workers wages. It meant negotiating the political program of Solidarity.

The government entered into a prolonged negotiation with Solidarity. The negotiations began in February 1989 and continued until April 5, involv-ing hundreds of negotiators on both sides, negotiating virtually every aspect of Polish life. The concluding document was over 400 pages.

Not every aspect of the negotiations led to agreement. Much of the 400 pages listed disagreements. But much, also, was settled.

The most significant results relegalized Solidarity and scheduled democra-tic elections for 35 percent of the seats of the existing chamber of Parliament, the Sejm. A second, advisory chamber, the Senate, was to be created. Its mem-bership was to be totally democratically elected. Elections were scheduled for June.

Solidarity was not what it was in 1980 and 1981. Before martial law, Solidarity was a mass movement of ten million people uniting the non gov-ernmental sector. There was virtual unanimity that Solidarity was the appro-priate vehicle for channelling opposition sentiment.

The seven years of illegality that Solidarity suffered led to the radicaliza-tion of some, and the apathy of others. Substantial debate in nongovernmen-tal circles took place in 1988 as to whether Solidarity should have entered into the round-table talks at all. Solidarity itself was an aging group, its leadership intact, but without significant infusion of new blood.

The apathy of the opposition is the flip side of the deterioration of power caused by the years of repression. The situation in Poland had been so bad for so long, the hopes of 1980 and 1981 so convincingly squelched, the vestiges of tyranny so clear, the liberalization so half-hearted, that people developed a cynical wait-and-see attitude. The liberalization of 1989 could not compare in its enthusiasm and its mobilization of hopes with the liberalization of 1980 and 1981.

In many aspects – for freedom of expression, for freedom of association, for due process in the courts – the round-table discussions coincided with, benefited from, and reinforced a liberalization of the Polish state. Yet to talk of liberalization was to use a misnomer. A more apt characterization of what was happening was disaggregation of tyranny. Some elements of the state were committed to liberalization. Others carried on as if nothing had happened.

An early example of this disaggregation was the Nowa Huta strike of steelworkers in April and May of 1988. Strikers had occupied the steel works illegally, and sat in occupation for days. Management refused to negotiate with the workers because management refused to recognize the right to strike or the leadership of the workers.

The minister of the interior, Cz Kiszczak, accepted an offer of a Solidarity delegation to serve as an intermediary between the workers and management. On May 5, the delegation entered the steelworks, talked with the workers, and then with management. As a result of this intervention, management agreed to begin talks with the workers.

That night the police raided the steelworks. The strikers were arrested and jailed, and a dozen workers were brutally beaten by the police.

Afterwards, the minister of the interior was apologetic. He arranged for the quick release of the detained workers from jail. But no disciplinary or punitive action was taken against the raiding police.

It is, of course, possible that the minister of the interior planned the events. A more plausible explanation was that the left hand did not know what the right hand was doing. The leadership wanted to be liberal, but those it had turned to in the past to be violent just acted out the old patterns.

This disaggregation of repression was manifested in a graphic way with the occurrence of beatings. Beatings of dissidents by the authorities had occurred in Poland with such frequency, violence, and pervasiveness that they had every appearance of being a state policy.

The Polish Helsinki Watch Group, in its report for 1988, tabulated 190 names of people harassed by beatings by the authorities. The actual cases known to the Group for that year exceeded that number: there were beatings by prison guards of those detained; officers of the militia and secret service beat people in the streets, in their cars, and in their homes; police and security forces beat people during peaceful demonstrations and meetings; there were beatings associated with strike breaking; and there were beatings by unknown perpetrators in circumstances that led the Group to believe the police were responsible.

The number of known beatings was greater in 1988 than 1987, but that fact does not in itself contradict the perception that Poland was a more liberal country in 1988 than in 1987.

It is one of the perverse effects of liberalization that, in its early stages, it leads to increased victimization. When repression is at its most severe, very little is permitted. Transgressions are punished with severity. As a result, very little is attempted.

As repression eases, people attempt to assert and expand their new freedom. They test the boundaries of the new dispensation. Some components of the state ease their repression. Others do not. There are cross currents of increased tolerated activity and increased brutality at one and the same time.

As liberalization in Poland solidified, beatings became more selective. Warsaw, the capital, a centre for international visitors and the international media, was spared. Well-known figures were treated with respect. But in university towns, and against politically active students and young professors, the pattern of beatings continued as before.

The Polish Helsinki Watch Group, in a report presented to the annual general meeting of the International Helsinki Human Rights Federation held in Warsaw April 21 to 25, 1989, detailed a mass attack by police on demonstrators as late as April 2nd. Two thousand demonstrators had gathered for a peace demonstration. Police blocked all exits to the square where the demonstrators gathered. Fights broke out with the police when demonstrators tried to leave the square. The police attacked with truncheons. They dragged people away. People were beaten as they were leaving the square. The Watch Group listed twenty victims of beatings, six of whom were so severely beaten they had to be taken to hospital.

Political killings, even at the height of martial law, had not been a common occurrence. The best-known case was that of Father Jerzy Popieluszko, murdered in 1984 by three high-ranking officers of the interior ministry. The priest had been the chaplain of the Solidarity movement.

Yet, by the end of January, 1989, there were already two deaths reminiscent of the murder of Father Popieluszko. Father Stefan Niedzielak was found dead January 21st. The autopsy revealed a fracture of the spine. Father Stanislaw Suchowolec was found dead January 30th. The official story was he died of carbon monoxide poisoning. Both had been involved in independent activity. Father Suchowolec had been the victim of two prior attacks. There had also been a pattern of anonymous threats and attacks by unknown perpetrators on other independently minded priests. Many people in Poland believe the deaths of these two priests were politically caused.

Perhaps the best way to see the pattern in the waltz of tyranny in Poland is to look at political prosecutions. Again, the partners in the dance seemed to be stepping on each other's feet.

There were no political prisoners in Poland in 1989. Political imprisonment ceased, by and large, in 1986. Even before then, the sentences for political imprisonment were gradually decreasing. In the summer of 1986, the jurisdiction for political offences was transferred from the general courts (under the jurisdiction of the ministry of justice, which sentenced those convicted of political offences to jail) to the misdemeanour courts (under the jurisdiction of the ministry of the interior, which impose fines on those convicted of political offences). There was an amnesty for political prisoners then currently detained.

The 1986 shift was an obvious improvement, but not a complete one. When penalties for such offences as transporting illegal publications or producing illegal publications became less severe, the volume of prosecutions increased dramatically. Under the new dispensation, people would be prosecuted for having a couple of issues of an illegal magazine in their possession, something that did not happen under the old procedures.

As well, the misdemeanour courts were a travesty of due process. Even the regular penal courts gave serious cause for concern because of the lack of independence of the judges from the state. However, in political cases, even though the result may have been a foregone conclusion, in the penal courts there was at least some semblance of due process. The prosecution presented its case. The defence presented its case. And the judge decided.

In the misdemeanour courts, in political cases, there was no due process. The defence was not allowed to present evidence or argue its case. The prosecution did not bother to present evidence against the accused. All that was presented was the allegation. And the court convicted.

The trial took place in the absence of the accused if he did not appear when notified, no matter how justifiable the reason for his absence. If the accused did appear and asked for an adjournment to retain counsel, the adjournment request was denied. If the accused appeared with counsel, the tribunal often did not allow counsel to take part in the hearing.

The misdemeanour court, besides having the power to impose fines, had the power to impose forfeiture. What was forfeited was not only illegal literature, or publications. Anything that contained or displayed the illegal literature was confiscated. Sometimes the confiscated items were of great value. Their confiscation involved a substantial loss. The confiscation of cars containing illegal literature was commonplace. Computers with illegal messages in their memories were confiscated. The government even reserved the right to confiscate apartments and houses used for illegal publishing.

What was illegal was not just political literature. Ecological or environmental literature was subject to prosecution. As long as the publication itself was not sanctioned, if its point of view was different from that of the state, the person in possession was subject to prosecution.

Appeals from these misdemeanour convictions were possible, but only to a second level misdemeanour court. Reversals on appeal were rare.

Many of the misdemeanour court judges had no legal training and no security of tenure. They were bureaucrats in the interior ministry.

A prosecutor's office inspection report confirmed these problems. According to a news story of this report, "Hearing of witnesses for the prosecution is a rare event. Not even one case of calling for evidence [by the prosecution] was observed … it was never checked [by the court] whether the accused wanted to be assisted by counsel for the defence."

Some lawyers boycotted political prosecutions in misdemeanour courts. They felt that their very presence gave an aura of legitimacy to these courts they did not deserve. Those lawyers who continued to attend had a frustrating, impossible task on their hands.

Misdemeanour courts dealt with far more than political offences. In 1988 they processed some 600,000 cases a year, about three times the number of the higher courts, but of that 600,000 only about 1,000 were political prosecutions. The legalization of Solidarity and the round-table agreement on elections meant that much of the literature that was illegal before was now legal. People had been prosecuted, as well as beaten, by the authorities, for carrying Solidarity literature and slogans. That stopped happening. The political prosecutions tapered off (in the first three months of 1989, there were sixty political prosecutions) but these cases manifested all the worst features of the misdemeanour courts.

On April 12 Marek Jasinski was convicted in Breslau of possession of subversive literature. He was a leader of the Czech-Polish Solidarity movement. At the time of the charge, a Czech counterpart in the movement was visiting Jasinski. The Czech was evicted by the Polish authorities to the Czech border; Jasinski's library of Czech and English literature was seized and confiscated; and he was fined 80,000 zlotys.

On April 21 a client of Piotr Andrzewski, a legal member of the Polish Helsinki Watch Group, was convicted in Warsaw. The penalty included costs against the accused plus confiscation of books for which the prosecution was launched.

Solidarity raised the question of the misdemeanour courts in the round-table talks. Their proposal was to transfer the courts from the ministry of the interior to the ministry of justice, which is responsible for the administration of the superior courts. The theory was that, with that transfer, the misdemeanour courts would acquire those elements of due process used by the superior courts. The government rejected the proposal. The matter was not resolved by the talks.

During the talks, Jerzy Ciemniewski, a member of the Polish Helsinki Watch Group and a participant in the talks, raised the case of an illegal publishing office which had 300 copies of Karl Popper's *The Open Society and Its Enemies* seized by state officials. The book itself was not banned and was available in Polish book stores. The answer Ciemniewski got was that the books had been destroyed, so his intervention was pointless.

Immediately after the International Helsinki Human Rights Federation meeting in Warsaw, I joined an International Helsinki Federation delegation that met, on April 24, with officials of the interior ministry, including the deputy minister, General Brigadier Zbigniew Pudysz. At that meeting the International Helsinki Federation raised its concerns about the functioning of misdemeanour courts.

International Helsinki Federation representatives asked that the courts be made independent of government, that the prosecution be required to prove its case, the defence be allowed to present evidence, that there be a right to counsel. We asked that political prosecutions cease, pending cases be discontinued; confiscated literature and other seized material returned; and that political offences be repealed from the misdemeanour code.

The response the International Helsinki Federation got was less than satisfactory. The attitude of the officials to the concern for independence of the judges was that the principle of independence was already in the law. A planned reform of the misdemeanour courts included a reaffirmation of that principle.

However, while the principle of the independence of the courts was indeed in Polish law, so were other principles which undercut and contradicted that principle. Besides independence, the law articulated the principles of unity of power and the leading role of the Communist Party. In the legislated hierarchy of tasks of the courts, first came its task as custodian of the political system of the state. Second came its task to protect the achievements of the working people, i.e. the state. Protecting rights of citizens was far down the list. A judge was considered an advocate and co-author of socialism. The notion that a judge could be disengaged from politics was considered a "bourgeois fiction."

Practically, the dependence of the judiciary on the state was shown in a number of different ways. There was no security of tenure or security of compensation. A dismissal procedure without due process was based solely on the state's judgment of the judge's personal suitability.

The International Helsinki Federation pressed the matter of independence with interior officials, expressing the position that independence required security of tenure and security of compensation. Declarations of principle were not enough. That position was met with silence.

The concern the International Helsinki Federation expressed about the lack of due process met with an equally unsatisfactory response. On the one hand, officials acknowledged there were procedural problems in these courts. The draft reform of the misdemeanour law addressed the question of increasing procedural guarantees, of requiring the court to allow the participation of the defence. The officials informed the meeting that instructions had recently been sent to the misdemeanour courts instructing them of the necessity to observe procedural guarantees, including the right to defence.

On the other hand, officials talked about the need to retain informality in the courts that deal with petty offences. Officials said there was no desire to have a procedure as complicated as in the superior courts. The very fact that instructions could be given to these misdemeanour courts by the interior ministry on procedural guarantees highlighted the lack of independence of these courts from the ministry. The rejection of defence evidence was, itself, justified by officials on grounds that the defence counsel and accused often attempt to introduce into court evidence that was inadmissible according to the rules of evidence.

Polish Helsinki Watch members presented the concern that books were being seized and burned. That concern was met with the response that books were being pulped, not burned, as if the manner of destruction mattered.

In response to the Helsinki Federation's request that political prosecutions cease, officials said that the law must be respected. When there is activity against the law, there should be activity to restore the law. There has to be a sanction for each infringement; law cannot just be ignored. The Helsinki Federation's suggestion that the law itself was wrong and should be repealed met with no response at all.

The April 24 meeting itself was long (two hours with the officials, and another hour with the deputy minister) and frank. At times, the exchange between the officials and the Helsinki Federation delegation was testy. One official complained that the Polish members of the delegation were taking advantage of the fact that international members were present to put forward their own agenda. Another official asserted that the Polish group should establish its status according to Polish law. (Polish law requires registration of associations.) The officials, as a group, criticized Polish Helsinki Watch reports as being often inaccurate in their facts.

Marek Nowicki, one of the Polish members of the delegation, had been taken forcibly to the interior ministry building three years earlier by the authorities. He had been detained for forty-eight hours and interrogated about his Helsinki Watch involvement. It was a measure of how much matters had changed that he was now meeting with the deputy minister to discuss the very matters about which he had been interrogated. While appreciating the progress that had been made, the International Helsinki Federation delegation, nonetheless, rejected the criticisms that had been offered.

The delegation asserted that officials should be meeting and discussing with Polish Helsinki Watch group members about human rights violations in Poland, whether there were international guests present or not, and that the Watch Group should be free to register or not under the law of associations as it saw fit.

The disadvantage of registration was that it allowed state control, through the courts, of registered associations. The state had the right to rummage through the books and files of registered associations to see what they were doing and whether or not it conformed to what they were "supposed" to be doing. There had been prosecutions for deviation from the objects and stated plans of registered associations. At the round-table talks, state control of non-governmental organizations was a bone of contention. It remained one of the unsettled issues, the state insisting on maintaining this control, despite Solidarity objections.

Finally, the International Helsinki Federation delegation noted that the same set of facts can lead to different interpretations. Particularly when there is a violent clash between citizens and authorities, the citizens and the authorities often come away with differing testimony of the event. The International Helsinki Federation delegation stressed that there has to be room for differing appreciations of these events. The authorities' version cannot always be treated as factual, and the citizens' version cannot always be treated as false.

Freedom of expression and freedom of association manifested this same half-hearted development that due process showed. The round-table talks generated an improvement in the situation, but not as much as had been hoped. Solidarity was then able to publish, legally, union newspapers and periodicals. However, the censorship laws, the power to censor, remained in force.

The ban on bringing in single copies of publications from abroad was lifted. However, the ban on bringing in multiple copies remained.

Television and radio remained virtual state propaganda monopolies. The only concession was that thirty minutes a week on TV and sixty minutes a week on radio was allowed for the expression of views other than state positions. There was to be no opposition participation in management of radio and TV.

Rationing of paper for printing was maintained until January 1, 1990. With rationing, state printing houses got the overwhelming percentage of the rationed paper. The Catholic press got only 4 percent of the paper available.

For freedom of association, a main bone of contention had been the Scouts. Scouting has been traditionally popular in Poland. The communists took over scouting and turned it to a paramilitary communist youth movement. The thaw of 1980 and 1981, which saw the growth of Solidarity, also saw a renaissance of traditional scouting. It became a rallying point for youth, much like Solidarity had become for adults. The imposition of martial law did not lead to a total reassertion of communist control over the scouting movement. Nominally, communist patterns of authority were reasserted, but scouting activities were conducted more in line with traditional scouting than with communist ideals.

The liberalization led to a breakaway scouting movement. Fifty independent scoutmasters, at a meeting in Warsaw on February 12, 1989, decided to set up an independent scout union, separate from the Communist Party. Scouts from this breakaway scouts movement provided the organizational infrastructure for the International Helsinki Federation meeting in Warsaw in April.

The right of the breakaway scouts union to function as an independent organization was a subject of the round-table talks. The authorities refused to accept the principle of pluralism in scouting. Government spokesmen insisted that the official Polish Scouts union maintain the monopoly over all scouting symbols.

Poland is a land of the dead. There were more Polish Jews killed in the Holocaust than Jews from any other country. Fully one half of the six million Jews killed in the Holocaust, 3.1 million, were Polish Jews. The Nazi massacre of the Jews in Europe started with Einsatzgruppen killing units, shooting Jews where they were found. That, as a technique, turned out to be too slow for the Nazis, who turned to a concentration-camp and death-camp system, with killing by poison gas, Zyklon B. The concentration camps, such as Buchenwald and Dachau in Germany, Theresienstadt in Bohemia, and Auschwitz in Poland, were multiple-purpose camps: for prisoners of war, for slave labour, as well as for killing. The death camps specialized in killing alone. All of the six Nazi death camps – Birkenau, Treblinka, Chelmno, Belzec, Majdanek and Sobibor – were in Poland.

It is impossible to talk of human rights in Poland without reference to the Holocaust, which formed the origins of the post-war human rights movement. The ghosts of the Holocaust hover over Poland, haunting the contemporary human rights debate.

The Nazi killing machine could not have functioned anywhere without locals who knew the language, the geography, the identity of the Jews in the population. Poland had its share of collaborators, war criminals, mass murderers.

The Polish record of resistance to the Holocaust compares with that of other nations. There is also a long list of Polish nationals who risked their lives to save Jews. There are more Poles in Yad Vashem, more Poles honoured by the Heroes and Martyrs Remembrance Authority in Israel, for saving Jews, than nationals of any other country.

The bulk of the population neither collaborated nor resisted, but simply watched in horror. Now they remain bewildered that the horrors they saw could have happened.

Anti-Semitism and insensitivity to the nature of anti-Semitism remain a problem in Poland. In 1968 there was a wave of state-sanctioned anti-Semitism, a purge of Jewish Poles from official positions, and many surviving Jewish Poles left Poland. The Jewish community that remains behind is small and aging.

A Polish Helsinki Watch group member reporting to the International Helsinki Federation annual general meeting in Warsaw in April, 1989, when asked about anti-Semitism in Poland today, responded that there is no reason for it at this time. The unthinking implication of that response is that there was reason for anti-Semitism in the past, and there may be reason for anti-Semitism in the future.

Because I was a speaker at a public symposium in Warsaw in 1989 on the independence of the judiciary, I was given a petition by a member of the audience. The petition read that a certain named person "is a victim of the evil will of international Jewry's Polish section." I was asked to help the victim of this Jewish persecution.

A culture grows from variety. It dies from uniformity. Promoting and enhancing minority cultures is not only of value to the minorities themselves. It is of value as well for the energizing effect it has on the majority culture.

The violation of the human rights of a cultural minority can be approached from two different extremes: forced assimilation or total rejection. Official Poland, even today, for the memory of its Jewish minority killed in the Holocaust, oscillates between these extremes.

When I was there in 1989, Official Poland did not deny the Holocaust. But it denied the Jewish nature of the Holocaust. At Auschwitz, where the Polish government has established a museum, the state signs talked of four million victims of Hitler's genocides of Polish and other nations, killed at that place.

The Auschwitz museum located at Auschwitz I, the concentration camp of the Auschwitz complex, has five buildings with general displays and nine buildings displaying the persecution of fourteen different nations. One of the buildings is devoted to persecution of the Jews. A person who missed that building would have had little idea of what the Holocaust or Auschwitz was all about.

Birkenau, the death camp of the Auschwitz complex, a much larger facility than Auschwitz I, has no museum or display at all. It is a poorly maintained and deteriorating site. Birkenau is a vast sea of chimneys. While some buildings still stand, most have disappeared through neglect, decay, or destruction. All that remains is their chimneys. When I visited, Auschwitz it was busy with Polish school children. Birkenau was empty.

The purpose of this official forced assimilation in death was not so much anti-Semitism as communist propaganda. The communists portrayed themselves as the liberators of Auschwitz, the liberators of Poland from Nazism. The official guide book of Auschwitz warned of the danger of revival of Nazism in West Germany, a revival that could lead to a re-invasion of Poland. Communists apparently felt that their warnings and message of salvation would be diluted if the official story of Auschwitz talked of Polish Jews being killed rather than just Poles.

The desecration of the Jewish dimension of the Holocaust, the attempt to make the memory of the Holocaust Judenrein, was symbolized by the establishment of a Carmelite convent at Auschwitz I in 1984. The convent was housed in a building that the Nazis used to stock Zyklon B gas for mass extermination. Catholic leaders agreed with Jewish leaders, in 1987, to relocate the convent. But the convent remained. In 1989, opposing the relocation, 1,375 Polish citizens of the town of Auschwitz (called "Oswiecim" in Polish) signed an open letter.

The other extreme, of rejection, is manifested by the mourning of the dead. What was lost in the Holocaust was not only the lives of the victims. What was lost was survivors to mourn the victims. The Jewish cemeteries in Poland, where the Jewish dead from before the Holocaust are buried, have fallen into disrepair. Gravestones have crumbled and toppled; weeds and bushes have grown over the sites. For those Jews who died both before and during the Holocaust, there is no one left to mourn.

At the time the International Helsinki Federation was meeting in Warsaw, there were two significant anniversaries. One was the name day of Father Jerzy Popieluszko. April 23, the day of Father Jerzy's patron saint, is the day on which his death is commemorated. April 19 is the anniversary of the commencement of the Warsaw ghetto uprising.

The two events were remembered in very different ways. St. Stanislaw Kostka church, where Father Jerzy Popieluszko is buried was, on April 23, thronged. It has become a shrine, a destination for pilgrims. It is filled with plaques and gifts from all over Poland.

The Monument to the Heroes of the Warsaw Ghetto was, on that same day, by comparison, abandoned. It is significant that the Monument memorializes only those who fought in the revolt, not all those who were massacred. A few floral wreaths at the foot of the monument were the only indication there was any contemporary interest in Poland in commemorating the event at all.

The genocide of the Jews of Poland has forced Poland into a cultural homogenization. There has been a downward spiral in the Polish cultural dialectic, which makes it difficult for those who remain to appreciate or to understand what was lost. An article in that April 23, 1989, issue of the

Warsaw Voice, an official English-language newspaper, referred to a recent revival of Polish interest in Jewish culture as "rather boring."

Virtually everyone in Poland has his own story of personal tragedy from the war. Each has his own relatives or friends to mourn. To move beyond that, to mourn what Poland has lost as a whole, has become an insurmountable task.

The background of the Holocaust has had a muting effect on the contemporary Polish human rights debate. There is a muting effect on the indignation and sense of wrong. Present wrongs pale in comparison to past wrongs.

There is a muting affect on passions. The extravagance of the results of past passions makes the players cautious now about being too heated in the pursuit of current causes. There has been a muting effect on hopes. When so much has already been lost beyond retrieval, what is to be gained in the future is only relative. There is no paradise waiting in the future, only a movement from hell to limbo. Poland is now free from communism. However, the shadows of the past, both Nazi and communist, cloud the Polish present and dim the future.

CHAPTER SIX

THE SOVIET UNION:
JUNE 1990

The boldest and most significant of the forays of the International Helsinki Federation into Eastern Europe was its annual general meeting in June 1990. Surrounding the meeting days, the International Helsinki Federation held two days of public hearings, as well as several private meetings with officials, in which the Federation thoroughly canvassed the contemporary human rights situation in the Soviet Union.

By 1990 there had been dramatic improvements in the human rights situation of the Soviet Union. The Soviet Union was a drastically different place from what it once had been. The very fact that the International Helsinki Federation could have had its meeting there was significant. We were the first nongovernmental international human rights organization to hold a meeting in the Soviet Union.

Despite the progress that had been made, a whole host of problems remained. There were difficulties of three sorts. There were difficulties the International Helsinki Federation suffered. There were more general human rights problems that were a continuation, in lessened form, of the problems of the pre-Gorbachev era. And there were new problems that had arisen because of the changes that had occurred.

First there were the problems the International Helsinki Federation suffered. In a general sense, the Soviet system was one of total administrative discretion. There was no rule of law. The courts performed no independent supervisory function over the administration to assure that it conformed to the law. The leading role of the Communist Party meant that the authorities did whatever they thought fit. Socialism meant that the authorities interfered in virtually all components of everyday life. Revolution meant that violence was to be used to realize state aims whenever necessary.

One of the most intrusive aspects of this interference in daily living was interference with freedom of movement. This interference had three components to it: obstacles to entry to the Soviet Union, obstacles to exit from the Soviet Union, and obstacles to movement within the Soviet Union.

For the International Helsinki Federation, the problems focused on entry to the Soviet Union. Western Europeans and North Americans needed visas for entry to the Soviet Union. Eastern Europe did not need visas, but needed invitations. They were advised to get visas as a matter of practice, to ensure their entry at the border, even though they were in principle not required.

Visas for those attending the International Helsinki Federation meeting were given out at the last minute, hours before scheduled flights, and in some cases only after flights had been postponed or cancelled. Visas were delayed, even for people who had made visa requests months in advance. Consular officials balked at giving visas. It was only after repeated requests by the International Helsinki Federation headquarters, and the direct intervention of the ministry of foreign affairs that visas were obtained.

Every state has the right to require a visa policy, and deny a visa to whomever it wishes. What was reflective of the bureaucratic discretionary Soviet system was the last-minute way in which visas were issued. The Helsinki Federation held its annual general meeting in Moscow, immediately before the Copenhagen Human Rights Meeting, and one year before the 1991 Moscow Human Dimensions meeting. The reason was to test the waters for Moscow for 1991. We wanted to find out what the conditions would be, not only for us in 1991, but also for all nongovernmental organizations who wanted to attend and engage in parallel activities to the intergovernmental meeting.

Our finding was that conditions were nowhere near satisfactory. The meetings we had were held without harassment or intimidation. But simply getting there had been so difficult that the 1991 meeting could not have been held in the conditions to which we were subject.

A second problem the International Helsinki Federation suffered, which presents another facet of past Soviet oppression had to do with the Serbsky Institute of Forensic Psychiatry. In the late 1960s and 1970s, the Serbsky Institute was used as a prison for political dissidents. Dissidents arrested on political charges were systematically subjected to psychiatric examination. If they were diagnosed as mentally ill, and many of them were when there was no other symptom than their political dissent, then they were subjected to psychiatric detention.

Dr. George Morozov, head of the Serbsky Institute, propagated a theory of a disease he called creeping schizophrenia. Among its symptoms were dissemination of slander against the state, exaggerated belief in any religion, and excessive valuation of the West.

Despite the hollow nature of Soviet justice, prosecutors preferred psychiatric detention to a court trial. A court trial led to automatic conviction, but a case had to be prepared, and punishment was for a fixed period of time. Psychiatric detention did not require the prosecution to assemble a case, except of the most perfunctory nature, and detention was indefinite, until the patient was cured. The behaviour of the prisoner could be controlled with drugs. This drug control was a form of torture not practised in the ordinary Soviet prisons and labour camps.

The Soviet Psychiatric Association was expelled from the World Psychiatric Association because of the abuses of the Serbsky Institute. The World Psychiatric Association, at its October 1989 Congress, re-admitted the Soviet psychiatrists on condition that if psychiatric abuse for political purposes continued, the Association could again reject the Soviet Psychiatric Association.

The International Helsinki Federation, when it was in Moscow, scheduled a meeting with the Serbsky Institute to discuss past problems and the present situation. When the Serbsky institution learned that Soviet members of Helsinki Watch were part of the delegation, they asked that these Soviets not come to the meeting. The Institute said it refused to meet with "former patients." In fact, two of three Soviets who were part of the delegation had been examined by the Serbsky Institute for mental illness after being charged with political offences. But they had not been found insane and served their time for their political offences in the regular prison system.

When the Federation found that it could not bring the Soviet members of the delegation along, it felt compelled to cancel the meeting. The meeting did not take place.

The problems faced by the International Helsinki Federation were reflections of more general problems in the Soviet Union. Freedom of movement was still not a generally recognized right. There was a law under consideration by the Supreme Soviet that accepted, in principle, freedom of movement. According to this draft law, everyone was entitled to a passport on application. People in an employ where they learned state secrets could be denied exit visas, but only if they had been advised in advance of the exit problems their work might entail. The denial could only be for a period of five years after they got the work. Refusals were subject to review by the courts.

The law, itself, and this was a problem in general with human rights law in the Soviet Union, proceeded through the Supreme Soviet at a snail's pace. While the law was being considered, the policy behind the law was not being implemented.

Long-term refuseniks in the Soviet Union, people who were denied exit visas for ten years or more, appeared to have little or no knowledge of state secrets, even though that was the official reason for the refusal. And there was no court review allowed for the refusals.

At the Moscow meetings, I met one refusenik named Anatoly Genis, who has been refused exit for fourteen years, since 1976, because of simple calculations he did as an engineer, from 1970 to 1973, seventeen years previously. His wife and three children had been allowed to leave, to the U.S. So he was denied not only the right to leave, but also the right to be reunited with his family.

Another flagrant case, which the International Helsinki Federation mentioned to the Soviet authorities, both in Moscow and in Copenhagen, was the case of Irina Voronkevich, a seventy-eight-year-old grandmother. She had retired in 1976 as a professor of history. Yet she has been refused permission to leave on the grounds of knowledge of state secrets.

Emigration law, in 1990, besides imposing the obstacle of state secrets also imposed poor-relative and relative-invitation obstacles. A Soviet citizen could not emigrate unless he/she received an invitation from a relative abroad. The existence of a relative at home, who was dependent on him/her for support, could prevent the person from leaving the country.

The draft law retained the poor-relative obstacle, though it could be submitted to judicial review. The draft law removed the requirement of an invitation from a relative abroad, but the relative-invitation obstacle remained while the draft law was being considered. Internal refugees fleeing Armenia to Moscow had in many cases been given U.S. entry visas but denied Soviet exit visas, because no relative in the U.S. had invited them over. They remained stuck in Moscow.

As well, the new law was not retroactive. People refused permission to leave under the present law were not able to benefit from the new law even though, aside from timing, they fitted within its terms.

Freedom of movement was an internal as well as an external problem. There was an internal Soviet passport system. Soviets were allowed to take short trips from one part of the Union to another without permission. But actually moving from one place to another required the permission of the state.

Physically, there were no fences at republic border points, preventing people from moving from one place in the Soviet Union to another. But, if a person did move without permission, he/she would not be assigned a residence and would not be allowed to work. And the children would not be allowed to go to school. For a short while in Moscow, just before the International Helsinki Federation arrived, those who had no official status in Moscow were not allowed to buy food. To buy food, a person had to present a passport. Only those with Moscow passports were allowed to purchase food.

These restrictions on mobility posed a particularly acute problem for those affected by the Chernobyl disaster. There were large areas of the Soviet

Union affected by radioactive contagion. The authorities failed to provide full disclosure of the dangers people faced. And those who wanted to leave, to escape the dangers, were effectively prevented from doing so, by the internal restrictions on freedom of movement.

Problems with the Serbsky Institute and psychiatric abuse, as well, were problems more general than just what the International Helsinki Federation encountered. Political prisoners were detained on psychiatric grounds. The Moscow Helsinki Group identified forty-six cases of alleged psychiatric imprisonment in its list of political prisoners. Those responsible for past abuses should have been prosecuted. Instead, the leadership of the Serbsky Institute responsible for the worst abuses of psychiatry in the late '60s and '70s, including Dr. Morozov, remained in place. The legislation on psychiatric detention, though recently changed, still provided inadequate safeguards to prevent abusive psychiatric detention for political purposes.

The problem of political prisoners was not just a problem of psychiatric abuse. It was a more general problem encompassing people detained in the prisons and labour-camp systems. The purely political offences, anti-Soviet agitation and propaganda, and anti-state slander were removed from the Criminal Code. No one was being held in Soviet prisons for political offences alone.

However, there were from 50 to 188 cases of people detained for ordinary criminal offences, where the evidence of the commission of the offences was slight or nonexistent, and the motivation for the prosecution and detention appeared to be wholly political. The Federation, in Moscow, highlighted the case of Mikhail Kazachkov, arrested fourteen and a half years previously for wanting to leave the Soviet Union without permission. He had been detained in prison since then for standing up for the rights of prisoners. When originally convicted, he had had a secret trial. He was denied the right to counsel of choice. He was not allowed to present evidence in his defense. He never was allowed to see the judgment against him. Since his detention his parents had been denied family visits. He was denied access to his counsel both before his conviction and since. His Soviet counsel continued to be denied access to the government file and the judgment against him.

And regrettably, the case was not an isolated one. Release of political prisoners in the Soviet Union came as it always had, through pressure from the West. When foreign diplomats took up a case with the Soviets, the authorities would discuss it. When Soviet citizens, such as the Moscow Helsinki Watch Group, Soviet parliamentarians, or the person's own lawyer raised a case, they were met with a wall of silence.

Problems for political prisoners did not end when a political prisoner was released. There remained a need for rehabilitation. Prisoners, once released, remained with criminal records that could hamper them throughout their lives.

In a totally socialist state, the government is the employer for virtually all work. When a person has committed a crime against the state, getting work again commensurate with experience and training ranges from difficult to impossible. A convicted criminal not rehabilitated cannot hold public office or be published.

The massive nature of political imprisonment in the Soviet Union led to massive demands for rehabilitation, a finding by the state that no crime was committed, and that the person was exonerated. Since the advent of the Gorbachev era, there were close to a million rehabilitations. But many more still awaited their rehabilitation decrees. Like all other changes, rehabilitation came all too slowly, and without any explanation by the authorities in the meantime of what was happening with the case. Responding to the snail's pace of individual rehabilitations, Gorbachev, on July 13, 1990, ordered the blanket rehabilitation of all victims of Stalinist repression.

Rehabilitation was a problem not just for those sent to prison and labour camps, but as well for those found criminally insane. Psychiatric records needed to be cleared. False psychiatric diagnoses needed to be overturned. The Serbsky Institute, in this, as in other matters, proved recalcitrant.

The problem of political imprisonment does not begin and end with imprisonment itself. It includes the problems of treatment in prison.

Mistreatment of prisoners was not restricted to political prisoners. It was a general, widespread problem from which prisoners generally suffered, no matter what the nature of their crime.

Prisoners in Soviet jails and labour camps were treated in a manner that fell far short of the UN standard minimum rules. There was overcrowding and poor nourishment. Beatings were common. Those in prisons got too little exercise; those in labour camps got too much. Those sentenced to labour camps or to forced labour after trial outside of labour camps were subjected to conditions that amounted to slavery. There was inadequate medical care. Seventy percent of the tuberculosis cases in the USSR were prisoners or former prisoners.

Poor prison conditions are not unique to communist regimes. But the absence of any real control over the prison administration from outside meant that little, if anything, could be done about the worst prison conditions. The Soviet system had an institution called the procuracy, which was designed both to prosecute, and to exercise a supervisory role over the administration of justice, including the prisons. But the combination of functions in one office prevented the supervisory role from being effective. There was legislation proposed to separate the supervisory and prosecutorial role of the procurator's office, but like so many other legislative proposals, its realization was post-poned to the indefinite future.

The International Helsinki Federation made persistent attempts while we were in Moscow to arrange for prison visits by expert nongovernmental prison inspection teams. The attempts got nowhere.

There was a particular problem of supervision or control in relation to army deaths. Each year hundreds of soldiers died outside of combat, in unex-plained circumstances. The families of those killed alleged that they had been murdered by the army, through hazing or for protesting forced labour of sol-diers and conditions of military service. The army was not supervised by the procurator's office, but it had, instead, its own military procurator. The mili-tary procurator refused to investigate any of these allegations but just dis-missed the deaths as suicides of the mentally ill, or as accidents.

I have mentioned pending laws about the right to leave and the supervi-sion of the administration of justice. There were four other laws or pending laws about freedom of expression, about freedom of conscience, about free-dom of association, about judicial control of the administration that high-lighted four other Soviet problems.

The law on freedom of expression, passed June 12, 1990, abolished cen-sorship. It allowed individual citizens to set up newspapers. Immediately before the law was passed, the press in the Soviet Union was free, in the sense that it was allowed to print more or less what it wanted. But it was still illegal. Copies of independent newspapers were haphazardly confiscated by the authorities. Independent newspaper editorial boards, on occasion, were arrest-ed, then released. The newspapers cost many times more than state newspa-pers. Because printing was illegal, the printers charged for the risk of putting out the papers.

Paper for printing was hard to come by. Independent newspapers could not be sold at newspaper kiosks, which were government owned. There had been a number of alarming incidents where the offices of some of the inde-pendent press had been ransacked and burglarized. *Novy Mir*, a government authorized literary journal, but one of the most independent, for instance seri-alizing Alexander Solzhenitsyn's *The Gulag Archipelago*, had to shut down because the authorities refuse to allocate paper to publish it.

The problems of the press highlight the difficulties with having freedom in a socialist state. If a newspaper cannot buy paper on the open market, on the same terms as government newspaper, and if the allocation of newsprint depends on the government, then can there be a truly independent press?

The draft law on freedom of religion allowed for freedom of expression for religious beliefs, as well as religious education. It provided for alternative military service for conscientious objectors.

It is worth noting that the Soviet Union did not provide for conscientious objection. Those who objected to military service out of religious conviction could be sent to jail. There were an estimated 300 such prisoners of peace in Soviet jails in 1990. The detention of conscientious objectors continued while the draft law allowing for conscientious objection went through Parliament.

The draft law was not an answer to all the problems of religious oppression communism has posed. The Russian Orthodox Church was under the direct control of the state. Until the election of the patriarch in June 1990, church officials, bishops, and primates were, in effect, chosen by the state authorities. The church leaders have traditionally been servants of the state.

Immediately after World War II, the Ukrainian Orthodox Church was forcibly merged with the Russian Orthodox Church. There was a massive transfer of Church properties from the Ukrainian Orthodox Church to the Russian Orthodox Church. Before the war, there were only 250 Russian Orthodox churches in West Ukraine. By 1990 there were over 3,000. The increase was largely the result of an expropriation of the properties of the Ukrainian Catholic Church. The Ukrainian Catholic Church reemerged in the Soviet Union, though it was not legal until the draft law on freedom of religion passed. The Ukrainian Catholic Church had no means available, even under the proposed law, to get back the churches, sanctuaries, and monasteries taken from it.

The draft law on freedom of association allowed for any association to come into existence that individuals wished to form. There was to be a requirement of registration, but also a right to register. In 1990, associations were supposed to register. But there was no right of registration. Registration was discretionary. Historically, registration had been refused to any association whose goal did not coincide with the interests of the state. The leading role of the Communist Party meant not only the government, but also the leadership of every registered association, had to be communist. The ending of the leading role of the Communist Party has meant the ending of that requirement.

But the current law was not being operated in accordance with the policy announced in the new draft law. Associations which applied for registration were being rejected. The most significant example was "Memorial," a human rights association that played a key organizational role in the human rights forum that was part of the International Helsinki Federation annual general meeting in Moscow.

Unregistered organizations, nevertheless, functioned. The Soviet Helsinki Watch Group, was, itself, an unregistered association. But unregistered meant illegal. And illegal meant the organization was subject to official harassment and denied the official advantages which registered associations had.

For example, a registered association could invite foreigners to visit, at the expense of the Soviet association. An unofficial association could issue no such invitation. All foreign guests had to come at their expense, in foreign currency, even though the local association may have been both willing and able to pay all expenses in Soviet rubles. Or, to take another example, unregistered associations had great difficulty opening a bank account.

The leading role of the Communist Party continued, in lesser form. The party remained in charge of the military, the police, and the KGB. The party had political groupings, or cells in each of the units that, in effect, ran them. Rather than abolish these cells, reform attempts were directed to try to marginalize them. The policy departments of the forces were to be separated from Community Party cells. And other parties were to be allowed to form their own organizations within these forces as well.

The fourth law allowed for the courts to exercise control over the administration. The law took effect July 1, 1990.

The Soviet constitution said that "citizens of the USSR have the right to lodge a complaint against the actions of official state bodies and public bodies."[1] But until 1988, that was a right without a remedy. There was no legal institution designated by law to which a complaint could be made.

A 1988 law allowed for complaints to the courts against the actions of individual officials. The 1990 law, which superseded the 1988 law, allowed, as well, for the courts to consider complaints about collective decisions by official bodies.

The 1990 law had a number of procedural defects. For instance, when a decision was made on a complaint, the court did not tell the complainant. It told only the official against whom the complaint was made.

Aside from the procedural defects, there was a fundamental problem with making the law work – the historical absence of independence of the judiciary. Like so many other human rights violations in the USSR, the historical lack of independence of judiciary has a theoretical basis.

Traditionally, the courts in the Soviet Union were expected to give priority to the building of socialism and the implementation of Communist Party policy. According to communist jurist S. Kucherov, in case of collision between "the formal requirement of law and Party policy, the law must be subordinated to Party policy."[2] In practice, in politically important prosecutions, the Party would dictate both the verdict and the sentence.

The Supreme Soviet on November 2, 1989, passed a law penalizing interference with court proceedings. However, as a U.S. Helsinki Watch report noted, "Since nearly all judges in the USSR are members of the Communist Party long entrenched in the judicial system, they are capable of bias without any pressure from outsiders."[3]

Old habits die hard. Since the new noninterference law came into effect, judicial decisions at variance with state requirements were few and far between. A system of judicial review of the administration cannot function effectively without an independent judiciary, something the Soviet Union did not yet have.

These were problems of the past, that continued into the present. But there were a whole new set of problems, that did not exist in the days of Stalin, Khrushchev, or Brezhnev. These problems were the direct result of perestroika and glasnost.

Any country exists because of the will of its people, because of a common, shared idea of what the country is, and why it should hold together. For the USSR, that shared idea was communism. The USSR was the only country in the world without a proper name. "Union of Soviet Socialist Republics" was a designation without a geographic context. The USSR could have encompassed the whole planet, as at one time its leaders thought it would, or it could have shrunk to a fraction of its current size without any necessity for a change of name.

But the idea behind the country faded. The conviction in violent revolution ended. The belief in historical necessity, the constitutionally legitimized leading role of the Communist Party, the determination to mold men and women into the new socialist personality – these, too, went. There remained hard-core believers. But they ceased to be in control of events.

The Soviet Union was disintegrating. There was a real question whether the Union of Soviet Socialist Republics could survive an ending of the belief in soviet socialism. What was replacing it was national ethnic consciousness, within the borders of the various republics. It remained to be seen whether the Union of Soviet Socialist Republics could survive as simply the Union of Republics.

There were and are human rights problems associated with the rise in nationalist minority consciousness. Francis Fukuyama, a U.S. state department official, has argued that the collapse of communism and the end of the Cold War has meant the end of history itself.[4] According to him, the historical dialectic has worked itself out to its final synthesis of capitalist freedom.

I would argue that the reverse has occurred. Instead of history ending with the collapse of communism, history has begun again. The communist world was a world that accepted the theory of the Hegelian dialectic, that believed history had ended with communism. History, in a communist society, was in a state of suspended animation. In the Soviet Union since World War I, in Central and Eastern Europe since World War II, time has stood still.

Once the communist damper was lifted from the Soviet Union, Eastern and Central Europe, history returned in full unmitigated force. National groups are relearning their histories. They are filled with indignation about the human rights violations they have suffered. But it is indignation always directed against those from other groups. Armenians blame Azeris. Kirghiz blame Uzbeks. Macedonian Turks blame Georgians. Ukrainians blame Russians. And members from every group blame the Jews. In the former Soviet Union, it appears that those who learn history are condemned to repeat it. Communist repression, rather than ending nationalist conflicts, just pressurized them.

The ending of communism has not just meant the return of the historical dialectic at a stage that was interrupted by a communist interregnum. The intervening communist stage of history has become part of the dialectic, envenoming ethnic nationalism, giving it a virulence it would never have otherwise had.

On a practical level, former communist leaders looking for a constituency once the belief in communism had disintegrated, turned to the fanning of ethnic hatred. The red/ brown phenomenon, joining former communists and fascists, is not as paradoxical as at first blush it seems. It can be explained by the totalitarian temptation, the disdain for democracy that continued, once the belief in communism had collapsed. Cultivating rabid ethnicity became a means for former communists to continue in politics and in power.

Conflicts among national minorities have a violence even greater now than they did before communism put a lid on them. Much of the animosity, to communism, for its gross violations of human rights, is phrased in nationalistic terms.

This nationalistic reaction to the past wrongs of communism has led to its own set of human rights violations. During World War II, Stalinist forces deported a number of ethnic populations away from Soviet borders, suspecting them of disloyalty and moved them into the interior. In this respect, the Soviets behaved little differently than the U.S. and Canada, which deported its Japanese populations away from the West Coast inland after the bombing of Pearl Harbor.

Following the war, Americans and Canadians of Japanese origin were free to go back to the West Coast if they wished. Soviet controls over internal freedom of movement prevented their displaced ethnic populations from returning to their homelands. At the Helsinki Federation's public hearings in Moscow, we heard, in particular, from the Macedonian Turks, expelled from Georgia and the Crimean Tartars expelled from Crimea. The domestic populations of Georgia, and Crimea were hostile to the return of these expelled minorities. The leaders of the deported populations had been petitioning the Soviet authorities to allow the return of their ethnic communities, with little effect.

The nationalities conflicts that flared up throughout the Soviet Union created a large internal refugee population, an estimated 700,000 fleeing danger in their home republics and seeking protection in another.

The Soviet restrictions on internal movement caused problems for these people too. Internal passport laws did not prevent republic refugees from fleeing. But the laws ensured that these refugees led lives of misery, once they left their assigned places.

In Moscow there had been some temporary assistance to the Armenian refugees fleeing persecution by the Azeri majority in Baku, Azeribaijan. But the assistance ran out, for many. And, even at its best, it did not cover everyone.

Refugees in Moscow were forced into living outdoors, or on floors of buildings, without bedding. Aside from temporary emergency aid, they were not eligible for social assistance. Like anyone else who moved without permission, they could not work at their new locations, or go to school. They were not eligible to be assigned residences.

The international community does a good deal to help refugees, but only those who have left the state where persecution is feared. The mandate of the United Nations High Commission for Refugees does not extend to internal refugees. These internal refugees suffered from the worst of both worlds – the ravages of rampant nationalism, and the bureaucratic indifference of communism.

The ending of totalitarian repression did not mean the end of man-made danger in the Soviet Union. When people's lives cease to be controlled, they are free to do harm as well as good. No society can do without a functioning police force.

The authorities in the Soviet Union were in a totally unfamiliar situation, where they had to protect citizens from each other, rather than controlling their lives in all aspects in the interests of the state. In this new situation, the authorities did not know how to act. They either did too little or too much.

Crime in the former Soviet Union is rising astronomically, including ethnically based violence. Citizens are left unprotected. The ending of repression has been replaced by a power vacuum. Attack after attack occurs, and the authorities do nothing.

The most victimized by the Soviet failure to intervene to protect its citizens was the Jewish community. There was a mass emigration from the Soviet Union consisting mostly of Jews fleeing pervasive threats, threats that seem to emanate from everywhere.

Galina Starovoytova, a member of the Moscow Helsinki Group, and a deputy of the Supreme Soviet, in an address she gave to the public hearings of the International Helsinki Federation in Moscow in 1990, said that there was greater support for anti-Semitism in the Soviet Union than there was in the Weimar Republic in Germany at the time that Hitler began his rise to power.

A survey in Moscow in 1990 showed that 44 percent of the population was not prepared to reject the proposition that "Jews have too much influence over Russian culture," and 23 percent actually agreed with that. Sixty-two percent were not prepared to reject the statement, "When it comes to choosing between people and money, Jews will choose money," and 33 percent actually agreed with it.[5]

Abusive language against Jews was found everywhere. Graffiti against the Jews could be found on buildings, in elevators. Jews were identified as Jews in their internal Soviet passports. At a time when passports had to be shown in Moscow in order to buy food, the presentation of a Jewish passport meant, for many, being the subject of scornful remarks.

Acts of violence and incitement to violence against Jews went unpunished. In mid-January 1990, a group of members of Pamyat, an anti-Semitic society, broke into a meeting of a writers' association shouting anti-Semitic slogans. The Soviet government had opened an investigation into the incident and announced that there would be prosecutions. But when the International Helsinki Federation was in Moscow in June no prosecution had yet been launched.

Smirnov-Ostashvili, a person identified by the prosecution office in a meeting I had with them in Moscow, as someone to be prosecuted, published, with apparent impunity, while I was in Moscow, a broadsheet calling for the killing of the Jews. Smirnov-Ostashvili went on trial for the January attack on July 24, 1990, for the charge of inciting intolerance.

Anti-Semitism in the Soviet Union, as in the Weimar Republic had developed an intellectual pseudo-respectability. Right-wing writers' associations in Leningrad and Moscow claimed Jews had too much influence over Soviet culture.

Whenever ethnic violence flares up in one of the republics, whoever else is in danger, the Jews are always at risk. For instance, when Azeris and Armenians were fighting in Baku, Jews in Baku were forced to flee.

The Soviet leadership remained silent about the rise in anti-Semitism. While Mitterand went to the Carpentas cemetery to protest anti-Semitism in France, Gorbachev, in contrast, appointed to his advisory Presidential Council, Valentin Rasputin, a known anti-Semite.

In the days of Stalin, Jews were blamed for thwarting communism. Now that communism is itself the target, Jews are blamed for causing communism.

The danger of anti-Semitism in the former Soviet Union was not just a danger to the Jews. It represented a threat to the Soviet Union itself, in the same way that the Nazis of the 1920s represented a threat to the Weimar Republic.

Pamyat is more than just an anti-Semitic minority. It is a right-wing political and ideological grouping that uses anti-Semitism as a strategy to win power. The Jewish community realized the dimension of the threat, as its mass emigration showed. But the former Soviet government did not.

I have said that Soviet authorities did either too little or too much in relation to ethnic violence. When the authorities eventually did intervene to protect a beleaguered community, they overreacted. States of emergency were declared in a number of republics because of ethnic rioting. Military intervention under states of emergency were accompanied by widespread reports of military abuse. Unnecessary and exaggerated force was used against peaceful elements of the population. There were repeated allegations of troops firing without warning on unarmed protesters.

There was no procedure for investigation of allegations of abuse inflicted under states of emergency. The Soviet legal system for remedying state abuse was flimsy at best. In times of states of emergency it was virtually non-existent; the repressive nature of the state apparatus returned in all its former horror. What tentative controls were being developed in the Soviet Union just disappeared.

Russia and the other republics of the former Soviet Union today present a mixed and troubled picture. The increased respect for human rights, the joining of the West and East in a common relationship of what human rights means are cause for hope. But the disintegration, the emotional nationalism, the virulent anti-Semitism are cause for deep concern.

CHAPTER SEVEN

THE HELSINKI PROCESS

The Helsinki process for the protection of human rights presents a paradox. No other process for the promotion of human rights has been as dramatically successful as the Helsinki process. Yet, and this is paradox, this process has had no institutional machinery for the promotion of human rights, no right of petition, no committee of experts, no compliance-reporting requirement, no specialized rapporteurs or working groups, none of the systems we have come to expect in the international human rights arena.

However, the transformations in Eastern Europe, the collapse of the Berlin wall, glasnost in the old Soviet Union, the election of Václav Havel in Czechoslovakia, can all be traced in part, to the Helsinki human rights process.

No other nongovernmental organizations have been as successful as the Helsinki Watch committees of Eastern Europe. Some of the most well-known human rights activists in the world are or were part of the Helsinki Watch movement. Yelena Bonner, Anatoly Sharansky, and Yuri Orlov were all part of the original Moscow Helsinki Watch Committee. Václav Havel was part of the Czechoslovak Helsinki Watch Committee. In Poland, the Czech Republic and Hungary, virtually the whole of the Watch Committees have moved into government or parliament.

Even the standards articulated are rudimentary. The Final Act of the Conference on Security and Cooperations in Europe runs to 67 pages. Of these pages, only one, of eight paragraphs, deals with human rights.

The Final Act has three baskets of provisions: the first deals with questions relating to security in Europe; the second relates to cooperation in the field of economics, science and technology, and the environment; the final is called "cooperation in humanitarian and other fields."

The first basket on security in Europe has two components: a declaration of principles governing relations between states, and a document on confidence-building measures for security and disarmament.

The declaration of principles sets out ten principles. These principles talk about such things as territorial integrity, peaceful settlement of disputes, sovereign equality, and other principles normally related to security. Only Principle

VII relates to human rights. It is titled "respect for human rights and funda-mental freedoms, including freedom of thought, conscience, religion or belief."

Principle VII says first of all that the participating states will respect human rights and fundamental freedom, including freedom of thought, con-science, religion or belief, without distinction as to race, sex, language, or religion. States will promote and encourage the exercise of civil, political, economic, social, cultural, and other rights. States will recognize and respect the freedom of the individual to profess and practice religion or belief acting in accordance with the dictates of his own conscience. States will respect the rights of persons belonging to national minorities to equality before the law. States recognize respect for human rights is an essential factor for peace. States confirm the right of an individual to know and act upon his rights. States will act in conformity with the Universal Declaration of Human Rights and any international agreements by which they may be bound. And that is it.

There are a number of striking features of Principle VII. One is that there are absolutely no mechanisms at all. The whole Helsinki process is a process of intergovernmental meetings, each meeting deciding when the next will be. Until the Charter of Paris of November 1990, there was no permanent secre-tariat. Each host country served as the secretariat for the meeting it hosted.

The Helsinki meeting of 1975 was followed by a Belgrade meeting in 1977, a Madrid meeting that ended in 1983, and a Vienna meeting that ended in 1989. In between the general meetings there were specialized meet-ings on particular subjects. All meetings, specialized and general, functioned by consensus. If there was no consensus, the specialized meetings would sim-ply break up without a result. The general meetings would continue until consensus was reached. The Madrid meeting went on from November 11, 1980, to September 9, 1983, because of a prolonged deadlock. The Vienna meeting went on from November 4, 1986, to January 19, 1989, for the same reason.

The specialized meetings were often billed as meetings of experts. But they too were all intergovernmental. Countries were represented by delega-tions taking instructions from their governments. They were expert only in the sense that governments sent their civil servants who were knowledgeable in the subject matter.

The second feature of Principle VII is incorporation by reference. By and large Principle VII is devoid of standards as well as mechanisms. It just incor-porates other standards set out in other instruments, in particular, the Universal Declaration of Human Rights, and, as well, any other agreements by which state parties may be bound.

Third: in so far as any standards at all are mentioned, there is an emphasis on freedom of conscience. Even the title of the Principle specifically mentions that freedom. Of the eight paragraphs in Principle VII, three specifically assert freedom of conscience, including the right of the individual to know and act upon his rights. In so far as the drafters of the Helsinki Accord saw one right or freedom as the engine for the realization of all rights and freedoms, that engine was freedom of conscience. And that freedom has been the engine of change. Change has come about in the way that it has in Eastern Europe because of the assertion of conscientiously held beliefs by the Helsinki committees and others in Eastern Europe.

This book elsewhere argues that nongovernmental organizations are the implementation arm of human rights instruments. In the Helsinki Accord, that concept was almost explicit. Those that exercised in their full plenitude the freedom of conscience, the right to know and act upon their rights, were nongovernmental organizations, and in particular the Helsinki committees. It was almost as if the drafters of Principle VII envisaged what would happen and planned that activity as the implementation mechanism of the Helsinki Accord.

Planned or not, envisaged or not, that was what happened. Helsinki Watch groups sprang up in Eastern Europe immediately after the Helsinki Final Act, and because of the Helsinki Final Act. They became the conscience, the compliance assessment mechanisms, of Principle VII of the Accord.

Fourth: the human rights part of the Helsinki Accord is not part of the humanitarian basket, as we might expect. It is, instead, part of the security basket. For the Final Act of the Conference on Security and Cooperation in Europe, human rights were considered part of security in Europe, and not part of cooperation in Europe. The humanitarian basket deals with human contacts, including family reunification, which has an obvious human rights component. It also covers access to information, cultural exchanges, and education exchanges. While bits and pieces of human rights are within the humanitarian basket, human rights as a concept and principle are elsewhere.

The insertion of human rights in the security basket explains the paradox of the success of the Helsinki Final Act. Principle VII was so successful, the Helsinki Watch groups of Eastern Europe were so successful, precisely because of this linkage between security and human rights. It was this linkage that was new and different about the Helsinki Final Act.

Human rights as a concept had been accepted by the signatory states of the Helsinki Final Act before the Final Act was signed. All the signatory states have accepted the Universal Declaration of Human Rights, and virtually all the International Covenant on Civil and Political Rights (though the U.S. did not ratify this Covenant until 1992).

All signatory states are part of the UN human rights system. But the acceptance of these instruments and their attendant mechanisms had nowhere near the impact of the Helsinki Final Act, because these instruments and mechanisms were free-floating instruments and mechanisms, without linkages to security.

Two other of the ten security principles, besides respect for human rights, are inviolability of frontiers and territorial integrity of states. In themselves, as principles, inviolability of frontiers and territorial integrity of states are unexceptionable. But one of the signatories to the Helsinki Final Act was the German Democratic Republic. Another was Poland, whose border had been shifted by the Soviets 150 miles to the west. A third was the Soviet Union itself, which had swallowed Lithuania, Latvia, and Estonia whole after the war. A fourth was Romania whose province of Moldavia had been moved into the Soviet Union.

There had never been a peace treaty after World War II recognizing the boundaries of the states set up after the war in Eastern Europe. There had certainly never been any official Western acceptance of Soviet domination of Eastern Europe. The Helsinki Accord came as close to a Western acceptance of the Soviet view of the boundaries of Eastern Europe as the Soviets were likely to get. To the Soviets, the Helsinki Accord was a prize document. The ten basic principles of the Helsinki Accord, including the one on human rights, were put into the Soviet constitution. The Soviet constitution of October 7, 1977, states:[1] "The USSR's relations with other states are based on observance of the following principles." The ten Helsinki principles are then listed.

Because the Helsinki Accord was such a prize to the Soviets, human rights activists had a great deal of leverage when using it. If Principle VII on human rights was not being respected, as the Helsinki Watch groups argued it was not, then all the other principles, including the principles of territorial integrity and inviolability of frontiers need not be respected.

If, for the East, the Helsinki Final Act was a prize, for the West, it was a weapon. Allegations of human rights violations are often used by governments for political purposes, to attempt to discredit and delegitimize their political opponents. The Helsinki Accord and, in particular, Principle VII, gave the West a platform to attack and criticize the East. Anti-communism and allegations of human rights violations in Eastern Europe formed a cocktail which the West mixed heartily and drank with glee. The leverage the Helsinki Final Act gave to promotion of respect for human rights in Eastern Europe was used as enthusiastically by Western governments as by the Helsinki committees themselves. While nongovernmental organizations could not address the intergovernmental meetings directly, there was invariably a government willing to raise their concerns.

The Helsinki process became a human rights battlefield, which is why the Madrid conference took almost three years, and the Vienna conference took more than two years. The Soviets could not afford to walk away from a process that meant official Western acceptance of the then current boundaries of Eastern Europe. And yet the Soviets certainly were not respecting human rights, which meant agreement at each of these conferences was so hard to get.

The International Helsinki Human Rights Federation was created in 1982. Its founding meeting was in Bellagio, Italy. It was created by Western Helsinki committees in support of and in response to the Eastern Helsinki committees that were harassed, disbanded, and imprisoned by their home governments.

Each component of the International Helsinki Federation has considerable latitude in how it operates. The headquarters, in Vienna, does its own human rights work, following its own agenda. But so do each of the components of the Federation, each setting their own agenda. The International Helsinki Federation in 1988 won the Council of Europe Human Rights prize and in 1989 the Bruno Kreisky Foundation's human rights prize.

The typical Helsinki committee has a board of about two dozen eminent persons in the field of human rights. It produces researched, in-depth reports on the human rights situations in the various Helsinki process countries. The Canadian Helsinki Watch Group has produced reports on Canada, Hungary, Poland, Yugoslavia, the USSR, and on transition in Eastern Europe generally.

In some countries there is professional staff doing Helsinki Watch work. The U.S. and Norway, in particular, have substantial, professional staffs. Both the International Helsinki Federation and the national groups undertake missions, and write reports on the missions. As well, organized delegations visit officials in countries of concern and make representations.

There is, as with any human rights organization, advocacy of issues, and adoption of particular, acute cases of concern. But the general method of operation is to emphasize fact finding and publication.

Now that the Iron Curtain has lifted and the Cold War has ended, the dynamics of the Helsinki process have changed substantially. For one, a human rights mechanism has been launched.

The Vienna Conference's concluding document of January 1989 set up a rudimentary process of interstate complaints. Human rights, fundamental freedoms, and issues of a humanitarian character were lumped together and labelled the human dimension of the Conference on Security and Cooperation in Europe. The participating states agreed, in January 1989, to respond to requests and representations made to them by other states on questions relating to the human dimension of the Conference on Security and Cooperation in Europe. They agreed to hold bilateral meetings with participating states that request examination of questions relating to the human dimension of the Conference on Security and Cooperation in Europe, including specific cases.

Of course, states are free to raise bilaterally with other states whatever they want. So the mechanism set out in the Vienna concluding document did not amount to all that much. Still, it was a sign of what was to come.

The concluding document out of Vienna proposed a series of conferences on the human dimension, one in Paris in 1989, a second in Copenhagen in 1990, and a third in Moscow in 1991. The holding of a human rights conference in Moscow was a matter of controversy. It is only as the human rights situation in the Soviet Union improved that the controversy abated.

The Charter of Paris provides for new procedures involving the services of experts or a roster of eminent persons experienced in human rights issues, which issues could be raised under the human dimension mechanism of the Conference on Security and Cooperation in Europe. Participating states undertook to provide, in the context of the mechanism, for individuals to be involved in the protection of their rights. They decided to develop further their commitments at the Moscow meeting on the human dimension. The Charter members decided on the creation of an office for free elections in Warsaw to exchange information on elections within participating states.

The Moscow Human Dimensions conference in October 1991 adopted a new mechanism for the promotion of human rights amongst member states. Or rather it decided to enhance the effectiveness of the mechanism established by the Concluding Document of the Vienna Conference on Security and Cooperation in Europe. The mechanism that was developed, although promising, is not a human rights compliance assessment mechanism.

The technique endorsed is either a mission of experts or a mission of rapporteurs. The mission of experts is not activated by individuals. It is activated by the violating state. The Moscow Concluding Document states that a participating state may invite the assistance of an expert mission.

The mission has the power to submit observations, and these observations, presumably, may be that on the particular question, the inviting state complies with or violates the Helsinki Accord. However, the observation would be subject specific. The mission is "to facilitate resolution of a particular question or problem." The mission would not cover all issues of compliance or violation.

There is, as well, an interstate complaints mechanism. Either six states, when the relevant state has not satisfied their inquiries, or ten states, directly in extreme circumstances, may send a mission of up to three rapporteurs.[2]

The rapporteurs may make observations but only observations of fact. Compliance assessment would not normally be considered an observation of fact and presumably could not be made by the rapporteurs.

The belief that neither rapporteur missions nor expert missions are meant as compliance assessment devices is reinforced by the provision in the Moscow Document that says states remain free to raise any issue of implementation of the Helsinki Accord within the Conference on Security and Cooperation in Europe process, even once these mechanisms are engaged. If the mission of experts or rapporteurs was a true compliance assessment mechanism, one would not expect to see such a saving provision.

Another change in the Helsinki process, coincident with the ending of the Cold War, was the legalization and depopulation of Eastern European Helsinki committees. The human rights movements of Eastern Europe attracted the most principled, the most articulate, the most incisive minds of their societies. Before glasnost, human rights was the intellectual and cultural focus of the Eastern European world.

Now human rights activists have moved on to politics and to government. Human rights is rapidly becoming a backwater. The human rights movement in the East has suffered heavy losses, of a sort not likely to be recouped soon. The Eastern European intellectual and moral leadership sees the period as a time for politics, not for human rights.

Human rights was a political strategy used by those whose first concern was not human rights but political power. Exposure of human rights abuses served the purpose of criticizing and delegitimizing a regime which was opposed not only for its human rights abuses, but for political, nationalistic, or ideological reasons as well.

When legal opposition was not possible, when the struggle for power was in an incipient stage, the agenda of political opposition groups and human rights activists coincided. Once the achievement of power by opposition groups became a real possibility, their human rights colouring disappeared. The Ukrainian Helsinki Watch Group became, for instance, the Ukrainian Republican Party. One cannot say that opposition groups ceased to believe in human rights. It is just that human rights ceased to be their only or even main concern.

If the political aim was national independence or democracy in totalitarian times, the goal seemed radical, even absurd. Respect for human rights was a reasonable, realistic target. Although, in practice, human rights activists were repressed, in principle not even the communist leaders could object to the human rights aims.

Human rights was an umbrella that could cover all the opposition, across the whole political spectrum. It was a unifying force when the opposition needed the strength of unity. It articulated a vocabulary of minimal demands on which all could agree.

The human rights movement in Eastern Europe was an uneasy coalition of political opposition and human rights activists. As soon as power became achievable for the opposition groups, the coalition broke apart.

In general, nongovernmental organizations cannot sustain themselves as nongovernmental organizations if they are filled with people seeking to be part of government. It is essentially a false position for nongovernmental organizations to have.

Nongovernmental organizations, to be credible and effective, have to be nonpolitical. Yet once they are fronts for opposition parties, they are anything but nonpolitical.

On a personal level, nongovernmental organizations cannot function, once they are stalking horses for would be government members. For eventually, the opposition succeeds. It gets into government. And the nongovernmental organization collapses.

However, in an Eastern Europe context, one cannot say that human rights activists were taken advantage of by opposition groups. If opposition groups had a strategy of adopting a human rights facade, human rights activists had a strategy of inculcating the ethics of human rights into opposition. Opposition to repressive governments would have existed whether there was a human rights movement or not. The use of human rights as a focal point of opposition had the value of educating opposition groups about human rights values.

Operation of an opposition party in a totalitarian atmosphere has a degrading effect. There is a temptation to function underground, in secret, simply for self-preservation. The opposition becomes dishonest, deceptive.

Opposition in a repressive society is tempted not just to secrecy, but also to violence. The violence of the state inexorably suggests violence in the minds of the opposition. Revolution, it is thought, must come from rebellion.

Melding human rights with opposition has three effects. Human rights focuses on means, rather than ends. Human rights activists, even at great personal danger to themselves, are prepared to stand up publicly for the values in which they believe. They counteract the naturally secretive tendencies of opposition forces in repressive societies, holding governments up, and at the same time holding themselves up, to public standards, public scrutiny.

The human rights movement, as well, counteracts the penchant for violence. The human rights movement is a nonviolent movement. Change may come more slowly through peaceful means. But it is more deeply rooted, more long lasting, and more respectful of the values those who advocate change attempt to promote.

On a moral level, the human rights movement is an antidote to the moral debilitation from which an underground opposition would otherwise suffer. A secretive, violent opposition is unlikely to form a government that will respect human rights values. A human rights movement that pulls opposition away from this amoral abyss has a value that persists once the opposition comes to government.

Once opposition groups can operate freely, they part company with human rights activists. But the loss for the human rights movement is not total. The opposition retains the human rights values it has learned in more repressive times.

One reason that in Eastern Europe the changes have occurred, by and large, without violence, that the revolutions have been velvet revolutions, is that the opposition has learned human rights lessons from its human rights phase. In Romania, the former Yugoslavia, the former Soviet republics – where there is violence associated with change – these are the areas where the human rights movement was weakest in the totalitarian era.

Human rights nongovernmental organizations in Eastern Europe can take satisfaction from what they achieved, not only in being an engine for change, but also for the form and manner of change. Now, instead of having antagonists in power, they have friends in power, people who believe in human rights.

Whatever the reasons for intermingling of human rights and politics in Eastern Europe in the past, and there were many, those reasons, with the shift to democracy, have ceased to be relevant.

Human rights nongovernmental organizations must distinguish themselves more clearly from political activists than they have done. Even once the opposition succeeds in achieving their aims of taking power, the work of the human rights movement continues to be needed. One future task for human rights nongovernmental organizations is to extricate themselves from association with those with a purely political agenda.

These problems are the problems of success. When human rights violations decrease, it is understandable that concerns about violations decrease as well. Nonetheless, because violations never cease altogether, because even if they did perpetual vigilance is necessary to prevent their recurrence, we must be aware of this weakening of the human rights monitoring capacity and compensate for it.

The movement of human rights activists into government in the East represents an opportunity as well as a problem. Having so many government leaders who were, until recently, victims of human rights violations, who are steeped in the vocabulary of human rights, bodes well for the promotion of human rights around the world.

Before, Eastern Europe Helsinki committees were brutally repressed. Now they are free to meet, to organize, to publicize. The International Helsinki Federation now has several constituent members from within Eastern

Europe, including Russia, Poland, Hungary, and the Czech Republic. During the height of the Cold War, although the International Helsinki Federation was set up in solidarity with Eastern committees, formal links with them were impossible.

For these Eastern committees, however, human rights no longer has the centrality to Eastern European political discourse it once had. Human rights activists have moved on to parliaments and governments. They have not, hopefully, left human rights behind. But they have left the nongovernmental community behind. A whole new group is needed to fill the gap. It will be a group that may have neither the background, nor the experience, nor the history of commitment that the old group had.

The most important change in the Helsinki process following on the end of the Cold War is that the linkage between respect for human rights and security has gone. The value of the Helsinki Final Act to Eastern Europe did not disappear, but it changed substantially. The value is no longer, for the former Soviet republics, respect by the West of territorial integrity and inviolability of their frontiers. It is German recognition of Polish borders that has become important rather than Conference on Security and Cooperation in Europe recognition of Polish borders.

Because the linkage between security and human rights has gone, the leverage human rights had in the Helsinki process has also gone. Of course, all this happened in a context where respect for human rights in many countries of Eastern Europe has improved dramatically. But respect for human rights is never complete and entire, anywhere. The means that are left are fewer; the people that are left are less used to coming to grips with the violations that do occur.

We are in a situation, for security reasons, where the West is as anxious to have the transformations in Eastern Europe succeed as the Eastern European governments themselves are. Politically, Western governments are no longer motivated to try to discredit Eastern European governments by pointing to human rights violations. The tendency is the contrary, to avoid embarrassing these governments.

The political wind has gone out of the sails of the human rights component of the Conference on Security and Cooperation in Europe process. The West enthusiastically raised human rights concerns at Helsinki meetings when the West wanted to criticize and embarrass Eastern European governments. Equally grave and even more serious violations committed by Turkey, a NATO ally, went unremarked by Western governments. The West did not wish to embarrass its ally.

The political dynamic that once worked in favour of Turkey is now working in favour of all the Eastern European governments. The West wants to encourage and support the political changes that are taking place in the East. There is a tendency to sweep under the carpet incidental or anomalous violations of human rights that occur along the way. Where there once was enthusiasm about raising human rights issues, now there is reluctance. The Conference on Security and Cooperation in Europe process as a weapon in the battle of respect for human rights is in danger of being lost.

Governments can no longer be counted on to raise nongovernmental concerns at international meetings. In this context, the role of nongovernmental organizations as watch guards for human rights assumes particular importance, because the vigil they are holding may be lonelier than it ever has been.

PART III

APARTHEID IN SOUTH AFRICA

CHAPTER EIGHT

APARTHEID AS A ROOT CAUSE OF HUMAN RIGHTS VIOLATIONS

To write of apartheid as a root cause of human rights violations may seem unduly kind to apartheid. It might be more accurate to say apartheid is a human rights violation. And indeed there are key elements of human rights that apartheid violated, just by being what it was. Dr. N. Diedrichs, a former South African minister of finance, said in 1948 that apartheid and human rights were "two outlooks on life fundamentally so divergent that a compromise is entirely impossible."[1] Apartheid and human rights could not live together.

The reason I refer to apartheid as a root cause of human rights violations rather than just calling it a human rights violation of its own is that apartheid led to violations of human rights above and beyond those advocated by the apostles of apartheid. Apartheid advocates discrimination. One cannot say it leads to discrimination. It is discrimination. The advocates of apartheid preached discrimination.

The advocates of apartheid did not, however, preach human rights violations such as torture, arbitrary detention, or extrajudicial execution. Apartheid led to these violations. One cannot say the promoters of apartheid saw them as part of an ideal they were working to achieve.

When I write about apartheid as a root cause of human rights violations, the point I am trying to make is that apartheid generated abuses that horrified even those who once believed in apartheid. And it is these abuses, stemming from apartheid, that led to the end of apartheid in South Africa.

What is apartheid? It is, first and foremost, racist. The advocates of apartheid talked in terms of the white race and the non-white races. Apartheid was a philosophy of the Afrikaner, or the Boer, the descendants of the original Dutch settlers in South Africa. It was part of a nationalist movement, but it did not just encompass the Boers or Afrikaners. It spoke in more general terms of the white race, to include non-Boers as well as Boers.

Believers in apartheid saw white and non-white as not only skin colours but, as well, as cultures. To believers, there is a white culture and civilization. And there are non-white cultures and civilizations. Afrikaners used the term "European civilization" to refer to the civilization of the white race.

This division between whites and non-whites was linked to religion. In the words of a school textbook published for the Transvaal schools, "God himself made the diversity of peoples on earth."[2]

Apartheid moved on from this perception of racial diversity and cultural diversity that is racially based to the assertion that the white race is superior to the non-white races. Again in the words of the Transvaal textbook, "The white stands on a much higher plane of civilization and is more developed."[3] Dr. Diedrichs said, in 1967, of the white race in South Africa, "We are the bearers of the values that made the West great."[4]

If whites are at a higher level of civilization, the corollary is that the non-white races represent a lower level of civilization. A pamphlet put out by the Institute for Christian National Education in South Africa in 1948 refers to "the cultural infancy of the native."[5] The Transvaal textbook mentioned earlier warned against whites sinking to the cultural level of the non-whites. The notion of non-whites as uncivilized, as less civilized, permeated apartheid discourse. Natives were stereotyped as primitive and illiterate.

The apartheid notion that whites are superior to non-whites has a number of consequences. One is racial purity. Whites may not marry non-whites. Whites must not socialize with non-whites. They should not eat or drink or visit together. Socialization may lead to intermarriage and an end to the white race. The Nationalist Party, at its Congress in 1938, decided, "[This Congress] declares that it must be the earnest and determined struggle of that race [the white race] to preserve its racial purity." There are constant warnings against race suicide.

A second consequence of the notion of white superiority is masterdom. Apartheid advocates believed the white race should rule the non-white races. J.G. Strijdom, Nationalist prime minister of South Africa from 1954 to 1958, said, "Our policy is that the European must stand their ground and must remain baas [masters] in South Africa."[6] In 1948 the *Cape Times* reported a speech that Strijdom gave before he was Prime Minister. In that report the paper wrote, "The main principle of apartheid as he [Strijdom] saw it was the continuation of European supremacy."[7]

Tied up with the notion of white supremacy is the colonial notion of white man's burden. Because whites are superior, they must survive and be in a dominant position not only for their own benefit but also for the benefit of non-whites as well. So, the head office of the Nationalist Party in the 1947 pamphlet previously mentioned said that the task of promoting the happiness and well-being of its citizens, non-whites as well as white, "can best be accomplished by preserving and safeguarding the white race."[8]

If whites are masters, what follows is that blacks are akin to slaves. They cannot be allowed to strike, because according to B.J. Schoeman, minister of labour in 1953, they "have not the faintest conception of the responsibilities of trade unionism."[9] Natives do the menial work of the South African economy under the direction of white masters.

The need to preserve the white race, the need to maintain racial purity, the need to maintain white culture or European civilization requires separation of the white and non-white races. Avoiding social contact between the races is not enough. There has to be segregation. Segregation has to be maximized. It does not just mean separate facilities for non-whites and whites. It means territorial separation. The only guarantee of purity is isolation.

A pamphlet issued by the head office of the Nationalist Party in 1947 said, "The policy of our country should encourage total apartheid as the ultimate goal of a national process of separate development." "The Bantu [natives] should be regarded as migratory citizens." "The process of detribalization should be arrested."

As early as 1912, a newspaper, the *Star*, reported General Hertzog, the then minister of native affairs in South Africa, as saying that segregation of black and white was the only solution. The Bantus would not be allowed to have land in the white man's territory. They (the government) would place natives in those parts where there were already large masses of their compatriots.[10]

Total separation means, of course, separation in education. It means, however, more than that. Apartheid requires a lesser education for non-whites than whites. According to H.G. Verwoerd, minister of native affairs and then prime minister from 1958 to 1966, training the Bantu to do more than menial labour does nothing but mislead him "by showing him the green pastures of European society in which he is not allowed to graze." He said, "Education must train and teach people in accordance with their opportunities of life. Higher education for the Bantu means he becomes frustrated and rebellious. Native education has to be controlled to prevent the native from being drawn away from his own community."[11]

That, in outline, is apartheid as a belief. How did this belief manifest itself? The requirement of racial purity meant laws against mixed marriages and interracial sexual relations. The Mixed Marriages Act of 1949 prohibited marriages between whites and non-whites.[12] Any such marriage outside of South Africa was void in South Africa.

An Immorality Act of 1927 prohibited intercourse between whites and Bantus. An Immorality Amendment Act of 1950 expanded the prohibition to a ban on intercourse between white and non-whites.[13] In 1957, legislation increased the penalty for an "immoral" act to seven years imprisonment and added the offence of soliciting the commission of an "immoral" act.

It was not until 1985 that these statutes were repealed. While they were on the books, thousands were prosecuted for their violations.

The notion of white superiority led to the denial of the vote to non-whites. J.G. Strijdom, the former Nationalist prime minister, asked, "If the franchise is to be extended to non-Europeans and the non-Europeans are given representation and the vote and the non-Europeans are developed as the same basis as the Europeans, how can the Europeans remain master?"[14]

The Union of South Africa was founded in 1910 as a federation of the Orange Free State, Transvaal, Natal, and the Cape. The Orange Free State and Transvaal were Boer republics defeated by the British in the Boer War, 1899 to 1902. The Union provided for a non-racial franchise in the Cape and Natal, but a suffrage restricted to whites in the Orange Free State and Transvaal.

Nationalists divided non-whites into three subcategories: Asians, coloured and Bantu. "Coloured" consisted of those of mixed racial descent. "Asians" consisted largely of descendants of Indian immigrants. "Bantu" were also called Africans or blacks or natives.

The demographics are such that coloured and Asians could have had a vote without threatening white majority rule. However, giving blacks (Bantus) the vote would have meant the end of white dominance.

Once the Nationalist Party got elected in 1948, it began a prolonged legal, political, and legislative struggle to restrict the vote to whites alone. The struggle involved packing the Appeal Court, which had declared one legislative effort as unconstitutional because of entrenched voter rights in the 1910 constitution. By 1971, the effort was successful. The House of Assembly elected in that year was chosen by white votes alone.

A constitutional change of 1983 introduced a House of Representatives for coloured people and a House of Delegates for Asians. There were separate voter rolls for white, coloured, and Asians. Each House dealt with "own affairs," with matters pertaining to its own community. General affairs, as well as any conflict amongst the Houses, fell within the purview of Parliament as a whole in which the House of Assembly, the white House, had an overall absolute majority. There was no elected House for Bantus.

Basic to this legislative structure, as well as to apartheid as a whole, was the Population Registration Act. Under this Act, every South African was classified as belonging to a particular racial group. Without this legislation, separate voter rolls, as well as much of the rest of the system of apartheid, would have been impossible.

If, politically, the division between whites and non-whites was a division between ruler and ruled, economically the division was between master and servant. African trade unions were not outlawed, but neither were they recognized. The Native Labour (Settlement of Disputes) Act of 1953 prevented strikes by African unions.[15] Bantus had no effective power to resist employer demands.

Even more pernicious than the inability to strike was the concept of job reservation. Job reservation applied to Bantus, coloured, and Asians. The notion behind job reservation was that the best, the most highly skilled jobs, should be reserved for whites. The 1951 Native Building Workers Act provided that no Bantu might be employed as a skilled building worker outside of a Bantu area. The Industrial Conciliation Act of 1956 gave the government power to reserve certain types of work for any racial group. The Act was used, for instance, to reserve for whites the posts of fireman and traffic policeman above the rank of constable in the Cape Town area, or to reserve for whites skilled work in the wholesale meat trade.[16]

These provisions remained in effect until 1981. In that year, the Black Labour Relations Act gave all unions the right to strike and abolished the system of job reservation.

Superiority and inferiority, mastery and serfdom, are not just inherent. They had to be preserved. Education was structured to prevent blacks from learning enough to enable themselves to improve their skills and capacities. The Bantu Education Act of 1953 gave the minister of native affairs unrestricted powers to decide what schools should exist, what the conditions of service for teachers should be, and what the content of African education would be.[17]

That power was used to lower the already low pay scale for teachers of Bantu students, to decrease the percentage of African students in training, vocation, and technical training, and to require only the most basic level of education, in the vernacular (native languages).[18] Even the government notion of basic education was frustrated by insistence on use of the native vernacular. Mathematics, in particular, was not adequately translated into the vernacular. As well, the standard of English declines considerably when education is in the vernacular only.

Basic to apartheid is separation. This separation consisted of petty apartheid and grand apartheid. The legal foundation for petty apartheid was the Reservation of Separate Amenities Act of 1953. That legislates permitted any person in charge of any public premises or public vehicle to reserve the vehicle or premises for the use of any race. The law was used to provide for such things as racially segregated public toilet facilities, or whites-only beaches and public parks. As apartheid receded, many of the reservations were removed. The law eventually allowed for multiracial use of facilities once restricted to whites. The law itself remained on the books, and still applied to some amenities, such as beaches, or national sporting events, until June 1990. The then president of South Africa, F.W. de Klerk, announced, June 1, 1990, that the government would ask Parliament to repeal the Separate Amenities Act. The Act was repealed June 19.

Two legal foundations for grand apartheid were the Group Areas Act and the Land Act. The Land Act dated from 1913. It prohibited Bantu ownership of land outside of certain areas set out in a schedule to the Act. In itself, the Land Act was only an economic measure, joining other measures that prevented Bantus from achieving economic equality.

What made the Land Act a cornerstone of apartheid was the complementary Group Areas Act of 1950. That Act provided for the establishment of racial ghettoes, where not only ownership but occupation of land could be restricted to a specified population group.[19] The Act forced people to live in specific zones proclaimed for their racial group.

In general, the Act was used to exclude all non-whites from the central areas of towns and cities. In 1985, the law was changed to allow non-white professionals to occupy premises in the centres of cities for work. But at night they had to go back to zones reserved for their housing.[20]

The Group Areas Act was reinforced by the Prevention of Illegal Squatting Act of 1951. That Act empowered the authorities to remove squatters from land where they had no right to be and move them elsewhere at the discretion of the authorities. The same law empowered demolition of squatters' buildings.

The Black Communities Development Act of 1983 allowed for disestablishment of any land on government discretion. Disestablishment meant the residents become illegal squatters.[21]

The Black (Urban Areas) Act of 1945 and then the Native Laws Amendment Act of 1952 prohibited Bantus from remaining in prescribed areas without permission. The effect of these laws was to set up a migrant labour system. Male Bantus would be given permission to come to urban areas to work. They would be required to leave their families behind. The system was labelled influx control. The Abolition of Influx Control Act of 1986 ended the system. But influx control remained in effect because of the Group Areas Act, the Prevention of Illegal Squatting Act, the Black Communities Development Act, and the Bantustan system.

The notion of separate development reached its zenith with the concept of homelands, Bantustans, as separate black states within South Africa. The Promotion of Bantu Self-Government Act of 1959 abolished all Bantu representation in the South African Parliament and replaced it with a devolution of executive powers to territorial authorities in the areas where black land ownership was allowed.

There were ten homelands in South Africa. They were not ten separate tracts of land, but instead a patchwork of scattered bits and pieces. Over time, new bits and pieces were added to the homelands by decree.

The Bantu Homelands Citizenship Act of 1970 assigned every Bantu in South Africa to one or other of these homelands. The idea behind the law, according to Connie Mulder, minister of Bantu administration, in 1978, was that, "There will be not one black man with South African citizenship."[22]

Every black (Bantu) became, initially, a dual citizen of South Africa and his/her assigned homeland. The Bantu Homelands Constitution Act of 1971 allowed the South African president to make each homeland independent by declaration. Four out of the ten Bantustans – Transkei, Bophuthatswana, Venda, and Ciskei – were the targets of such a proclamation. The effect of the proclamations was that every Bantu assigned to one of these "independent" homelands ceased to be a citizen of South Africa, and became a citizen of the homeland alone.

The homelands were not recognized internationally, nor were they truly independent from the government of the Union of South Africa. The main effect of this denationalization of black South Africans was to subject them to foreign worker laws and alien controls. Foreign workers cannot work in South Africa without permission. Violation of the Aliens Act laws led to summary arrest and deportation to the homeland.[23]

A Restoration of Citizenship Act of 1986 restored the citizenship of some but not all of these who lost it by virtue of the "independence" of the homelands. Those who lived in the homelands, those who became migrant workers in South Africa since "independence," remained denationalized until the collapse of the homelands in 1994.[24]

The creation of the bantustans led to forced removal of denationalized blacks to their designated homelands. This forced movement consisted in large measure of women. Bantu men had work permits allowing them to be outside the homelands. Bantu women, by and large, did not.[25]

A migratory labour force, with women living in the bantustans, and men allowed to live and work outside, meant family separation. Black men were forcibly separated from their families eleven months at a time, living in labour camps.

Denationalization was not the only reason for forced removal to the Bantustans. Removal was also generated by abolition of labour tenancies on white farms, laws prohibiting squatters from living on white farms, elimination of black spots (the suppression of property rights vested in Bantu in land situated in white areas), relocating black urban townships in neighbouring reserves, or expulsion of black workers from urban areas because of pass law offences or simply because work permission has been withdrawn. As of 1980, over six million people had been forcibly removed to Bantustans.

Location and movement of black labour throughout South Africa was tightly controlled. Pass laws were designed to enforce this control. Blacks were required to carry passbooks to show identity, place of residence, and place of work. Anyone not in possession of a passbook, or in a place which, according to the passbook, he/she should not have been was subject to prosecution.

The pass laws were abolished in 1986. However other laws, and in particular the Group Areas Act and the homelands policy, effectively prevented freedom of movement in South Africa.

So far, what I have been describing is what apartheid was, the human rights violations inherent in apartheid. Piled on top of these indignities were the violations to which apartheid inevitably led.

It is impossible to compartmentalize respect for human rights. Human rights are an indivisible whole. The converse is also true. It is impossible to compartmentalize human rights violations. One set of human rights violations inexorably brings on others.

Government can function in only one of two ways. It can base itself on the consent of the governed. Or it can base itself on repression.

Apartheid, by its very nature, cannot function by consent. The notion of superiority and inferiority are central to apartheid. While it may be easy for a group of people to consider itself superior, it is unrealistic to expect any group to consider itself inferior. It is especially unrealistic when this alleged inferiority is based on something as superficial as skin colour.

Some whites may have actually convinced themselves that they benefitted blacks by dominating them. Few if any blacks were likely to be convinced that domination by others was for their benefit.

For apartheid to function, it needed more than just segregation. It needed repression. On top of the structure of apartheid, there developed a whole superstructure of repressive laws and practices.

The Suppression of Communism Act of 1950 was drafted so widely as to cover not only communism in the traditional sense, but as well any organization that promoted racial equality. Communism was defined in the Act to include any doctrine "which aims at the encouragement of feelings of hostility between Europeans and non-Europeans races of the Union," the consequences of which were calculated to further the achievement of political, industrial, social, or economic change within the Union by the promotion of disorder.[26]

The Act was used to ban a whole host of organizations committed to ending apartheid, including the International Defense and Aid Fund for South Africa, an organization whose object was to provide legal aid to those accused of criminal offences for political reasons. According to the law, a banned organization has no right to notice or a hearing before the banning is proclaimed.[27]

Despite the wide definition of communism in the Suppression of Communism Act, the government eventually came to find it was not broad enough. Parliament in 1960 passed the Unlawful Organizations Act, which authorized the banning of any organization which in the opinion of the government threatened public safety or order. The African National Congress was banned under this legislation.

Both the Suppression of Communism Act and the Unlawful Organizations Act provided for listing and banning. Listed members of prohibited organizations could not be Members of Parliament or lawyers. They could be prohibited from involvement in any of a long list of organizations, including parent-teacher associations, and restricted to the cities in which they lived.

The Suppression of Communism Act and the Unlawful Organizations Act were replaced by the Internal Security Act of 1982. Banning, as it existed before 1982 and as provided for in the 1982 Act, was a form of civil death. A banned person could be prevented from attending gatherings, from publishing any statement, from staying in any place, from absenting himself or herself from any place, from receiving visitors, from communicating with any person, from performing any specified act.

Banning affected not only the person concerned. A banned person prohibited from attending gatherings could not be quoted. Quoting any utterance, past or present, of a banned person was an offence punishable by up to three years imprisonment. The practice of banning ended with President F.W. de Klerk's address to Parliament on February 2, 1990.

Banning has to be distinguished from banishment. Banishment, or the power to order any Bantu or any tribe from one district to another, was a power that existed since the Native Administrations Act of 1927. Banishment could be without trial. A 1956 amendment allowed banishment orders to be served without prior notice to the person concerned.

The Criminal Law Amendment Act of 1953 created severe penalties for otherwise minor offences committed with a political motive, "by way of protest or in support of any campaign for the repeal or modification of any law" or the administration of any law. People involved in passive resistance to apartheid became subject to years of imprisonment, and whipping.

The General Law Amendment Act of 1962, also known as the Sabotage Act, covered virtually any act deemed to endanger the maintenance of law and order, including just trespass.[28] Once the act was committed, the burden was on the accused to show that the act was not done with the intention of furthering any political aim.[29] Possible sanctions for violation of the Act included house arrest, and the death penalty.

The possibility of detention without trial was a commonplace of South African law. The General Law Amendment Bill of 1963 provided for detention for interrogation without trial for ninety days. This law also allowed someone sentenced to jail for a political offence to be kept in jail after the expiry of his/her sentence at the discretion of the government.

The Terrorism Act of 1969 allowed for indefinite detention without trial. Terrorism was defined to include even a lawful act, to encourage change, in cooperation with an international body. There was no requirement of intent. The offence could be punished by the death penalty. The Internal Security Act of 1982 updated the crime of sabotage, the crime of terrorism, the power of indefinite detention.

The dehumanization of blacks involved in the ideology of apartheid made torture all too easy to commit. From 1960 to 1990, there were seventy-three deaths in detention, apparently from torture.[30] The International Commission of Jurists concluded, in 1988, that "Torture and brutality are virtually routine for security forces" and that "torture of detainees who have been convicted of no crime [is] at best condoned by the government."

South Africa had a comprehensive networks of censorship laws. Books, films, plays, art, and newspapers were all subject to banning. The laws were used to ban any work that so much as displayed blacks and whites together, talking to each other. Even artists or writers whose works were not banned were subject to subsequent attack if they published any false information about the police or prisoners.[31]

As if all of these police state powers were not enough, the Public Safety Act of 1953 gave the authorities extraordinary powers if a state of emergency was declared. Except for three months, South Africa was under a state of emergency, in whole or in part, from 1985 to 1990.

A state of emergency allowed the government to function by decree. It did not need to pass legislation through Parliament. Although the Internal Security Act already allowed for detention without trial, the arrest had to be authorized by an officer of or above the rank of lieutenant colonel. The state of emergency allowed for detention without trial by even the most junior police officer.

Repression existed to enforce apartheid. In turn, apartheid itself was used to assist in repression. A Bantu who was allowed to live outside of his/her Bantustan could be deported, because of political activity, to his/her homeland and required to remain there. If the Bantustan was one of the four independent homelands, deportation followed upon revoking whatever status the Bantu had outside of his/her homeland. If the Bantustan was one of the six that never became independent, South African citizenship was revoked, and then the Bantu was deported to his/her homeland.[32]

The nature of human rights violations in South Africa was unique. There were other countries where the number of cases of arbitrary detention, extra-judicial executions, or torture were as great or greater. There were other countries where human rights violations may have been more gross. But there was none where human rights violations were more flagrant.

In South Africa, human rights violations were perpetrated by means of a visible legal structure. South Africa was a state dedicated to the violations of human rights, built upon the principle of human rights violations. As the Soviet Union abused psychiatry for political reasons, South Africa abused the laws for its political agenda. In South Africa, law and the rule of law were totally divorced.

The nature of human rights violations in South Africa led to apartheid being defeated on its own terms. Advocates of apartheid justified the system on the basis that whites represent a higher plane of civilization than blacks. Yet South African apartheid society was the least civilized, the most barbaric in the modern world. Apartheid is universally repugnant to modern civilization. South Africa stood alone not, regrettably, in the violation of human rights, but in its refusal to accept the concept of human rights as valid.

N. Diedrichs, who said that no compromise between apartheid and human rights was possible, was right. But human rights is nothing less than respect for the inherent dignity and worth of humanity. Denial of human rights is denial of human nature. Believing in apartheid means, in a fundamental sense, ceasing to be human. South Africa drew out the logical consequences of apartheid to the fullest. It found out, through its own laws and practices, what apartheid truly meant. And that discovery of the true meaning of apartheid meant a realization that apartheid must end.

CHAPTER NINE

BLACK-ON-BLACK VIOLENCE

We all read the stories from South Africa. The headlines said "Tribal Bloodbath,"[1] "Latest Bloody Zulu – Xhosa Round Claims 27,"[2] "Rival Black Factions Rampage,"[3] "Zulu Inkatha War Rages."[4] These stories talked of black-on-black violence, of Zulus attacking Xhosa, and Xhosa attacking Zulus, of battles between factions loyal to the African National Congress, led by Nelson Mandela, and factions loyal to Inkatha, led by Kwazulu homeland chief Mangosuthu Buthelezi.

These headlines masked a reality that was rarely reported, if reported at all – the story of state complicity. This so-called black-on-black violence was really a continuation of the state policy of oppression through apartheid in another form.

There were a whole set of facts that led to this conclusion. They were:

- The police allowed Inkatha supporters to bear arms; but seized arms from Inkatha opponents, from African National Congress supporters. Vigilante attacks by Inkatha supporters often followed close on the heels of a police seizure of arms from African National Congress supporters.

- There was a pattern of Inkatha aggression followed by African National Congress supporter arrests. The overwhelming majority of the attacks, although by no means all, were Inkatha initiated. The overwhelming number of those arrested, on the other hand, were African National Congress supporters.

- Under South African law it was an offence to possess a firearm without a licence. It was an offence to possess any dangerous weapon which was not a firearm. The concept of dangerous weapon was broad enough to cover any object whatsoever which could cause harm.[5]

This law was enforced against African National Congress supporters, but not against Inkatha supporters. Inkatha warriors attended rallies visibly armed with spears, knives, fighting sticks, and home-made guns. The police did not seize them or charge anyone, on the grounds that the weapons were merely cultural weapons. In August 1990, after fighters had killed thousands with these "cultural weapons," a situation which argued for the enforcement of the weapons law against cultural weapons led to nothing of the kind. Instead, the weapons law was amended to allow possession of these cultural weapons.

- The police failed to prosecute Inkatha warlords involved in violence, despite abundant eyewitness testimony. From 1987 to 1990 there were 3,500 killings in black-on-black violence in Natal province alone. From July to October 1990, there were 800 more killings in Transvaal. Yet there were less than a handful of successful prosecutions against Inkatha perpetrators. There were no prosecutions even in cases where coroners inquests found Inkatha members responsible for murder.[6]
- Lawyers in private practice, for some Inkatha murders, did the paperwork police or state prosecutors failed to do, taking all the necessary statements, locating the witnesses, providing the documents necessary for prosecution. Still no state action was taken.
- The police failed to protect witnesses, complainants, or court applicants. Witnesses and complainants were murdered or disappeared. It became increasingly more difficult to persuade surviving witnesses to bring cases to court because of this failure of protection.
- In the few cases where Inkatha warlords were arrested and taken into custody, they were systematically released on bail shortly after arrest. These releases increased the risks to the complainants and witnesses.
- There was no effective police disciplinary procedure. The police force in South Africa is nationwide, not municipal. The police functioned as a paramilitary force whose primary target was counter-insurgency. There were no structures at all by which the police could be held accountable to the black communities. Even white civilians had little effective control over the police.

The Police Act prohibited comments about the police which were untrue. The onus was on the publisher to establish he had reasonable grounds for believing the allegations to be true.[7] The law had the effect of stultifying criticism of police behaviour. The law was one reason why reporting of police complicity in black-on-black violence was so rare.

Ministers of law and order were themselves not completely in control of the police. The police did not fully inform ministers of their activities, and, on occasion, actively misinformed them.

South African law provided for prosecution when the police acted outside the power given to them by law. As well, the government was liable for unlawful actions of members of the police, and for their failure to act when there was a duty to act. However these controls disappeared in a state of emergency or state of unrest. During those periods, regimes had an indemnity, indemnifying the government and the police from liability for unlawful or reckless actions committed by them in the good faith exercise of their emergency of unrest powers.[8]

From 1987 to 1990 Natal was under a state of emergency. When the state of emergency expired in South Africa generally in June of 1990, it continued in Natal. After the violence started up in Transvaal in July of 1990, the government, on August 24, 1990, declared nineteen districts in Transvaal unrest areas for the purposes of the state of unrest legislation.[9]

There were, as well, no effective internal controls over the police. The police, historically, had failed to discipline or expel members who had been guilty of assault or torture. On the contrary, many of those identified as being involved in assault or torture were promoted.[10]

- When police arrived after a conflict between Inkatha and the African National Congress, police used Inkatha forces to identify African National Congress supporters. Those identified as African National Congress supporters were handed over to Inkatha for disciplinary action.

- On other occasions, when police arrived at the scene after a conflict between the African National Congress and Inkatha, ANC supporters were arrested after Inkatha identification, and Inkatha members were not. African National Congress supporters were arrested on the grounds that they contributed to the violence.[11]

- When Inkatha supporters were armed aggressors and African National Congress supporters were passive victims, the police failed to intervene, and in effect, granted the aggressors immunity for their violent behaviour.

    Police did not act to prevent the crimes. If they were actually present, they stood by and did nothing when crimes were being committed by Inkatha against the ANC.

- If police did intervene it was to facilitate Inkatha attacks rather than to prevent them. When residents of townships congregated to defend themselves against an anticipated Inkatha attack, the police arrived to disperse the residents. When Inkatha supporters assembled, there was no similar dispersal.

- Interdicts or injunctions were granted against the South African Police, ordering them to stay away from particular people and communities. The interdicts were granted on the basis of court findings that the police stood by while Inkatha warlords committed crimes.

- Interdicts granted against Inkatha warlords were not enforced by the police. Inkatha warlords violated court orders of interdict with impunity.

- Inkatha members were trained in the use of weapons and the use of force in South Africa Defence Force camps.

- Inkatha violence was perpetrated by three groups: vigilantes – self-organized groups established for the purpose of violence; warlords – part of the organized political structure of Inkatha; and the Kwazulu Police. The Kwazulu Police were, in theory, the police force for the Bantustan or homeland of Kwazulu, which Inkatha controlled. In practice, they were the armed wing of Inkatha. The minister of police was the head of Inkatha, Chief Buthelezi. The Kwazulu Police did not function as neutrals in the conflict between Inkatha and the African National Congress, but instead battled openly on the side of Inkatha. The Kwazulu Police were required to be members of Inkatha. Interdicts were granted against a number of Inkatha warlords and Kwazulu police.

The homeland or Bantustan policy, itself, was a progenitor of violence, creating an armed force that was a police force in name only. The Kwazulu Police were used for forced recruiting into Inkatha amongst the Zulu populations of Natal. The Kwazulu Police themselves needed to be disarmed if the violence was to end. The apartheid South African government did nothing about the police violence coming from the homelands.

- The Kwazulu Police routinely disobeyed interdicts against them. Residents of areas from which the Kwazulu Police were interdicted died in the custody of the Kwazulu Police.
- Inkatha distributed political literature through a fax machine owned by the South African Police Security Branch in Peitermaritzburg, the capital of Natal. The literature was traced to the police fax.
- Spent bullets found at the scene of violence in the days following a carnage were identified as police-issue ammunition.
- Inkatha warriors were transported to the scenes of attacks in police personnel carriers.[12]
- Whites, in civilian clothes, wearing masks, or blackened skin participated in Inkatha violence, alongside Inkatha warriors. In light of the other elements of police complicity, it was alleged that those whites were themselves members of the police force.
- The police covertly financed a sequence of Inkatha rallies, in November 1989, March 1990, and January 1991. President de Klerk, in July 1991, admitted the funding, but announced it had stopped as of March 1990. At the same time he announced the shuffling of Law and Order Minister Adriaan Vlok and Defence Minister Magnus Malan out of their portfolios to minor posts in the cabinet. Evidence of the funding of the January 1991 rally came out in November 1991, after the de Klerk announcement.

Why was this violence happening? Why was Inkatha attacking the African National Congress, and why were the police actively supporting Inkatha in this battle?

From the white racist perspective, Inkatha is a more moderate political force than the African National Congress. The ANC boycotted all the institutions of apartheid. Its supporters refused to participate in the white power structures in any form, either at the level of the administration, the legislature, or the judiciary.

Inkatha, on the other hand, was an active part of the apartheid system in place. Inkatha formed the government of Kwazulu, one of the ten homelands or Bantustans in South Africa designated for blacks. Inkatha participated in apartheid by forming the government of Kwazulu.

As well, at a time when the African National Congress called for armed struggle against apartheid, Buthelezi and Inkatha opposed armed struggle. That opposition to armed struggle against apartheid was ironic in light of the enthusiastic embrace by Inkatha of violence against the African National Congress.

Inkatha opposed sanctions against South Africa as an element in the international struggle against apartheid. Buthelezi echoed the arguments of the then South African government that sanctions hurt the poor in South Africa without deflecting apartheid from its course.

Inkatha was capitalist. The African National Congress was socialist. The ANC called for nationalization of a number of industries. Inkatha opposed these nationalizations. The ANC was not communist, but had many prominent communists amongst its leadership, including Joe Slovo, the former head of the Communist Party of South Africa. Inkatha portrayed itself as the champion of free enterprise.

It is easy to see why Inkatha was preferred by right-wing whites in South Africa to the African National Congress. Political differences of opinion cannot, in itself, however, explain a resort to violence.

Inkatha was the governing force in Kwazulu ever since its creation in 1972. Initially, its power within South Africa was unchallenged. The African National Congress was banned in 1960, and by 1972 was operating outside of South Africa almost entirely.

Black-on-black violence was not a feature of apartheid. It was a feature of the ending of apartheid. With the end of apartheid, there was a disintegration of the power structure on which Inkatha had relied.

Within South Africa, even before the African National Congress was unbanned, in 1990, there developed political movements in sympathy with the ANC. The United Democratic Front, founded in 1983, opposed, as the ANC did, participation in apartheid institutions. So did the Congress of South Africa Trade Unions, founded in 1985.

The United Democratic Front and the Congress of South African Trade Unions quickly developed a following that showed that Inkatha was no longer in control of the black community of Natal. In May 1987, the United Democratic Front and the Congress of South African Trade Unions called for a protest of all white parliamentary elections then being held. Blacks were asked to stay at home and stay away from work. In effect, a one-day strike was called.

The stayaway call was effective. Blacks remained home. The stayaway, in itself, was not directed against Inkatha. But it demonstrated to Inkatha that blacks in Natal were prepared to follow the United Democratic Front and the Congress of South African Trade Unions, rivals and opponents of Inkatha. The stayaway was followed by the murder of bus drivers who were supposed to bring the blacks to work, by a forced recruiting drive into Inkatha, and by an ever escalating cycle of violence.

The violence, of course, was not all on one side. There were African National Congress revenge and retaliation killings in response to the Inkatha killings. The point I am trying to make is that the police were engendering, manipulating, and escalating a conflict for their own ends.

From 1987 to 1990, the black-on-black violence was contained in Natal, one of four South African provinces. Natal is the South African province where Kwazulu is located. Although South African black-on-black violence was often portrayed as a tribal conflict, Natal violence was not a tribal conflict. Both perpetrators and victims were from the same tribe – Zulu. All that differentiated the participants was their political affiliation.

The violence in Transvaal, which began in July of 1990, was intertribal, between Zulus and Xhosa. The violence began in Seboking on July 22, one day after Inkatha launched itself as a national political party. Up to that time it had been a political party only in Natal, seeking power only in the Kwazulu homeland.[13]

The black-on-black violence served the political interests of Inkatha, because it gave it a power and a strength through force. More importantly, however, the black-on-black violence served the political interests of the white, right-wing community. The violence helped to discredit the notion of black majority rule. The violence created a perception of a black community incapable of governing itself, of needing a white force of law and order to keep warring black communities apart.

The black-on-black violence terrorized whites as well as blacks, who feared a black-run South Africa would be a violent South Africa dragged into civil war. The existence of tribal warfare reinforced the racial stereotypes whites in South Africa held about blacks for decades – primitive, violent, dangerous, and incapable of self-government.

Although I have used the term "black-on-black violence," because that is the way the violence was reported, that description is as misleading as calling

World War II white-on-white violence. The violence was political rather than racial or tribal.

The Inkatha attacks on the African National Congress were, in reality, police attacks on the African National Congress through intermediaries. Repression became privatized. ANC activists were arrested, beaten, and even killed. ANC structures were destroyed without the police being seen to be responsible.

Inkatha became a willing partner in a police strategy of masked repression. One can draw a parallel with the countries of Latin America where off-duty police dressed as civilians and perpetrated death-squad killings and disappearances, for which the state disclaimed all responsibility.

Lawlessness of the police, state-organized violence, does not end simply because the leadership changes direction. Structures of repression have to be removed. Police have to become subject to the rule of law.

Right-wing elements of the police and the Inkatha movement each had their own political agenda, which was threatened by the ending of apartheid. Security bureaucrats within the police wanted to see a continuation of apartheid. They wanted, at all costs, to avoid black majority rule. Inkatha, while opposing apartheid, wanted to maintain its dominant political position within the Zulu community, a position generated by the creation of the Kwazulu homeland and the boycott by the African National Congress of apartheid institutions. So both security bureaucrats and Inkatha joined together to use violence to achieve what they appeared to be losing through the then impending democratic dispensation.

Given the political motivation of the police to perpetrate atrocities, the question remained, why did the police use Inkatha for its repression, rather than doing the job themselves? To use a phrase of Clive Plasket, a South African attorney: Why were the police subcontracting the dirty work?[14]

One reason is that vigilante activity destabilized opposition to apartheid far more effectively than directly imposed state repression could do. Direct state repression has a mobilizing, rather than a disorganizing effect. The immediate targets may be neutralized. But a community of support swells to protest their victimization. Directly imposed state repression is counter-productive. It accelerates cohesion and commitment in the victim community.

Vigilante activity does not provide the same visible target for community resistance. The repression, by appearing to come from within the community, rather than from the outside, does not have the same cohesive effect on the community. On the contrary, vigilante activity from within divides the target community rather than unifies it.

Like much state repression, vigilante repression is not just a strategy. Rather it comes from a theory, a theory of low-intensity conflict. Low-intensity conflict theory suggests war must be fought by a combination of hard and soft measures. Soft measures are development aid, the building of such things as roads, schools and churches. Hard measures are violence through surrogates to replace the local hostile leadership with a local friendly leadership.

An opposition political force, according to low-intensity conflict theory, is not to be defeated through direct repression and confrontation, but instead with co-option of the leadership and counter-organization at the grass roots. This counter organization, rather than the military itself, becomes the arm of violence in the struggle to defeat the opposition. The opposition, instead of being confronted, becomes reconstructed.

For this low-intensity conflict theory to work, there have to be forces on the ground willing to function as surrogates of the military establishment. Generally, in South Africa there were no such surrogate forces, except in Natal. Inkatha was a willing and eager partner in the police counter-insurgency strategy, not for the reasons the police had, of continuing apartheid, but for its own political ends.

The South African Defence Forces had already applied low-intensity conflict theory in Mozambique, using Renamo as a surrogate. What happened in Natal and Transvaal bore an eerie resemblance to that.

Low-intensity conflict is a misnomer. The level of violence is, if anything, higher under low-intensity conflict than with direct state repression. Indeed that is, from the point of view of the perpetrators, one of its advantages. The political damage, both locally and internationally, the state suffers from low-intensity conflict is much less than it would suffer from a comparable level of directly imposed state repression. In reality, what is of low-intensity, in low-intensity conflicts, is not so much the conflict as the visible state involvement in the conflict.

Surrogate violence, rather than creating a demand to end state repression in the way visible state-imposed violence would, creates a demand for state repression. In Natal, the so-called black-on-black violence justified the continuation of the state of emergency after it had ended elsewhere in South Africa. In Transvaal, the violence justified the imposition of the state of unrest "Operation Iron Fist." Emergency law, unrest law, and Operation Iron Fist gave the police total and complete control, without legal supervision, and with a seeming justification.

The transition to democracy provided another justification for the use by the police of surrogate force. Directly imposed repression was no longer available as an option because it was rejected by the political leadership. Police rule could come about only in response to an emergency. So the police had to create one in order to restore their former dominion.

Now the African National Congress is the leading partner in a government of national unity. Nelson Mandela, leader of the ANC, is the president of South Africa. Legal apartheid has ended. South Africa is a democratic state. The homelands have disappeared. Inkatha continues in a democratic South Africa as a political force. But it is no longer a law unto itself. The police are subject to black control as well as white control. A Commission of Inquiry chaired by Richard Goldstone is investigating past police involvement in black-on-black violence.

This episode of violation of human rights standards is closing. But while it was ongoing, it cost thousands of lives. But it is important to focus on what happened and why it happened. For only then, can we learn from the tragedy.

CHAPTER TEN

PROSECUTION OF CRIMES AGAINST HUMANITY

For decades South Africa was a horror chamber of atrocities. That country was the leading violator of human rights in the world, not because of the number of those killed or tortured, but because apartheid rejected the very concept of human rights as valid. Now there is democracy. Apartheid has ended.

What is to be done about the crimes that were committed, the murders, the torture, the crime of apartheid? Albie Sachs has said: "If the price of peace in South Africa is that those involved in these terrible murders go unpunished, it is worth it."[1]

I do not quarrel with the conclusion, but I think that before we jump too readily to it, we must make an assessment. If democratic South Africans are going to pay a price for peace, they should know what the price is.

There is a duty in international law to prosecute torturers, mass murderers, criminals against humanity, grave violators of humanitarian law, and perpetrators of apartheid. The Torture Convention commits signatories to prosecute torturers wherever they are found.[2] The UN principles on extra-legal executions states that governments shall bring to justice persons who participate in arbitrary and summary executions, in any territory.[3] The UN principles on war crimes and crimes against humanity states that persons who have committed war crimes and crimes against humanity, wherever they are committed, shall be subject to arrest, trial, and, if found guilty, to punishment.[4]

So, the first price that has to be paid, is violation of international standards. If South Africa were not to prosecute torturers, murderers, and criminals against humanity as the price for peace, it would be violating international human rights law, not in the same way as it did when it perpetrated apartheid, but in another way.

Indeed, it is generally recognized that the duty to prosecute crimes against humanity is a peremptory norm of international law, or *jus cogens*. According to the Vienna Convention on the Law of Treaties, peremptory norms of international law take precedence over treaty obligations.[5] By refusing to prosecute, South Africa would not just be violating a rule of international law, it would be violating a rule of international law of the most basic and fundamental character.

The second point I would make is this: the duty to prosecute is not just a duty on South Africa; it is a duty on all states. If a South African torturer is found in Canada, then Canada has a duty to prosecute that torturer, whether South Africa prosecutes or not, whether South Africa grants an amnesty or not. Canada has recognized that duty and legislated the offence of torture in its Criminal Code.[6] The law gives Canadian courts universal jurisdiction. A South African torturer, who committed his crime in South Africa against a South African victim, will be prosecuted in Canada, provided only that he is physically present there.

The same is true of criminals against humanity. The duty to prosecute criminals against humanity is a universal duty, incumbent on all states. Canada, again, to take an example of my own country, has a duty to prosecute South African criminals against humanity, if they are found in Canada. And it has acted on that duty by providing for prosecution of any criminal against humanity found in Canada, no matter what the nationality of the victim, no matter what the nationality of the accused, no matter what the location of the crime, no matter whether the crime was committed before or after the passing of the law.[7]

This universal jurisdiction creates a second price associated with a South African amnesty. It is the price of making South Africa a haven for its own international criminals. Outside South African these criminals can and should be prosecuted. Within South African they will not be.

Local amnesties for international crimes have no status at international law. The criminals remain subject to prosecution outside South Africa, whether they can be prosecuted inside South African or not. A South African amnesty would have the effect of keeping criminals against humanity and torturers within South Africa. Only in South Africa would they be safe from prosecution.

We must also look at the issue from a purely practical level, from the point of view of the perpetrators, and from the point of view of the victims. Albie Sachs, who lost on arm to a car bomb in 1988, said he would have no problem if he met on the street the people who placed the bomb and tried to kill him.

The sentiments of Sachs are noble ones. If he wishes, personally, to forgive the crime done to him, if he wishes to show mercy to those who have done him wrong, I applaud him for it. I, myself, like to think I am prepared to forgive quite a lot that is done to me.

But I have no authority to forgive what is done to others. For those who have been murdered, the person who can forgive is gone. It would be impudent of me to forgive the murder of another. It is not my place to forgive. The United States organization Human Rights Watch has put it this way: "It is not the prerogative of the many to forgive the commission of crimes against the few."[8]

On the contrary, forgiving a murder victimizes the dead person twice over. First his life is desecrated. Then his death is desecrated. By denying the dead justice, we make their deaths meaningless. We impose a posthumous cruelty on them. The memory of the victims should be hallowed. By saying we shall do nothing about their deaths, we instead degrade the memory of their victimization.

There is a converse effect on the perpetrator. Doing nothing about a grave and flagrant crime emboldens and justifies the perpetrator. Doing nothing about torture, extra-legal killings, or crimes against humanity makes their reoccurrence more likely.

Perpetrators of these crimes in South Africa were and are members of the police force, the army, the security service. They remain in positions where they can, in the future, commit other atrocities. Past amnesties create expectations of future amnesties. The message an amnesty or immunity law gives is that these crimes are acceptable, that the perpetrator runs no risk by committing them, that no matter what the law says, an amnesty will rescue the perpetrators.

After decades of apartheid, torture and extra-legal killings became institutionalized as police and defence force practices. The ending of apartheid, by the force of circumstances, ended the use of torture and death squads to support apartheid. But it does not inevitably follow that the use of torture and the death squads by the authorities will disappear.

On the contrary, the experience has been, in other countries where an amnesty or law of immunity has accompanied a transition to democracy, that torture and arbitrary executions remain. They are no longer used for political repression. They are, nonetheless, used, to fight common crime.

Amnesty International, for instance, in August 1990, conducted a campaign against torture and extra-judicial executions in urban Brazil. Amnesty believes that the use of torture by the police in urban Brazil is endemic. Amnesty states that the police have taken "the law into their own hands torturing and killing ordinary criminal suspects and prisoners." An Amnesty report adds, "Brazilian police frequently act as if they are beyond the law, torturing with impunity and increasingly resorting to extra-judicial executions."[9]

The Amnesty report notes there were no prosecutions for widespread abuses, such as torture and disappearances, which occurred during the two decades

of military rule from which Brazil emerged in 1985. In 1979 an amnesty law
was passed that benefitted those accused of political crimes and members of the
security forces implicated in human rights abuses. The report concludes that
the lack of thorough investigation and prosecution for serious abuses in Brazil
effectively condones such nations. And so it would in South Africa.

Of all the atrocities in South Africa in recent years, the worst have been
centred in Natal province. Between 1987 and 1990, over 4,000 people were
killed in state-encouraged and -supported Inkatha violence directed against
the African National Congress, and in ANC retaliation killings.

Nicholas Haysom, a South African criminal lawyer, has said that a few
vigorous prosecutions at the beginning of the violence would have effectively
stopped the cycle of killings.[10] The police and the courts, however, refused to
prosecute because the violence served the purpose of the regime then in
power. Inkatha, which the apartheid regime favoured over the African
National Congress, as a black political option tolerant of apartheid, was
allowed to intimidate and murder African National Congress supporters. The
whole notion of black-on-black violence served the regime's purpose of discrediting black politics.

For an amnesty to cover these crimes committed in Natal, in light of their
genesis, would amount to a fit of collective amnesia. The legal profession
fought valiantly to bring this Natal violence to the courts, through interdicts,
civil actions, and pressure for prosecutions, in the face of official obstruction,
intimidation, and murder of witnesses. An amnesty would mean a capitula-
tion in this struggle for law and justice.

The Natal violence was white manipulation of black political division.
One cannot assume it was the only or the last such manipulation. Rivalry continues under a new democratic dispensation. Democracy has to protect itself
against those who try to discredit it and achieve their own ends through violence. An amnesty that embraces Natal violence bodes ill for the protection of
a future democracy throughout South Africa.

The best way justice systems have devised for preventing abuses is investigation, arrest, trial, conviction, and punishment. Surely the worst way of preventing atrocities is blanket absolution, forgiveness, and forgetfulness no matter how serious or flagrant the abuse.

If we step outside the frame of reference of perpetrator and victim, and
look at society as a whole, the effect of an amnesty is equally harmful. Doing
nothing in the face of flagrant international crimes is a violation of the principles of justice and the rule of law.

By bringing the perpetrators to justice, we assert the values that the perpetrators denied to their victims. The murder, the torture, the crimes that have
occurred in South Africa were wrong because they were unjust. Prosecution of

South Africans criminals cannot bring the murdered victims back to life or heal the wounds that were inflicted. But it brings justice back to life, and heals the wounds to the justice system.

Albie Sachs reminds us that the objective of punishment is not to satisfy a desire for vengeance. That, of course, is quite so. But it does not follow that we can abandon punishment because we do not believe in vengeance.

The difference between vengeance and justice is the difference between the tyranny of individual emotions and the rule of law. Vengeance is emotional. Justice is the rule of law. Justice should be tempered with mercy. It should not be hardened with vengeance. However, if we abandon punishment through an amnesty, we abandon an important part of our justice system, that like crimes be treated in like manner. A murder tomorrow will be punished. A murder yesterday will not be punished.

The quality of justice tomorrow depends upon the quality of justice today. Justice today is the foundation for justice tomorrow. When we amnesty past crimes, we knock the foundations out from under future justice. We perpetrate injustice.

The symbol of justice is a blindfolded woman holding scales. Justice is blind to whether crimes were committed yesterday or today. It is also blind to whether crimes were committed by those in government or those in opposition.

There is an assumption behind the notion of trading off peace for justice: that the atrocities were all on the side of the apartheid regime. The justice that is being abandoned is being given up by the opponents of the apartheid regime.

That assumption may not be true. There have been allegations of abuses perpetrated by those involved in armed struggle against the apartheid regime. Whether or not those who oppose apartheid can or should forgive the former government of South Africa for government-perpetrated atrocities, they have no moral claim to forgive themselves for any atrocities they themselves may have committed.

A blanket amnesty covers all. It covers apartheid's opponents as well as the former apartheid regime. It prevents the ill-founded charge from being dissipated. It prevents the well-founded charge from being substantiated.

The pursuit of justice uncovers all. Wild and unsubstantiated accusations against the opponents of apartheid can be dispelled. And for the well-founded charges, it cannot be said that apartheid's opponents used the peace process to cover up their own crimes.

An amnesty born out of political expedience does not put an end to the desire for justice. After World War II, the Allies stopped prosecuting Nazi war criminals in mid stream. Kurt Waldheim and many others were awaiting prosecution when the trials were halted abruptly for political reasons.[11]

The political reasoning at that time was that it was important to have West Germany as an ally in the then developing Cold War with the Soviet Union. The British, who led the charge to abandon prosecutions in 1948, linked, I believe falsely, the necessity of bringing West Germany on side in the Cold War and the ending of the prosecutions.

Prosecutions did end in 1948, as the British had proposed, but only to start up again, in one country after another, years later. The desire for justice would not be stilled. Prosecutions began again throughout continental Europe, including West Germany.

The United States set up an office of special investigation in 1979 to deal specifically with Nazi war criminal cases. Canada, in 1987, and Australia, in 1988, both passed legislation to allow for prosecutions of Nazi war criminals found in their territories. Even the United Kingdom's Parliament finally passed such legislation. The legislation was initially defeated in the House of Lords by some of the same people who were responsible for the 1948 do-nothing policy. But the government reintroduced the bill into the Commons. The Lords could not defeat it a second time. So it became law.

This push for justice for the crimes of the Holocaust came, in many instances, from people who were not even born during World War II, from people who had no connection with the victims of the crime. Decades later, the logic of the political compromise that led to the abandonment of prosecutions, if it ever existed, was forgotten. The cry for justice, on the other hand, became ever louder.

South Africa runs the risk of living through this same dynamic. If there is an amnesty, now, for political reasons, of the worst crimes of apartheid, there may well be, twenty, thirty, even forty years from now, persistent efforts to bring the criminals to justice. The desire for justice will not be quashed by political compromise. It will resurface in South Africa, as it has resurfaced worldwide in relation to the crimes of the Nazi Holocaust.

The costs of an amnesty I have been listing are costs that exist everywhere. There is one cost that is unique to South Africa. It has to do with the crime of apartheid.

There is an international convention on the suppression and punishment of the crime of apartheid. In that convention, the state parties declare apartheid is a crime against humanity.[12] The states parties undertake to prosecute, bring to trial and punish persons responsible for the crime of apartheid.[13]

There is, as well, an international convention on the non-applicability of statutory limitations to war crimes and crimes against humanity. That convention states that no statutory limitation shall apply to the prosecution and punishment of the crime of inhuman acts resulting from the policy of apartheid.[14]

The draft code of offences against the peace and security of mankind, under consideration by the UN International Law Commission, lists apartheid as constituting a crime against humanity.[15] According to the draft code, every state has a duty to try or extradite any perpetrator of the crime of apartheid arrested in its territory.[16]

As well, there is a whole list of United Nations General Assembly resolutions to much the same effect. The cumulative effect of the resolutions, declarations, draft codes, and amnesties has been to lead some jurists to argue that the crime of apartheid has reached the level of a norm of customary international law. The duty to prosecute the crime falls not just on convention signatories, but on all states.

Customary international law is sometimes divided into *lex lata* and *lex ferenda*, law generally accepted and law in the making. The crime of apartheid as a crime of universal jurisdiction in international law for which there is a duty to prosecute is not generally accepted. The Government of Canada, for one, does not accept it. Canada has not signed the Convention on Suppression and Punishment of the Crime of Apartheid nor the Convention on the Non-Applicability of Statutory Limitations to War Crimes and Crimes Against Humanity. This second convention defines apartheid as a crime against humanity. Canada has a number of universal jurisdiction offences in its Criminal Code, allowing for prosecution provided that the perpetrator is found in Canada. However, apartheid is not one of the universal jurisdiction offences in the Code.

The crime of apartheid represents a trend in human rights and humanitarian law. What effect will an amnesty in South Africa have on this trend? If the crime of apartheid is international law in the making, then an amnesty in South Africa will mean the unmaking of this law. If the crime of apartheid is not to be prosecuted in a democratic South Africa, where realistically can it expect to be prosecuted? An amnesty in South Africa runs the risk of causing the collapse of the whole international legal structure built up around the crime of apartheid. At the very least, current trends will be reversed, and current legal doctrine put in question.

While there is an unequivocal duty to prosecute torturers, death-squad killers, and traditional criminals against humanity in international law, it is arguable that for the crime of apartheid there is a power to prosecute, but not a duty to prosecute. However, if no one does prosecute this crime, the existence in international law of even the power to prosecute is cast in doubt. It would be ironic if the staunchest advocates of the development of the crime of apartheid would be the instrument of its undoing.

Humanitarian law and, in particular, Protocol I to the Geneva

Convention for the Protection of Civilians in Times of War require prosecution of the crime of apartheid. Specifically, the Protocol requires repression of
grave breaches.[17] The practice of apartheid is regarded as a grave breach of the
Protocol.[18] Grave breaches are, according to the Protocol, to be regarded as
war crimes.[19]

In 1980, Oliver Tambo, then president of the African National Congress,
submitted a declaration to the Red Cross in which he asserted the ANC
intends to apply the Geneva Conventions and Protocols whenever practically
possible. He said, "The African National Congress intends to respect and be
guided by the general principles of international humanitarian law applicable
in armed conflicts."[20]

The rejection of this Protocol would cause a problem to the African
National Congress, for a reason that is separate but linked to the issue of prosecution of the crime of apartheid. That is the issue of prisoners of war.

According to the Geneva Conventions, a combatant in an international
armed conflict cannot be punished by a party to the conflict solely for being a
combatant. A combatant can be prosecuted for war crimes and/or crimes
against humanity. A combatant cannot be prosecuted simply for taking part in
the combat.[21]

According to Protocol I of the Geneva Conventions, an armed conflict in
which people are fighting against racist regimes in the exercise of their right of
self-determination is considered an international armed conflict covered by
the Conventions. By the terms of this protocol, a person cannot be prosecuted
for fighting against apartheid, but only for committing atrocities in the fight
against apartheid.[22]

ANC members who were prosecuted in South Africa courts for their
armed struggle relied on this Protocol. The argument was rejected by the
courts, but that to does not change the fact that it was put forward by the
African National Congress.

If the ANC accepts humanitarian law, if it accepts Protocol I of the
Geneva Conventions, it is hard to see how it can pick and choose amongst its
provisions. If the ANC rejects the duty to prosecute, it, at the same time,
undercuts the claim that anti-apartheid combatants should have had prisoner-
of-war status. When the authority of one part of the Protocol is lessened, the
legal weight of the whole Protocol is lessened. By turning a blind eye to prosecution of the crime of apartheid, the African National Congress would make
its position that anti-apartheid combatants should have had prisoner-of-war
status that much less clear.

As I wrote at the beginning, I agree with Albie Sachs that if the price of
peace is that atrocities go unpunished, it is worth the price. The point I would
make though is that the price to be paid is a steep one. By not punishing these

atrocities, South Africa would be giving up quite a lot. It is a price that should not be paid in a spendthrift, extravagant manner.

It is, first of all, not at all clear that the price of abandonment of prosecutions has to be paid for peace. There should be no automatic assumption that such a price has to be paid. The regime under President de Klerk and the National Party appointed a judicial commission to investigate allegations of death squads in the South African police and the South African defence force. The implication, from the very appointment of this commission, is that the National Party regime would be prepared to bring the perpetrators of death-squad authorities to justice.

Second, if the price for peace is an amnesty, then there should be only so much of an amnesty as is needed to pay the price of peace. It may be that the parties would accept the notion of prosecution of those involved in extra-legal killings, but not the prosecution of those involved in torture. It may be that the parties would accept the prosecution of torturers, but not the prosecution of those perpetrating the crime of apartheid. If the price for peace is abandonment of the pursuit of justice, generosity in paying more of a price than is asked is misplaced. The price that is required should be paid, and no more.

As well, the choice South Africa faces is not a choice between prosecuting for past atrocities and doing nothing. There are other remedies available besides the criminal courts. Reparations or compensation can be paid to the surviving victims, their heirs, or the collective institutions that represent the communities from which they came. A work of investigation, of history, of reconstruction of events can be done.

If forgiveness for past violations is appropriate, and I have doubts that it is, it should not be blanket forgiveness in advance, without knowing who committed the abuses and in what circumstances, without knowing whether the disappeared are alive or dead, without knowing where the dead are buried, and how they died. It should be forgiveness only after the truth is known, only after what is being forgiven is publicly disclosed.

Peace may not be attainable with prosecutions, but may coexist with reparations, with investigation and public disclosure of past abuses. It would be irresponsible profligacy not to pursue these remedies, if the abandonment of the pursuit is not a required price for peace.

There is a reluctance to prosecute not just from the prior regime but from the African National Congress itself. Nelson Mandela, in June 1990, said: "Indulging in self-righteous indignation and finger pointing serve no useful purpose." He added: "Today we wish to concentrate on the future."[23] As well, at a Johannesburg meeting of a conference of newspaper editors held the week of August 2, 1990, he said: "Our attitude is to let bygones be bygones."

There is a fear within the ANC that a prosecution, after a peaceful transition, launched against the main architects of apartheid, would be viewed as political vindictiveness rather than the pursuit of justice. Any intention to prosecute that the ANC manifests will make the transition more difficult to accept.

Of course, these considerations just state the political reality the African National Congress faces in another way. The ANC has made a virtue of necessity. It has internalized what the prior regime itself would have wanted. Prosecution complicates transition to democracy. Transition to democracy is the main goal. Therefore, for the ANC, prosecution is to be avoided.

However, conceptually, virtue and necessity are distinct. From the point of view of principle, we must extricate one from the other. The necessary is not always virtuous. What is right and wrong must not be decided on the basis of what is politically practical. Once we remove political factors from our consideration, there is little or nothing to be said for inaction on gross and flagrant international crimes.

The notion of trading off peace and justice is very much a political one. It may well be that politics requires such trade-offs. We, all of us, have to recognize that in our daily lives it is difficult or impossible to realize our ideals.

However, that does not weaken or invalidate the ideals that we have. The African National Congress may have to trade-off peace against justice. But, human rights activists do not. Human rights activists can continue to assert the ideal, which is peace and justice, peace with justice, whether the ideal can be realized in South Africa or not.

The price that has to be paid for peace is not a price that human rights activists have to pay. Human rights organizations must not lose sight of the ideals worth pursuing, no matter what the limits of the political reality are. Selling off justice for peace may, in South Africa, in any country where there is a peaceful transition from tyranny to democracy, be a political reality. But it will, I humbly suggest, never be right.

PART IV

STATE REMEDIES

CHAPTER ELEVEN

SOVEREIGNTY AND THE RIGHTS OF THE INDIVIDUAL

In a conflict between sovereignty of the state and human rights of the individual, which is to prevail? That question assumes that sovereignty of the state and individual human rights are in conflict and asks us to pick one over the other. If for no other reason than that I am an individual and not a sovereign, I would prefer human rights of the individual over sovereign rights. But I do have a number of other reasons.

But first, I want to point out that there are two important respects in which the initial assumption is not true, in which sovereignty and human rights of the individual do not conflict.[1]

One has to do with the nature of sovereignty. Sovereignty of states is not absolute and unconditional. Sovereignty is limited by the restrictions states have imposed upon themselves. Once a state signs a treaty, it is bound by that treaty and cannot plead sovereign rights to violate it. For it has willingly limited its sovereignty by signing that treaty. Once the community of nations has developed a customary international law, through practice viewed as legally binding, then every state is bound by that law, as a member of the community of nations. The rights of sovereignty are one set of a package of rights defined by customary international law. The whole package of rights has to be examined to determine what sovereignty means and how far it goes. No state can pick one element of the package, sovereignty, and expect other states to recognize it to the exclusion of the rest of the elements of the package.

The rights of the individual are extensively defined and elaborated both by treaty law and by customary international law. The treaties which states have signed that articulate fundamental human rights are now a legion. To list only a few, there is the International Covenant on Civil and Political Rights; the International Covenant on Economic, Social, and Cultural Rights; the Convention on the Elimination of All Forms of Discrimination against Women; and the Convention on the Elimination of All Forms of Racial Discrimination.

One cannot say that these treaty rights conflict with sovereign rights. States, exercising their sovereign powers, have chosen to be bound by them. Rather here, sovereign rights and the rights of the individual are in consort. They stand together in the same corner of the ring.

There are two corollaries that follow from this observation. Everyone, presumably, wants to minimize the conflict between sovereign rights and the rights of the individual. In so far as that is so, we would want to encourage as many states as possible to sign and ratify as many international human rights instruments as possible. The more international human rights instruments states accept, the more their sovereignty is limited by the obligation to respect the rights of the individual.

Secondly, we would want to see as many international human rights instruments developed as possible. New instruments can articulate new standards that become acceptable to the international community. New instruments, even if they just re-articulate old standards in different ways, produce a combination that will generate signatories, which the old standards in their old combinations do not have.

It is arguable that all of the human rights of the individual, articulated in the Universal Declaration of Human Rights, are already part of customary international law. The Charter of the United Nations states that one of its basic purposes is promoting and encouraging respect for human rights and fundamental freedom for all. The Universal Declaration of Human Rights elaborates what that purpose means. The Declaration was accepted unanimously by all states when it was passed in 1948. Simply by being part of the United Nations, a state can be understood to have accepted and committed itself to respect for the Universal Declaration of Human Rights.

The Universal Declaration of Human Rights is a comprehensive human rights instrument. It covers economic, social, and cultural rights as well as political and civil rights. That does not mean that all human rights resolutions, declarations, conventions, covenants, and treaties that have followed are superfluous. In some respects they go beyond the Universal Declaration in the standards set. They provide for implementation mechanisms. They specify and clarify exactly what the standards in the Universal Declaration are.

But even if we are dealing with a state which has signed none of the international human rights instruments, the existence of the Universal Declaration and its incorporation into customary international law leaves very little room for sovereignty and the rights of the individual to conflict. By and large, what sovereignty means in this context is what states can do once they respect international human rights. The notion of sovereignty, as limited by international law, simply does not allow for state violation of the rights of the individual.

International law has the concept of *jus cogens* or peremptory norms of international law. According to the Vienna Convention on the Law of Treaties, peremptory norms of international law cannot be violated by treaties.[2] Where a treaty and a peremptory norm of international law conflict, then it is the peremptory norm of international law that prevails. And the rights of the individual are considered to be one of the peremptory norms of international law.

What that means is that states cannot violate international human rights standards, either individually or in consort. Even if states sign a treaty involving the violation of the rights of the individual, it is the rights of the individual, and not the treaty, that take precedence.

Sovereignty internationally has assumed the role of patriotism domestically. Sovereignty, like patriotism, is the last refuge of a scoundrel. Patriotism does not justify the violation of human rights domestically. And sovereignty does not justify the violation of human rights internationally. When sovereignty is invoked to shield against international protest of human rights violation, it is a verbal obfuscation rather than an assertion of a meaningful right.

That is not to say that sovereignty in this context is not invoked. It is invoked, and invoked frequently. I regret to say it has even been invoked by Canada. Native leaders have used the international mechanisms to assert aboriginal rights. And the Canadian government response has traditionally been one of opposition, lobbying against international action, arguing for restrictive interpretation of the instruments, and asserting that the issue is Canada's business alone, that the international community has no right to be involved.

For instance, at the time of the Oka crisis, Ross Hughes, for the Government of Canada, made a statement at the UN Working Group on Indigenous Populations in Geneva that the Oka crisis, including the food and medicine blockade of the Kahnesatake and Kahnawake reserves, were a domestic issue and not properly the concern of the United Nations. The UN ignored this statement by Canada, as it ignores all invocations of sovereignty in a human rights context, and proceeded to consider the issue.

Even the name of the Working Group, the Working Group on Indigenous Populations, is noteworthy. Canada has lobbied for the name "populations" and not "peoples" because the Government of Canada does not want the name of the group to suggest that aboriginal peoples can invoke the generally acknowledged international human right to self-determination of peoples.

The point is that virtually every state, including Canada, is tempted to hide behind the screen of sovereignty when it comes under attack in the international human rights arena. The appropriate response, legally as well as morally, is just to push that screen aside.

I wrote that there are two respects in which sovereignty rights and human rights of the individual do not conflict. The second has to do with which sovereignty we are discussing.

The relevant rights of sovereignty, in so far as they exist, are not just the rights of the violating state. They are also the rights of the nonviolating state concerned with the violations. There is much that a concerned state can do, in the exercise of its sovereignty, that does nothing to contravene the sovereignty of the violating state.

For instance, aid: there is nothing inherent in the concept of sovereignty that requires aid to be given to a human rights violator. It is not an interference with the sovereignty of the violating state to cancel or reduce or direct that aid because of the violations. On the contrary, it is part and parcel of the sovereignty of the donor state to direct that aid, if it wishes, in such a way as to maximize the realization of human rights, or to cancel aid altogether if need be.

The same can be said of trade, arms sales, diplomatic relations, diplomatic representations, and public statements. It is inherent in sovereignty that states are free to have diplomatic relations with whomever they want, to trade with whomever they want, to refuse to sell arms to whomever they want, to say whatever they want both privately in diplomatic contacts and publicly. The assertion of these sovereign rights to promote respect for human rights abroad means sovereignty and rights for the individual are working in tandem.

Again, this is an area where Canada could be doing more than it is. In foreign affairs, by and large, human rights is considered a multilateral, not a bilateral affair. Canada is a strong and effective voice for human rights in the UN Commission on Human Rights, and the Conference on Security and Cooperation in Europe. Even here it could be stronger. Canada could, for instance, sign and ratify the Inter-American Convention on Human Rights, but it has not yet done so.

However, when it comes to bilateral relations, the byword is silence. It is rare for human rights to be raised in Canadian interstate contacts. Organizationally in the Department of Foreign Affairs, human rights comes within the UN Division. There is no direct line relationship between human rights and the geographical desks. The results is that the geographical desks can and often do bypass human rights concerns.

To give but one example, I have for years tried to have the minister of foreign affairs raise the case of Raoul Wallenberg in interstate meetings with the Soviet Union and now with Russia. Despite the fact that Wallenberg is Canada's only honorary citizen, and his disappearance within the former Soviet Union is one of the great human rights violations of this century, to my knowledge, the matter has not been raised.

Be that as it may, given the two caveats I have just mentioned (that sovereignty does not include a licence to violate human rights, and that states can raise human rights concerns as part of the exercise of their own sovereignty), there is not much scope for conflict between sovereign rights and the rights of the individual. The only areas in which I can see that they conflict in a dramatic and obvious way, are in the issues of humanitarian intervention and aiding armed struggle.

Can states and should states send in troops to stop gross and flagrant violations of human rights by a sovereign state against its own people? Should states aid armed struggles of oppressed peoples against oppressor regimes? Here, there is no doubt that if states do, they are violating sovereignty in the name of individual rights.

According to international law, at least on one interpretation, it would be permissible to send in arms to aid the armed struggle of a national liberation movement combatting a colonial, racist, or alien regime[3] A national liberation movement is an organization representative of a people. The arms aid must be used to combat colonial, racist, or alien domination, and not to commit human rights violations. The human rights violations associated with the colonial, racist, or alien regime must themselves be of a gross and flagrant nature, to justify the arms aid. And the use of violence must be a last resort, when all hope of political accommodation has failed.

This international law doctrine is controversial. It is not universally accepted, but it is asserted by many. For those who accept it, the prototypical situation where it could have applied was the case of South Africa with its apartheid, racist regime. Apartheid involved the gross and flagrant violation of human rights. The African National Congress, before it was elected to power, was widely accepted as a national liberation movement and a legitimate representative of the South African people. The ANC renounced the use of terrorism and human rights violations as a means of armed struggle both in principle and in practice.

When it comes to actual armed intervention by one state against another in the name of human rights, there is another legal doctrine that is relevant, the doctrine of humanitarian intervention.[4] According to this doctrine, it is permissible for one state to intervene in another for humanitarian purposes, to prevent the infliction of gross and flagrant violations of human rights.

This doctrine is, if anything, even more controversial than the doctrine of aiding armed struggle of national liberation movements. It is noteworthy that the United States, which is perhaps that most interventionist government in this century, and has produced many weird and wonderful justifications for its interventions, has never invoked the doctrine of humanitarian intervention. On the contrary, the U.S. explicitly rejects the doctrine. The law officers of the U.S. Department of State reject it is a matter of international law.

A couple of situations where the doctrine could have been invoked illustrate its problems. The Vietnamese could have justified their invasion of Cambodia and the displacement of the Khmer Rouge Regime under Pol Pot in 1979 by the doctrine of humanitarian intervention. Tanzania could have justified its attack on Uganda to displace Idi Amin, also in 1979, by relying on the theory of humanitarian intervention.

The general unwillingness to accept the doctrine of humanitarian intervention is illustrated by the fact that neither Vietnam nor Tanzania relied on the doctrine for their actions. The Vietnamese claimed there was no invasion, that Pol Pot and the Khmer Rouge had fled because of the spontaneous uprising of the Cambodian people. Tanzania at least acknowledged they invaded Uganda, but justified it as a response to the prior invasion of Tanzania by Ugandan forces.

The Vietnamese invasion was widely seen as politically motivated. The new regime under Hun Sen was generally viewed as a Vietnamese puppet regime. The West, including Canada, continued to recognize a coalition of which the Khmer Rouge formed part as entitled to vote for Cambodia at the UN.

The Uganda problem was different. Idi Amin was replaced by Milton Obote. And Obote, in his own way, was as much a tyrant, as much a human rights violator as Idi Amin was. That was not the Tanzanian intention when they aided in Amin's displacement. But that was the result.

The Vietnamese situation illustrates the problem of politicization. It is a problem that both humanitarian intervention and aiding armed struggle share. Such assistance will inevitably be seen as political rather than humanitarian.

The way to overcome the taint of politicization is through internationalization. If there is to be armed intervention for humanitarian purposes, it is far better if it is done by an international force than by the forces of one country alone. At the very least, if the forces of one country alone are intervening, that intervention should be done with widespread international acceptance. The Allied intervention in Iraq to protect the Kurds can be justified as humanitarian, in part because of its widespread international acceptance.

The Ugandan situation illustrates the problem of control. An intervention may be able to topple an existing regime. It may be powerless to generate an indigenous regime that will be respectful of human rights.

This is a problem unique to humanitarian intervention. It is not shared with aiding armed struggle. When a state aids the armed struggle of a national liberation movement, the movement presumably is in a position to establish a successor regime. If the national liberation movement respects humanitarian and human rights principles in its armed struggle, as it should as a prerequisite for aid, then one would hope it would also respect these principles once in power.

But when there is humanitarian intervention, there may be no organized opposition at all. Indeed, for the most oppressive regimes, the mere existence of opposition, in any form, becomes impossible.

If there is to be humanitarian intervention, and I believe that in some situations there should be, it is not enough for the human rights situation in the country of concern to be bad. A conclusion must be reached that with an indigenous successor regime it could not possibly be worse. The level of human rights violations has to reach grotesque dimensions before armed intervention becomes justifiable. As well, no other course whether political or economic, must offer any hope. An example I would give is the Nazi Holocaust, the murder of six million Jews and the attempt to exterminate the whole Jewish people. Where the level of human rights violations does reach those dimensions, I would argue that humanitarian intervention is justifiable, and that individual rights must prevail over sovereign rights.

CHAPTER TWELVE

COMPENSATION

Amongst the remedies available for gross human rights violations are prosecution, extradition, revocation of citizenship, and deportation. Perpetrators may be prosecuted wherever they are found; they may be extradited for prosecution where the crimes were committed; their citizenship may be revoked, if they had been given citizenship in countries to which they fled; they may be deported from countries that they entered. Because I have written extensively about these remedies elsewhere,[1] this chapter discusses the remedy of compensation alone.

What has been the experience of obtaining compensation for victims of human rights violations? What lessons can we learn from that experience?

The Jewish community obtained compensation from West Germany for the human rights violations of the Third Reich.[2] The negotiation for compensation for West Germany was done entirely by a nongovernmental organization, the Conference on Jewish Material Claims Against Germany. The Conference was an umbrella group of various Jewish nongovernmental organizations set up specifically for the purpose of negotiating compensation with West Germany. The Conference was chaired by Nahum Goldmann, who became the chief negotiator for the Jewish Community with West Germany.

Negotiations focused on three aspects. One was individual compensation to be paid directly to the victims of the human rights violations, or their families. The second was compensation to the state of Israel. The third was compensation to the Jewish community as a group, outside of Israel.

The Claims Conference delegation reached agreement quickly with West Germany for legislation on restitution and compensation payable to individuals. That legislation was passed in 1953, and amended extensively in 1956 and 1965.

Compensation to Israel was not negotiated with Israel. Instead it was negotiated by the Claims Conference representatives. The negotiations presented the unusual spectacle of one state, West Germany, negotiating with a nongovernmental organization, the Claims Conference, as representative of another state, Israel. Direct contacts between West Germany and Israel were politically unacceptable to Israel at the time, so soon after the Holocaust. So the Claims Conference served as an intermediary.

Total payment to Israel was set at 3.45 billion marks. The schedule of payment was to be over fourteen years. Payment was a straight cash transfer. Israel, in return, undertook to buy goods in West Germany with Deutschmark amounts put at her disposal in West Germany and to export the goods to Israel. Goods purchased could be foreign as well as German goods.

The most difficult element of the negotiations was compensation to be paid directly to the Claims Conference itself for the Jewish community as a whole outside Israel. Initially German representatives to the negotiations were uniformly negative to this proposal. Eventually the concept was accepted and a sum of 450 million marks was settled on, which was to be used for the restoration of Jewish schools, synagogues, and cultural organizations and to allow Jewish writers, artists, and scholars to pursue their work.

The 1953 West German statute for individual compensation had two components. One was restitution of property seized. The other was compensation for injuries. For real property, there was a presumption of law that a sale was an unjustified deprivation. For personal property, purchase in good faith was protected, except for well-known, valuable objects.

Compensation was paid by the Government of West Germany directly to the victims or their families according to a strict set of eligibility criteria. Subsequently, a fund was set up for the distribution by the Claims Conference for those who had not benefitted from the law.

The law provided for compensation for damage to health. Yet illnesses seldom have one cause. A good deal of litigation in West Germany focused on whether the illness of the claimant was caused by the persecution or had some other cause.

West Germany received one and a quarter million applications for compensation. About half were accepted. More than 80 percent came from outside West Germany. Requests for restitution of property seized by the Reich totalled 4.25 billion Deutschmarks. Expenditure for compensation of claims was estimated at 70 billion Deutschmarks.

Victims who lived in countries occupied by West Germany were not compensated directly by West Germany. Instead, West Germany made lump sum payments to the governments of these countries. The individuals, in turn, claimed from their own governments. West Germany concluded treaties with twelve Western states for lump sum payments to be made for individual compensation. The total payment of West Germany under these treaties was 1 billion Deutschmarks.

None of the countries of Eastern Europe had indemnification treaties with West Germany. The West German statute allowed for Eastern European victims, once they left Eastern Europe, to claim for compensation.

East Germany, did not sign a compensation agreement with the Claims Conference. The government of East Germany took the position that it had no responsibility for the acts of the Nazi government of Germany. It changed its position only in early 1989, and agreed in principle to reparations. When East Germany was absorbed into West Germany in late 1989, the united Germany took over this commitment to reparations.

Austria did not sign an indemnification treaty with West Germany. West Germany viewed Austria equally as guilty of Nazi war crimes as the Third Reich. When Austria asked for reparations from West Germany, the reply was that West Germany would return to Austria the bones of Hitler.

Austria, on the other hand, viewed itself as the first victim of Nazism. It refused to accept responsibility for Nazi war crimes. The Claims Conference entered into negotiations with the Austrian government for a settlement similar to that with the West Germany. The Austrians provided a minimal indemnity for certain pressing claims. The difficult attitude of the Austrian government meant that Austrian Jews came out the worst in compensation of all Jewish victims. The World Jewish Congress asked Austria not to be admitted to the European Economic Community, until it agreed to pay reparations to survivors. The Austrian legislature in early 1990 passed legislation to pay $25 million U.S. to Jewish survivors of the Holocaust.

To this day, claims are still being made against the German compensation fund. There are offices throughout the world of the United Restitution Organization, a volunteer Jewish organization, assisting claimants in the processing of their claims. The headquarters is in Frankfurt.

In Canada, now, there are two offices, in Montreal and Toronto. There used to be offices as well in Winnipeg, Edmonton, and Vancouver. A Winnipeg staff member for the Winnipeg Jewish Community Council now does United Restitution Organization work for all of the West.

The German compensation system provides for changes in compensation when income changes, and when health changes. There is an annual reporting requirement. These reports of changes in circumstances, as well as new claims of those who have recently come out of Eastern Europe, provide continuing work for the United Restitution Organization.

The West German compensation scheme was unprecedented. Never before had a government paid out compensation to citizens of a former regime who at the time of payment were not citizens of that country. The legislation created a new legal concept. The compensation agreement represented an ethical victory.

The precedent was significant, not only because of what West Germany had done but, as well, because of what the Claims Conference had done. The Claims Conference, a nongovernmental organization, represented individuals at the international level and negotiated their legal rights with a state.

The Claims Conference and the United Restitution Organization have been crucial components of the compensation system for Nazi war crimes. The horror and criminality of the Holocaust bear no comparison whatsoever to the internment of Japanese North Americans during World War II. However, there are comparisons that can be made between the compensation schemes arising out of the two wrongs.

One point of contrast is the delay. Though the Luxembourg Agreement, that set out the settlement between the Claims Conference and West Germany, was not signed until 1952, West Germany accepted the principle of compensation immediately after the war. The notion of Japanese compensation took a long time to be accepted.

In this battle over compensation, the United States led Canada in several different ways. The United States legislated an Evacuations Claims Act as early as 1948.[3] The Act allowed for compensation for loss of real or personal property. But it did not cover losses resulting from death or injury, losses from hardship or suffering, losses of earnings. The Act also excluded claims from Japanese Americans who were deported from the United States. Approximately 26,000 claims were made and 37 million dollars were paid out. There was no similar statute in Canada.

In Canada, there was some immediate post-war compensation, but without a specific statute being passed for that purpose. The Emergencies Act, which received Royal assent July 21, 1988, requires that compensation shall be awarded to those who suffer damages as a result of the exercise of powers under the Act.[4] The War Measures Act, which preceded it, had no similar provision. The federal government set up a commission in 1949 headed by Mr. Justice Henry Bird to dispense compensation to Japanese Canadians. Compensation was limited only to losses resulting from the sale of property at less than fair market value. One thousand, four hundred people filed claims to the Commission. Nearly $2 million was paid out.[5]

Secondly, in the United States there was litigation about compensation.[6] William Hohri and eighteen others who were interned or descended from those interned sought damages in 1983 from the United States government. The United States government, in 1984, moved to dismiss the statement of claim. The U.S. government argued the statute of limitations, sovereign immunity, and the prior Evacuations Claims Act.

District Judge Oberdorfer of the Federal Court from Washington D.C.

accepted the government motion and dismissed the claim. The United States Constitution prohibits private property being taken for public use without just compensation. Except for compensation based on that constitutional provision, the court held the doctrine of sovereign immunity prevented the lawsuit.

United States statute law states that every civil action commenced against the U.S. is barred unless the complaint is filed within six years after the right of action accrues. The court held that because this action was begun more than six years after the internment, even for compensation for violation of constitutional rights, the action must be dismissed. Because of the decision on the time limit, it became unnecessary for the court to decide the U.S. government argument that the Evacuations Claims Act was an exclusive remedy, leaving room for no others.

The plaintiffs appealed to the U.S. Court of Appeals. At the Court of Appeals they were joined by a nongovernmental organization, the Japanese American Citizens League, who filed an *amicus curiae* brief arguing, with the plaintiffs, that the trial court judgment be reversed.

The Federal Court of Appeals for the District of Columbia circuit rejected the reasoning of the trial judge on the statute of limitations. The U.S. government had been guilty of fraudulent concealment. The government justified the internment of Japanese Americans both at the time, and during subsequent litigation, on the basis of military necessity. Yet the government had in its possession no professional intelligence analysis justifying the need for mass evacuation based on race. The only intelligence report it did have, which it concealed at the time, specifically rejected the need for mass evacuation based on race. This fraudulent concealment prevented the U.S. government now from relying on the statute of limitations.

The Federal Court of Appeals then said that the Evacuations Claims Act was not an exclusive remedy. If someone did not claim under the Act, he could now claim under the Constitution. However, the Act also had provision saying that if a person brought a claim under the Act he could be barred from all further claims. That finality clause, the court held, barred any further claims from anyone who received a benefit under the Evacuations Act.

In dissent, Chief Judge Mabbey reasoned that fraudulent concealment was not enough to overcome the statute of limitations. There had to more than mere silence. There had to be some misleading, deceptive, contrived scheme that was designed to mask the concealed information. Since that was not alleged, the action, in his reasoning, failed.

The case went to the U.S. Supreme Court. The Supreme Court held only that the wrong appeal court decided the case. The case on appeal should have been decided not by the Court of Appeals for the District of Columbia Circuit, but by the Court of Appeals for the Federal Circuit. At the U.S.

Supreme Court, the American Civil Liberties Union, the American Friends Service Committee, and the Anti Defamation League of B'nai B'rith filed *amicus* briefs.

The case went back to the Court of Appeals for the Federal Circuit. The judgment of the District Court was affirmed. Because, at the District Court, the plaintiffs had failed totally, the net result of the litigation was that the plaintiffs came away with nothing.

The litigation in the U.S. was unsuccessful. But at least it was attempted. In Canada, there has been no similar litigation.

Both countries, eventually, provided for more complete and adequate compensation than was given immediately after the war. The U.S. was first, passing legislation in 1988 that offered $20,000 to each Japanese American interned during the war. As well $50 million was to be set aside for education of the U.S. public.[7]

For Canada, the government announced, also in 1988, that $21,000 was to be given to each interned Japanese Canadian and $12 million was given to the National Association of Japanese Canadians, to contribute to the community. The government committed itself to spend $24 million to create a Canadian race relations foundation.[8]

As had happened with West Germany and the Claims Conference, the Canadian commitment came through negotiations with a nongovernmental organization, the National Association of Japanese Canadians. The government had, at one point, proposed only that $12 million be paid to establish a Japanese community foundation. The Japanese Canadian Association rejected the proposal. The government did not immediately accede. But at least it did not impose a unilateral solution. It was only after the Japanese Canadian Association accepted a government proposal that the government acted.

It is ironic that, in the case of West Germany and the Claims Conference, there was quick agreement on individual compensation. Only group compensation was a stumbling block. In the case of the Government of Canada and the Japanese Canadian Association, it was the opposite. The government, from the start, was willing to pay group compensation. Its objection was to individual compensation.

The Government of Canada felt that it was too late to obtain adequate evidence to support many individual claims. Lump sum payments, so the government said, would be arbitrarily established and unconnected to either actual loss or established need. The Japanese Canadian Association, nonetheless, persisted, the government relented, and agreement was reached.

Although both the West German/Claims Conference agreement, and the Government of Canada/Japanese Canadian Association agreement are important precedents, they are precedents that have been followed more in the breach than in the observance. War amputees have met with one obstacle after another in their attempts to obtain compensation for their injuries suffered at the hands of the Japanese government during World War II.

Chinese Canadians have been attempting to achieve compensation for the imposition of a head tax on Chinese immigration imposed from 1855 to 1923, by the Canadian government. The tax was imposed on Chinese immigrants and no others. It started off at $10 in 1886 and went up to $500 for 1904 to 1923. In those years, $500 was the price of a house.[9]

Because the head tax was imposed so long ago, the Chinese Canadian National Council is not asking for individual compensation. There are only a few surviving immigrants who paid the tax. Instead, the Council is asking the government to pay $23 million into a trust foundation for the community. A second group, the Toronto Chinese Head Tax Action Committee is, however, asking for individual compensation.

The head tax was blatantly discriminatory. The Chinese Canadian National Council has tried to rely on the Japanese Canadian settlement as a precedent. Many nongovernmental organizations have supported the Chinese Canadian National Council, as they had supported earlier the Japanese Canadian Association. The government, to date, has been unrelenting.

The German compensation scheme, though it has had many problems of implementation, and caused dissatisfaction in many individual cases, is at least important for its acceptance of the principle of compensation. In Canada, acceptance of that principle has been belated and inconsistent, applying to Japanese Canadians but not Chinese Canadians, and applying to Japanese Canadians only in 1988 for events of the 1940s.

Part of Amnesty International's twelve-point program for the prevention of torture is compensation. The program states that victims of torture and their dependants should be entitled to compensation.

Amnesty welcomed the Torture Convention provision that obligates state parties to provide compensation. The Convention, however, only applies to victims of torture narrowly defined. It does not apply to victims of cruel, inhuman, or degrading treatment or punishment which does not amount to torture. Amnesty recommended that the Convention compensation provision apply to victims of ill treatment which does not amount to torture. The organization regrets that the Convention was so limited.

In Canada, Amnesty International has been active in urging Canadian contributions to the United Nations voluntary fund for victims of torture. The fund distributes money to organizations offering humanitarian, legal, and financial aid to torture victims. The fund was established in 1981 by a UN General Assembly Resolution.

The Canadian contributions to the fund is the paltry sum of $10,000 (Canadian) a year. A few years ago Canada contributed $30,000 to the fund. There was a hope that this level of contributions would be maintained. But the government relapsed, returning to the amount of $10,000.

The Canadian contribution is small not only in absolute terms but in comparison to other donations. West Germany, for instance, in 1988 gave $150,000 U.S., France $76,000 U.S., Norway $75,000, the Netherlands $50,000.[10]

The fund each year gives to the Canadian Centre for Investigation and Prevention of Torture the sum of $30,000. I do not suggest that there should be a linkage between the money Canada pays to the fund and the money the fund pays to Canada. But the fact that Canada is receiving more from the fund than it is giving is another indication of how small the Canadian contribution is.

In sum, nongovernmental organizations have been involved in the issue of compensation for victims of human rights violations in a myriad of ways: as lobbyists, advocates, negotiating partners, legal interveners, recipients of funds, dispensers of funds for community institutions and individuals, and assistants to individuals making claims.

For the protection of international human rights generally, the contribution of nongovernmental organizations is indispensable. Their contributions is equally indispensable, in particular, for obtaining compensation for victims of human rights violations.

PART V

CANADA

CHAPTER THIRTEEN

CANADIAN COMPLIANCE WITH INTERNATIONAL HUMAN RIGHTS STANDARDS

Giving close scrutiny to Canadian violations of international human rights standards may seem pointless. Canada is one of the leading countries of the world in terms of human rights compliance. It may be that Canada violates some of its human rights commitments. However, Canadian violations are nothing compared to the gross and flagrant breaches committed by many countries.

Instead of being concerned with punctilious compliance on Canada's part, we may think we should be concerned with at least some measure of compliance from the worst violators. As long as international promises are violated in an egregious manner by other countries, what credibility does anyone have who insists that Canada comply with exactitude to every one of its promises?

International human rights agreements contain promises Canada has made to other signatory countries. Why should Canada pay close attention to whether it is keeping its promises, when other countries are openly violating theirs?

One reason Canada should be concerned with its own compliance is that Canada's keeping its promises is a strong argument for others to keep theirs. Canada can hardly ask other countries to keep their promises if Canadians show little concern for keeping theirs. Any complaints Canadians have about human rights violations around the world would lack credibility if Canada made no attempt to take its promises seriously.

A defence that signatory countries often raise to Canadian objections about international human rights violations is that the violations are a matter of domestic concern. Governments often rely on a clause of the United Nations Charter that says: "Nothing contained in the present Charter shall authorize the UN to intervene in matters which are essentially within the domestic jurisdiction of any state."[1] Canada can internationalize concern for human rights by tying its concern for human rights to its international promises. If Canadians say Canadian human rights issues are matters of more than domestic concern, Canadians can then say that foreign human rights issues are matters of more than foreign domestic concern.

International human rights promises are more than just promises between countries. They are promises to individuals as well. Individuals are not just the objects of international human rights accords. They are subjects, with their own rights. When Canada makes a promise internationally to respect human rights, it is not just a promise it has made to other countries of the world. It is, as much, a promise it has made to its own citizens. Canadians are entitled to bring their government to account for failure to comply with its international human rights commitments.

Ideally, Canada should be able to turn to international institutions to determine its compliance with international human rights standards. In practice, we have little choice. There are no institutions established to provide us with the assessment of compliance we should have.

There are, indeed, treaty-based bodies such as the Human Rights Committee established under the International Covenant on Civil and Political Rights. The Human Rights Committee receives reports from states that are party to the International Covenant on Civil and Political Rights on compliance with the Covenant for consideration of the committee.[2]

Because Canada has become a party to the Optional Protocol to the International Covenant on Civil and Political Rights, individual Canadians may complain to the Human Rights Committee of Canada's violations of the Covenant. The views of the Human Rights Committee, given after consideration of individual complaints, are not comprehensive enough to give Canada an assessment of its compliance with the Covenant. The individual complaints deal with only a few particular issues of compliance, rather than with all aspects of compliance.

The consideration given the Canadian compliance reports by the Human Rights Committee is comprehensive in nature. However, no conclusions are reached. The committees ask questions of Canada, but issue no judgments.

The Human Rights Committee, in 1980, discussed the whole question of assessment of state party compliance. The majority of the committee was of the view it should be making assessments. The minority was of the view that assessment was beyond the mandate of the committee. This view was that the committee was to assist state parties in the promotion of human rights. The function of the committee was not to pronounce whether states parties were implementing their undertakings.[3]

In the end, the committee agreed to make general comments to draw the attention of states parties to matters relating to the implementation of the Covenant. "General comments" means comments that do not refer to any individual country. These general comments are now being issued. They are no real substitute for assessment of state party compliance.

If we look at Canada's international obligations, and compare them with Canadian statutes, there are many differences. These differences may lead us to think that there are large discrepancies between Canadian international obligations and our domestic performance. However, that appearance would be deceiving.

Many of the differences arise from the Canadian legal tradition. Canadian law comes from a different legal tradition than do international instruments. Canadian common law, judge-made law, inherited from England, has traditionally emphasized remedies, not rights.

International instruments are profusions of statements of principle, but contain little in the way of remedies.

If Canada has a remedy that prevents an international right from being violated, it has met its international obligation. It need not have, in its law, a statement of the right as well. For instance, take slavery. Canada has committed itself internationally to prohibit slavery.[4] There is no statement in Canadian laws that slavery is prohibited. Yet Canada is not in violation of that obligation. There exists a set of remedies in Canadian law, such as the Criminal Code offences of kidnapping and forcible confinement, that prevent slavery from arising.

Even Canadian laws that articulate principles, Canadian human rights acts, the Charter of Rights and Freedoms, the Bill of Rights, have a far different appearance than international instruments. Canadian legislated statements of principle are meant to serve as symbols. The intention of the legislators is to have these principles expressed in simple, inspiring language, accessible to all.

International instruments, on the other hand, are political compromises of people from widely different legal systems, with different languages. They are exercises in verbosity elaborated to ensure there is no misunderstanding.

Canada is not in violation of its international obligations because Canadian law is succinct when the international obligation is prolix. The Canadian obligation is to meet its commitments, and not to reproduce international wording unthinkingly.

In a nutshell, Canada's strength, in its compliance with its international human rights obligations, is that Canada does by and large, comply. Canada is a country with an independent judiciary, a free press, and an elected Parliament. It respects basic human rights.

Canada's weakness is that compliance is more by circumstance than by design. Canada makes no systematic effort to match its domestic law with its international obligations.

In March 1979, Canada prepared a report on the implementation of the provisions of the International Covenant on Civil and Political Rights. It is a huge report, about five hundred pages. Canada prepared a supplementary report in 1983 of 162 pages, and a combined second and third report of 158 pages. These are, in reality, not reports of what Canada has done to implement the Covenant. They are not reports of Canadian design, but of Canadian circumstances. The reports attempt to show how the existing structure of Canadian law meets Canadian Covenant obligations.

Some countries, like the United States, have a direct reception of international obligations into domestic law. For the U.S., treaties are the law of the land. A person wishing to enforce compliance with a U.S. international obligation can go to court to ask the court to order compliance.

In Canada, there is no automatic reception of international obligations into domestic law. Incorporating international obligations into domestic law requires a separate step, domestic legislation. If the subject matter of the obligation is within federal jurisdiction, Parliament must legislate. If the subject matter of the obligation is within provincial jurisdiction, the provincial legislative assemblies must legislate.

Canada does, on occasion, legislate its international obligations. For instance, when the Charter of Rights and Freedoms was entrenched in the Canadian constitution, several provisions were included in an attempt to perform Canada's obligations under the International Covenant on Civil and Political Rights. One of these was the guarantee of the right to be tried in a reasonable time.[5] The Covenant obliges Canada to give such a guarantee.[6] Until the entrenchment of the Charter, that obligation had not been met. Until the entrenchment of the Charter, there was no such guarantee in Canadian law. The reason given for the entrenchment of that guarantee in the Charter was Canada's international obligation.

Another example is in the Immigration Act. The Immigration Act of 1976 legislated the definition of refugee that is in the United Nations Convention relating to the Status of Refugees. Canada has signed and ratified the Convention.

However, this sort of legislation is, by no means, comprehensive. The Charter did not entrench all Canadian obligations under the International Covenant on Civil and Political Rights. The Immigration Act does not incorporate all Canadian obligations under the Convention relating to the Status of Refugees and its Protocol.

Mostly, when Canada undertakes an international obligation, it does not legislate to comply. It relies on existing laws to demonstrate compliance. For instance, Canada is a signatory to the Convention on the Prevention and Punishment of the Crime of Genocide. The Convention commits us to preventing and punishing genocide.[7] The Criminal Code prohibits advocacy of genocide.[8] The Code has the crime of murder, war crimes, and crimes against humanity. As far as Canada is concerned, that is enough. The Government of Canada does not propose to introduce the crime of genocide into its laws.

Since Canada is abreast or ahead of the international community in most areas of human rights, this unsystematic fashion of compliance is, in general, successful. There is little or nothing it needs to do to comply with most of its international human rights commitments. However, given this absence of system to ensure compliance, it is hardly surprising that there are several areas where it does not comply. I shall review five of these: family reunification; cruel, inhuman, or degrading treatment; refugee protection; prosecution of criminals against humanity; and hate propaganda.

In what follows, I attempt to set out a few areas where Canada has violated its international obligations. The catalogue of violations is meant to be illustrative rather than exhaustive.

REUNIFICATION OF FAMILIES

Canada sponsored the Western proposal and led negotiations on family reunification at the Geneva negotiations leading up to the Final Act of the Conference on Security and Cooperation in Europe, signed in Helsinki in 1975. In view of Canada's leadership, it is particularly important that Canada comply with the commitment. Regrettably, Canada falls short of its commitment.

The Helsinki Final Act, says, in Basket III, on Cooperation in Humanitarian Fields, that participating states will favourably consider applications for travel for the purpose of allowing persons to enter their territory temporarily, and on a regular basis if desired, in order to visit members of their families. It also says that the participating states will deal in a positive and humanitarian spirit with the applications of persons who wish to be reunited with members of their family.

This provision is violated systematically in Canada for refugee claimants. Family members abroad of refugee claimants in Canada are not allowed entry to Canada. The Canadian system does not allow for it. They are not allowed entry as visitors on the assumption that, if they do come, they will claim refugee status. No one is allowed entry simply for the purpose of claiming refugee status.

Because refugee claims can take years to process, refugee claimants in Canada may be forcibly separated from their families for years. The problem is more acute for refugee claimants in Canada than for other foreigners. Other foreigners can at least be reunited with their families abroad. Refugee claimants who are real refugees do not have that option. Returning home for reunification may well mean persecution.

Prolonged family separations lead to family breakdown. The complexities and delays of the Canadian refugee determination system are unfamiliar to foreign spouses abroad. They often believe they have been abandoned, when the spouse claiming refugee status in Canada does not send for them.

The post traumatic stress syndrome that refugee claimants suffer is exacerbated when family separation is imposed in addition. The tension of waiting for a determination that may or may not be granted becomes harder to bear when the claimant does not have the family at hand as a support.

The Helsinki Final Act states that signatory states will deal with applications for family reunification as expeditiously as possible. Canadian families sponsoring their relatives abroad must, however, wait an inordinately long time before the foreign relatives arrive in Canada. Delays of two to three years are common. Processing is anything but expeditious.

The Helsinki Final Act states that special attention should be given to requests of an urgent character, such as requests submitted by persons who are ill or old. In Canada, such requests are not considered urgently. The ill are allowed into Canada, if at all, only after being delayed. Normally the ill are inadmissible, as medically prohibited. The Immigration Act prohibits admission of anyone with a contagious disease or an illness likely to place excessive demands on the Canadian health system.[9] If an ill person is admitted, it is only after extensive and time-consuming examinations and clearances.

The old are treated the same as the young. They are given no special treatment. Their applications are certainly not treated urgently.

The problem of family reunification is particularly acute for spouses, forced into separation for years. The Helsinki Final Act has a special provision for marriages between citizens of different states. The Helsinki Final Act states that the processing of documents required for spousal unification will be in accordance with the provisions accepted for family reunification, that is to say as expeditiously as possible. Yet, in Canada, spousal reunification, like family reunification is anything but expeditious.

A foreigner who while visiting in Canada meets and marries a Canadian may stay in Canada, pending the processing of the application for landing. A foreigner who meets and marries a Canadian abroad may not enter Canada to await the processing of the application for landing. The foreign spouse must wait out the processing abroad. As well, the Canadian spouse must be in Canada. Only a Canadian, resident in Canada, is allowed to sponsor a foreign spouse for landing in Canada.

The Helsinki Final Act says that until members of the same family are reunited, meetings and contacts may take place in accordance with the modalities for contacts on the basis of family ties. The provision about family ties states that participating states will favourably consider applications for travel with the purpose of allowing persons to enter their territory temporarily, in order to visit members of their families. In other words, while processing for family reunification is pending, family members should be allowed to visit.

For Canada, visiting is not allowed. Canadian immigration law divides applicants for entry into two rigid and mutually exclusive categories: visitors and immigrants. Visitors, after they enter, want to leave. Immigrants want to stay. It is impossible for a person to be both a visitor and an immigrant at one and the same time.

The Immigration Act prohibits entry of persons who are not bona fide immigrants or visitors.[10] A visitor who wants to stay is not a bona fide visitor.

A family member abroad who has applied to emigrate to Canada to be reunited with a family member in Canada cannot visit because the family member abroad is not considered a bona fide visitor. Once the family member abroad has applied to immigrate, the foreign relative has fallen into the immigrant category and out of the visitor category. Canadian law, at the least in the way it is applied, means visitor permission becomes an impossibility, a violation of Canadian law.

The prolonged delays in family reunification because of inordinately slow processing are compounded by this prohibition on visiting. Separation is more acute, more complete, because visiting is not allowed. Families often have to choose either a prolonged period of immediate separation, with reunification many years later, or periodic visits without permanent reunification.

The Helsinki Final Act states that participating states will lower fees charged in connection with family reunification applications, to ensure that they are at a moderate level. Applications for the purposes of family reunification may be renewed. Under such circumstances fees will be charged only when applications are granted.

Canada began charging $125 for applications for immigration, in 1986. Fees have increased regularly, and as of June 1, 1994, were $500 for an application. For each additional adult dependent, 19 or older, there is an additional fee of $500. If a person in Canada sponsors his/her parents and accompanying siblings, a separate fee has to be paid for the parents and for each sibling.

The fee has to be paid whether the application succeeds or not. The fee is for processing not for acceptance. If the application fails and the applicant reapplies, a new fee has to be paid.

Fees in Canada have not been lowered. They have been increased. It is a matter of judgment if $500, and in the case of accompanying adult siblings a multiple of $500, is moderate. In my opinion, $500 or its multiple is not moderate.

The obligation not to charge fees for reapplications unless the applications are granted is clearly and unequivocally wrong. The authorities have appeared to pay no attention at all to their Helsinki Final Act obligations in setting up the system of immigration fees.

CRUEL, INHUMAN, OR DEGRADING TREATMENT

The International Covenant on Civil and Political Rights, as well as the Convention against Torture, which Canada has also signed and ratified, prohibit cruel, inhuman, or degrading treatment. A brief prepared by the Inter-Church Committee for Refugees of the Canadian Council for Churches concluded that treatment of refugee claimants in the backlog was cruel, inhuman, and degrading.

Canada shifted to a new refugee determination system on January 1, 1989. All those caught up in the old system and not processed formed a backlog. Many of those in the backlog had been in Canada for years, waiting the determination of their claims. The government decided that those caught up in the backlog would have to be processed under the new system. Humanitarian landing of those caught up in the backlog could be allowed in only the most narrow of cases, for instance if a claimant married a Canadian. Successful establishment was not to be considered a ground for humanitarian landing.

The European Court of Human Rights had held, in the case of Soering,[11] that the U.S. death-row phenomenon amounted to cruel, inhuman, and degrading treatment. There was a risk of intense and protracted suffering of exceptional intensity and duration. The decision to extradite Soering from the U.K. to the U.S. to face a charge of capital murder was considered a violation of the European Covenant.

Refugee claimants in the backlog face something very much like the U.S. death-row phenomenon. They too face protracted uncertainty about their fate. For real refugees, the fate that awaits them on forced return to the country fled may be death.

The backlog consisted of 100,000 individuals. As of October 25, 1990, almost two years since the new law came into effect only 30 percent of the cases had been completed.

A survey of 200 refugee claimants in the backlog done by George Cram for the Canadian Council of Churches showed that 70 percent of those in backlog were suffering depression. For those who had been in Canada five years or more without their cases being decided, 63 percent had suicidal thoughts or feelings.

At the UN, members of the Human Rights Committee in 1990 noted that long delays to people who had suffered trauma could constitute cruel and inhuman treatment. The situation of refugees was one of the main problems in Canada still to be resolved. Asylum seekers should have the rights recognized in the Covenant, even if the question of asylum was not mentioned in it.

REFUGEE PROTECTION

The UN Convention on the Protection of Refugees, which Canada has signed and ratified, obligates Canada not to return any person to a country where his life or freedom would be threatened. This commitment is violated in a number of different ways, the most dramatic being by interdiction abroad. Canada operates an immigration control program at its overseas posts, employing some twenty-six officers. These officers both stop and train airline officials to stop refugee claimants coming to Canada. Some 9,000 persons are intercepted by the program each year.

Denial of access to Canada for the purpose of seeking refugee protection takes other forms besides interdiction. The combination of carrier sanctions (imposed on airlines for transporting those reported to immigration inquiries for violation of the Immigration Act on arrival), the imposition of visa requirements on refugee-producing countries, and denials of a visa to anyone who wishes to come to Canada to make a refugee claim stops many more than the interdiction program.

Interdiction, preventing a refugee claimant from ever coming to Canada to seek protection, is a practice that may lead to a refugee being forcibly returned to danger, or never being allowed to leave the country of danger. When an interdicted refugee is forcibly returned to the country of danger fled, then Canada shares the responsibility for that forced return, because of the interdiction, even if Canada is not the returning state.

Refugee determination procedures are deficient in a number of different ways.[12] Refugee claimants are denied access to counsel on their arrival. They may be interrogated about their claim, in the absence of a lawyer, by an immigration officer. What they say at the initial interview may then be used at their refugee hearings to throw their credibility into doubt.

The Executive Committees of the United Nations High Commission for Refugees has concluded that claimants should be given the benefit of an appeal, before they are required to leave, even for manifestly unfounded claims. In Canada, there is no appeal. There is only judicial review, restricted to technical, legal points.

At the time of writing this book, the absence of an appeal was under review by the government. Even if the government institutes an appeal, the fact remains that from January 1, 1989, refugee claimants were denied the benefit of any appeal, in violation of international standards. Many of those rejected in error without benefit of an appeal were forcibly returned to danger. Institution of an appeal system, even now, is too late to benefit them.

PROSECUTION OF CRIMES AGAINST HUMANITY

The Torture Convention obligates states, of which Canada is one, to bring torturers to justice. The UN principles on the prevention of legal executions calls on all states to bring perpetrators of extra-judicial executions to justice. The UN principles on war crimes and crimes against humanity calls on all states to bring war criminals and those who have committed crimes against humanity to justice.

Canada has fulfilled the obligations in form. It has passed laws allowing for the prosecution of torturers, of war criminals, of those who have committed crimes against humanity, no matter where the crimes were committed, no matter what the nationality of the victim, no matter what the nationality of the accused. All that is required is that the accused be found in Canada. In the case of war crimes and crimes against humanity, the criminal may be prosecuted even if the crime was committed before the law was passed, as long as the crime was a crime at international law at the time it was committed.

The issue that arises is the effectiveness of the laws. There are war crimes units in the Department of Justice and the Royal Canadian Mounted Police. To date, a few cases have been launched against alleged war criminals. However, a Commission of Inquiry on War Criminals said that there were twenty cases of alleged Nazi war criminals in Canada deserving urgent attention and 218 requiring further inquiry. The law was passed in 1987. So the pace of prosecutions is slow. To date, there have been no convictions.

As well the initiation of Nazi war criminal prosecutions is belated.[13] The duty to prosecute did not arise in 1987. It arose as soon as the criminals came to Canada after World War II. Canada delayed the bringing to justice of these accused for decades.

In principle the current laws are not restricted to Nazi war criminals. Any war criminal or any person who committed a crime against humanity found in Canada is liable to be prosecuted. Canada assumes the jurisdiction an international criminal court would have. However, there have been no cases launched outside of the Nazi war criminal area.

PROHIBITION OF HATE PROPAGANDA

An obligation to prohibit hate propaganda is in the International Covenant on Civil and Political Rights and the Convention on All Elimination of All Forms of Racial Discrimination, both of which Canada has ratified. The 1990 Concluding Document of the Copenhagen Human Dimensions conference in the Conference on Security and Cooperation in Europe process obligates the participating states to take effective measures, including the adoption of such laws as may be necessary, to provide protection against any acts that constitute incitement to violence against persons or groups based on national, racial, ethnic, or religious hatred.[14]

International conventions state, quite specifically, that hate propaganda shall be punishable by law. The Copenhagen Document talks about effective remedies, including laws. There is an assumption in the Copenhagen Document that the enactment of a law setting out an offence of hate propaganda will create an effective remedy. However, in Canada that has not been the case.

There have been a whole sequence of laws prohibiting hate propaganda in Canada, by various means. There are specific laws relating to the telephone, to the mail, to radio and TV, to importing. One provincial human rights act prohibits hate propaganda.[15] There is a prohibition in the Criminal Code.

The original importing provision under the Customs Act was not considered specific enough. It was struck down by the courts as unconstitutional, as being too vague.[16] It has since been replaced by a more precise law. The post office provision has turned out to be ineffective. In the one case where it was attempted, the tribunal that considered the case decided that there must be a criminal conviction before post office privileges of a hate propagandist could be suspended.[17] The Criminal Code provision requires the consent of the attorney general of a province before a prosecution can be launched. After the law was enacted in 1970, the Crown in Ontario launched one case in 1977 where it did not succeed.[18] Provincial Crowns in all provinces, for years after the failure, refused to give their consents to any more prosecutions.

The telephone prohibition law has functioned. Radio and TV prohibitions have been effective because of the regulatory control of broadcasting by the Canadian Radio-television and Telecommunications Commission. But the rest of the laws became dead letters for years, sitting in the statute books without effect.

Sabina Citron circumvented this system by launching a private prosecution under the false news section of the Criminal Code.[19] The hate propaganda provision of the Code does not allow for private prosecution, because it requires the consent of the attorney general. The false news section has no similar restriction.

Once it became apparent that the requirement of consent of the attorney general could be circumvented, consents started to be given. The attorney general in Alberta consented to the prosecution of James Keegstra, a school teacher who taught hate propaganda to his students as course material, which they had to learn and repeat for their essays and exams.[20] The attorney general of Ontario consented to the prosecution of Andrews and Smith of the Western Guard Party.[21] All of those accused were convicted, but the Alberta

Court of Appeal in the Keegstra case held in June 1988 that the statutory provision prohibiting hate propaganda was unconstitutional as a violation of freedom of speech.

The period of effectiveness was, therefore, short lived. After the Alberta Court of Appeal decision, prosecutions stopped again, not only in Alberta, but across the country. This ineffectiveness ended with the decision in December 1990 of the Supreme Court of Canada, in the cases of Keegstra, Andrews and Smith, and John Ross Taylor. Taylor was a person convicted of contempt of court for failing to obey an order, to cease hate propaganda by telephone, issued under the authority of the Canadian Human Rights Act. He too had challenged the constitutionality of that law.[22] None of these hate propagandists were successful at the level of the Supreme Court of Canada. All had their convictions upheld.

However, subsequently, the Supreme Court of Canada struck down the false news section of the Criminal Code as an unjustifiable violation of freedom of expression and unconstitutional. The safety valve which had allowed circumvention of the requirement of the consent of the attorney general, under the hate propaganda section of the Criminal Code, was shut off. Since it was shut off, consents for prosecutions under the hate propaganda provision of the Code have been difficult to get.

CONCLUSIONS

Canada is now or in recent years has been in violation of international human rights standards in a number of different respects. These violations are as follows:

- Refugee claimants are denied reunification in Canada with their families abroad.
- Reunification in Canada of Canadian citizens and permanent residents with immediate family abroad takes place only after inordinate, multiyear delays.
- Immediate family abroad are not allowed to visit relatives in Canada pending the implementation of the prolonged reunification procedures.
- Canada imposes visa charges on family reunification, whether the application is successful or not, whether the application is a first application, or a renewal.
- The delays in the processing of the refugee claims backlog were such as to amount to cruel, inhuman, and degrading treatment.
- Canada has denied protection to refugees by interdiction abroad, and by not providing adequate procedural safeguards for the determination of refugee claims.

- Canada did not begin prosecution of international war criminals and those who committed crimes against humanity in Canada till 1987. Since prosecutions have begun, the pace of prosecutions has been inordinately slow and ineffective.
- The Canadian obligation to prohibit hate propaganda has been respected only fitfully. From the time of the decision in the Keegstra case in the Alberta Court of Appeal on June 1988, till the decision of the Supreme Court of Canada in December 1990, the hate propaganda laws were completely ineffective.

Economic, Social, and Cultural Rights and the Canadian Charter of Rights and Freedoms

T he Canadian Charter of Rights and Freedoms focuses on civil and political rights. It says little or nothing about economic, social, and cultural rights. Canada is a signatory to both the International Covenant on Civil and Political Rights and the International Covenant on Economic, Social, and Cultural Rights. The International Covenant on Civil and Political Rights is largely reflected in the Charter. The International Covenant on Economic, Social, and Cultural Rights is ignored by the Charter.

The International Covenant on Economic, Social, and Cultural Rights, in brief, contains the right to work, the right to just and favorable conditions of work, the right to form trade unions, the right to an adequate standard of living, the right to health, the right to education, and the right to take part in cultural life.

The issue of economic, social, and cultural rights is very little discussed, nationally or internationally. The bulk of the time spent, for instance, at the UN Commission of Human Rights is spent on political and civil rights and not on economic, social, and cultural rights. The same, to take another example, is true of the Human Dimension component of the Helsinki process. Human rights nongovernmental organizations, by and large, pay attention to civil and political rights and not economic, social, or cultural rights. Amnesty International, Human Rights Watch, and the International Commission of Jurists rarely mention economic, social, or cultural rights. The academic literature also reflects this vacuum. Articles and books about political and civil rights are a legion. Articles and books about economic, social, and cultural rights are a handful.

The neglect is a studied one. There is a lot of opposition to the concept of economic, social, and cultural rights, despite the existence of the International Covenant on Economic, Social, and Cultural Rights and its widespread acceptance. The issue of the entrenchment of economic, social, and cultural rights in the Canadian constitution has shared the general oblivion to which economic, social, and cultural rights have been subject. Nonetheless, from reading the general objections that have been raised to the concept of economic, social, and cultural rights, it is possible to anticipate what a number of the objections would be to entrenching economic, social, and cultural rights in the Canadian constitution.

In what follows I attempt to anticipate these objections and respond to them. I believe that all the objections that could be raised to entrenching economic, social, and cultural rights in the Canadian constitution are ill founded. While applying the objection to the Charter debate is my own doing, all of these objections about economic, social, and cultural rights have been raised in other contexts. As a result, they have to be taken seriously, and answered. They cannot just be ignored.

The subject may be too little discussed to have developed a mythology. The myths listed here are really myths in the making. It is my belief that these are myths that should never take hold.

Myth Number One: Economic, social, and cultural rights are not really rights. According to this view, the use of the word rights in an economic, social, and cultural contexts is a moral or hortatory one. It is a political statement rather than the assertion of a legal right.[1]

The Reality: We are capable of making economic, social, and cultural rights legal rights in a Canadian context, if we wish to do so. There is nothing inherent in economic, social, and cultural rights that prevents them from being legal rights. At the international level, economic, social, and cultural rights are rights as much as political and civil rights. All are subject to international covenants. In form there is nothing to distinguish between the two covenants that leads us to believe that one, the Political and Civil Covenant, deals with legal rights, and the other, the Economic, Social, and Cultural Covenant does not. Both covenants are treaties, and treaties are considered a source of international law, no matter what the content of the treaty.[2]

Myth Number Two: We do not need to put economic, social, and cultural rights in the constitution, because there is no obligation, internationally, to implement these rights. Economic, social, and cultural rights are merely aims or goals which should be achieved progressively, rather than immediate obligations to be met.

The Reality: The Covenant on Economic, Social and Cultural Rights commits each state party "to achieving the full realization of the rights recognized in the present Covenant to the maximum of its available resources."[3]

That provision might excuse a poor country realizing the obligations immediately. It does not excuse a country like Canada, one of the wealthiest in the world. If any state, when devoting its maximum available resources to the realization of economic, social, and cultural rights, can realize those rights, then Canada can.

As well, there are many provisions of the Covenant, no matter what the level of resources available, which must be realized immediately by all. Limitation of resources can never excuse violation of the rights to equality in the enjoyment of economic, social, and cultural rights;[4] the right to form trade unions;[5] the liberty of parents to choose private education for their children;[6] freedom for scientific research and creative activities;[7] prohibition of employment of children in harmful work;[8] the rule[9] that marriage must be entered into with the free consent of the intending spouses.[10]

Myth Number Three: Economic, social, and cultural rights are variable in content. What they mean differs over time, and differs from one place to another. They depend on the level of economic development, the resources available to realize the right. Political and civil rights, on the other hand, are constant in their content. They mean the same everywhere all the time. It makes more sense to have rights in the constitution which are constant in content than rights which are variable in content. Putting rights in the constitution which are variable will cause unending problems for the courts.

The Reality: The mythological part of this objection is the notion that political and civil rights are constant. In the U.S. we have seen wild variations in court interpretations of the Bill of Rights over the years. Perhaps the most well-known instance was the case of *Brown v. The Board of Education.*[11] The U.S. constitution states that no state shall "deny to any person within its jurisdiction the equal protection of the laws."[12] Until 1954, and the case of *Brown v. Board of Education*, the courts had held that segregation was compatible with the U.S. Bill of Rights as long as the facilities offered, though separate, were equal in nature. In 1954, the U.S. Supreme Court reversed that jurisprudence and held that segregation itself was a denial of the right to equal protection of the law.

In Canada, the notion of variability in civil or political rights is imported into section one of the Charter, the reasonable limits clause. The Supreme Court of Canada has divided rights violations into two categories. There are those rights where the state is the singular antagonist of the person whose rights have been violated. Secondly, there are those rights where the violation involves the reconciliation of claims of competing individuals or groups. When the violation is of the second sort, the Supreme Court of Canada has said that all courts must show considerable flexibility. As long as the government has a reasonable basis for the second type of violation, the impugned legislation will stand.[13]

Myth Number Four: Political and civil rights instruments apply all their rights to everyone. Economic, social, and cultural rights instruments, on the other hand, allow for only certain rights to apply and allow for rights to apply only to certain aspects of the population. Rights that can be applied in so elastic a fashion do not properly belong in the constitution.

The Reality: The Economic, Social, and Cultural Covenant has a provision that allows developing countries to "determine to what extent they would guarantee the economic rights recognized in the present Covenant to nonnationals."[14] There is no comparable provision in the Civil and Political Covenant.

However, the Civil and Political Covenant allows for derogation, which the Economic, Social, and Cultural Covenant does not. Some rights, such as the right to life are nonderogable. But other rights, such as the right to liberty and security of the person, are derogable in time of public emergency and which threatens the life of the nation and the existence of which is officially proclaimed.[15] None of the economic, social, and cultural rights is derogable, even in times of emergency which threaten the life of the nation.

Secondly, despite the unqualified appearance of the rights in the International Covenant on Civil and Political Rights, state parties can sign the Covenant with reservations, as they can with any treaty. Canada has not attached any reservations to its signature. But many other countries have. The U.K., by way of reservation, excepted from its commitment under the Civil and Political Covenant the armed forces, prisoners, and foreigners.

Thirdly, the Canadian Charter of Rights and Freedoms allows for legislative limitations of the existing civil and political rights. The limitation must be reasonable and demonstrably justified in a free and democratic society. But it remains a limitation all the same. Political and civil rights cannot be considered absolute rights.

Fourthly, the Charter has been interpreted in such a way as not to apply to classes of people. In the case of *Ruparel*,[16] Mr. Justice Muldoon, in the Federal Court Trial Division, relying on the judgment of the Federal Court of Appeal in the *Canadian Council of Churches*[17] case, held the Charter does not apply to noncitizens outside of Canada. So an applicant for immigration applying through a Canadian visa office abroad could be a victim of discrimination on the basis of age, and the Charter could not help him.

The point is that it is simply wrong to think of political and civil rights as absolute and economic, social, and cultural rights as qualified. Political and civil rights are subject themselves to too many qualifications to make the distinction tenable.

Myth Number Five: At the international level, economic, social, and cultural rights are treated in a different fashion than are political and civil rights. Because the two sets of rights are treated differently internationally, it makes sense to have the two sets of rights treated differently domestically, with one set in the Charter and the other set outside of the Charter.

The Reality: There was a difference historically in the mechanisms established for implementing civil and political rights, on the one hand, and economic, social, and cultural rights, on the other hand. But the difference over time has diminished. The remedies for the two sets of rights have converged.

The Civil and Political Covenant establishes a Human Rights Committee of independent experts. States parties are supposed to file periodic reports with the committee on their compliance with the Covenant. The committee is supposed to study these reports and make general comments on them. As well, there are optional provisions for interstate complaints and individual complaints to the committee.

The Economic, Social, and Cultural Covenant, on the other hand, establishes no such committee. Compliance reports are to be furnished directly to the Economic and Social Council of the United Nations, a state representative body, and not an expert independent body. There is no interstate complaints option, nor an individual complaints option.

Even at the beginning, the difference in structure of implementation between the two sets of rights was more apparent than real. The main reason there was no expert committee for economic, social, and cultural rights was that there were a number of technical agencies reporting to the Economic and Social Council, such as the World Health Organization or the Food and Agricultural Organization, that already dealt with these rights. There was a concern that an economic, social, and cultural committee would be a duplication.[18]

Nevertheless, over time, as the compliance reports started to come in, it became apparent that an expert committee was needed. The Sessional Working Group of the Economic and Social Council established to consider state parties compliance reports went about its work in a manner that was, in the words of the International Commission of Jurists, "cursory, superficial, and politicized."[19] It neither established standards for examining reports nor reached any conclusion on the reports.

Specialized agencies of the Economic and Social Council were impeded from participation in the Working Group. The Group sat too little. Its membership kept changing. Members of the Group attended irregularly. The lack of expertise of Group members meant they showed little understanding of the issues or the reports themselves.

In consequence, the direct reporting to the Economic and Social Council was abandoned and replaced by reporting to an expert committee. The committee was established by a 1985 Economic and Social Council resolution. It held its first session in March 1987. It now functions very much like the Human Rights Committee established under the Civil and Political Covenant.[20]

Using differing forms of mechanisms domestically for implementing political and civil rights, on the one hand, and economic and cultural rights, on the other hand, would be repeating domestically the errors made internationally. Canada should learn from the international experience and not repeat its mistakes. The lesson the international experience gives us is that economic, social, and cultural rights, if they are to be treated seriously, have to be handled in much the same way as civil and political rights.

Myth Number Six: Economic, social, and cultural rights are not as important as political and civil rights. First priority should be given to the realization of political and civil rights. If we put economic and social rights in the Charter then we put them on the same level as political and civil rights. We end up confusing our priorities. We will dissipate our energies on the less important – the economic, social, and cultural rights. Political and civil rights will suffer.

The Reality: At international law, there is no ranking of economic, social, and cultural rights, on the one hand, and political and civil rights, on the other. Each is viewed as equally important. Pursuit of civil and political rights does not justify violation of economic, social, and cultural rights. Indeed, the two sets of rights are generally considered interdependent and indivisible. It is impossible to realize one set of rights while ignoring the other. The Universal Declaration of Human Rights contains both sets of rights and does not differentiate between them.

Myth Number Seven: The pursuit of economic, social, and cultural rights is used in many countries as a justification for violation of political and civil rights. By elevating the status of economic, social, and cultural rights in the Canadian Charter of Rights and Freedoms, we give credence to that justification.

The Reality: The argument is often raised that economic, social, and cultural rights must come first. We hear that you cannot have democracy if you do not have food. However, the argument that violation of political and civil rights leads to respect for economic, social, and cultural rights is specious. Tyranny does not lead to respect for economic, social, and cultural rights. Tyrannical governments are less able to deliver economic, social, and cultural rights than democratic governments. The answer to this objection is the same as the answer to the last one – that all rights are interdependent, indivisible, and equal in status.

Myth Number Eight: Economic, social, and cultural rights are Marxist in inspiration. They involve a commitment to government interference in the economy and a rejection of laissez-faire ideology.

The Reality: This objection is bad philosophy, bad history, and bad economics. Virtually every Western country has ratified the Covenant on Economic, Social, and Cultural Rights. The articulation of these rights has been a Western and Judaeo-Christian tradition. Economic, social, and cultural rights resemble more the programs of Mackenzie King in Canada or Franklin Delano Roosevelt in the U.S. than they do the programs of Marx or Lenin. The champions of these rights in the international scene have been Western Europe, Australia, and New Zealand.

As well, when we look at the Marxist economies or their remnants, the reality is that they have been a good deal less effective in realizing economic, social, and cultural rights than the free-enterprise economies. Marxism is neither an ideology of nor a prescription for the realization of economic, social, and cultural rights.

Myth Number Nine: It is inappropriate to have economic, social, and cultural rights in the constitution because their realization involves the expenditure of money. The realization of political and civil rights do not, on the other hand, involve the expenditure of money.[21]

The Reality: There are a number of political and civil rights that cost the state money to implement. There are a number of economic, social, and cultural rights that are cost free. It is impossible to distinguish between political and civil rights, on the one hand, and economic, social, and cultural rights, on the other, on the basis of expenditure.

For instance, both the right to a fair trial and the right to free elections, both political and civil rights, involve substantial state expenditure. In refugee law, the right to life, liberty, and security of the person in the Charter has required the Government of Canada to spend substantial sums of money on refugee determination procedures.[22]

To take examples from the economic, social, and cultural side, recognizing the right to form trade unions,[23] or equal opportunity for promotion subject to no consideration other than seniority or competence[24] involves no substantial commitment of state expenditures. Indeed, if promotion on the basis of competence is furthered, the result would be a saving rather than an expenditure of funds.

Myth Number Ten: What is important for the realization of economic, social, and cultural rights is the delivery of services. Putting economic, social, and cultural rights in the constitution is an empty formalism that accomplishes little or nothing.

The Reality: It is true that we do not have to entrench rights in the constitution in order to respect them. Canada was a democratic, tolerant country before we had the Canadian Charter of Rights and Freedoms. Nonetheless, the Charter has given Canadians a powerful tool to perfect the realization of rights they had before. Constitutional entrenchment cannot be the be-all and end-all for realizing these rights. But the constitution can be an important aid.

The constitution has a symbolic value. It articulates our aspirations. As well, it is a practical everyday instrument that can be used to assist in the realization of rights.

Myth Number Eleven: Economic, social, and cultural rights create positive obligations on the part of the state. They create a duty to act. Political and civil rights on the other hand create only negative obligations on the part of the state. They create only a duty to refrain from acting. It makes more sense to put in the Canadian Charter of Rights and Freedoms negative state obligations than positive state obligations.

The Reality: This objection is similar to the ninth objection and so is the answer. Several political and civil rights impose a positive obligation. The right to a fair trial would not be realized without the state being actively involved. The administration of justice is a state activity. The state can administer justice fairly or unfairly. It cannot administer justice by doing nothing at all.

Conversely, there are economic, social, and cultural rights that impose only negative obligations. Respecting the right to form trade unions does not require the state to do anything. All it does is require the state to recognize the right. The same can be said for freedom for scientific research and freedom for creative activity, and the right of parents to send their children to private schools.

Myth Number Twelve: Even if we are prepared to accept economic, social, and cultural rights in the constitution, we should not put all such rights in the constitution. We should limit ourselves only to the negative prohibitions. Although a few positive political and civil rights are in the Charter, most have been omitted. The same restraint should be shown for economic, social, and cultural rights.

The Reality: It is true that the positive political and civil obligations, such as the obligation to prohibit hate propaganda or the obligation to promote racial equality, have been omitted from the Charter. However, that creates an unhealthy situation that needs curing, even in the political and civil domain. It is not a situation that should be duplicated in the economic, social, and cultural domain.

The problem is that with the negative prohibitions inserted in the Charter and the positive obligations omitted, the negative prohibitions sit in judgment on the positive obligations. The positive obligations must pass Charter scrutiny of the negative prohibitions. Negative prohibitions and positive obligations are meant to co-exist, to be read together. They are all part of the same human rights package. By placing one set of rights in the Charter and omitting another, those rights inserted are given an artificial importance in relation to those omitted.[25]

We have seen challenges to the hate propaganda laws based on the

Charter guarantee of freedom of expression. For a time, in Alberta, in the *R. v. Keegstra* case,[26] the challenge succeeded, though the decision was eventually overturned by the Supreme Court of Canada. Only because the positive duty to prohibit hate propaganda is given a lower status in Canada than the negative duty to allow freedom of expression was the Alberta judgment possible. In order to avoid distortions such as these, once we start putting rights in the Charter, they all have to be there. Picking and choosing amongst them may well end up frustrating the ones we omit.

Myth Number Thirteen: The Canadian Charter of Rights and Freedoms controls governments. It does not control the private sector. The realization of economic, social, and cultural rights depends on more than just governments. It depends on what the private sector does and does not do. Putting economic, social, and cultural rights in the Charter will not help all that much in the realization of those rights, because the entrenchment would leave the private sector unaffected.

The Reality: The Supreme Court has indeed held that the Charter does not control private activity.[27] But there are several important limitations placed on that general principle. All legislation is subject to the Charter, even legislation that is invoked only in a private context, between two individual litigants. Because the Charter binds legislatures, any infringement of Charter principles in legislation is a violation of the Charter itself, even where the person or entity relying on the legislation is nongovernmental.

So the only area of law where the Charter does not apply is the common law (judge-made law). Even for the common law, the Charter applies when it is the government that is relying on it to justify its own actions. It is only where a private actor relies on the common law that the Charter has no effect.

Mr. Justice McIntyre, on behalf of the Supreme Court of Canada said, about this area of Charter immunity: "I should make it clear, however, that this [Charter immunity] is a distinct issue from the question whether the judiciary ought to apply and develop the principles of the common law in a manner consistent with the fundamental values enshrined in the Constitution. The answer to this question must be in the affirmative. In this sense, then, the Charter is far from irrelevant to private litigants whose disputes come to be decided at common law."[28]

As previously mentioned, economic, social, and cultural rights include in their number many rights which are positive in character. They require government action to realize the rights, even if it should intrude into the private sector. It is no defence to the denial of, say, the right to food, that the starvation is the result of the workings of the private sector. If the private sector fails to supply adequate food to all, the government must step in to meet the needs the private sector fails to meet.

Finally, the private/public distinction, although part of the present Charter, is not engraved in stone. There is no reason why it has to be part of a revised Charter, or a limitation on economic, social, and cultural rights. Even if it remains a limitation on civil and political rights, there is no justification for the private/public distinction in the Covenants themselves.

Myth Number Fourteen: Promoting respect for economic, social, and cultural rights is better left to experts than human rights systems and the courts. The courts have little or no experience with the protection of economic, social, and cultural rights. They are ill placed to be the defenders of these rights.

The Reality: That is an objection that could be raised equally to political and civil rights. If economic rights should be left to economists, then one could also say that political rights should be left to political scientists, and rights in criminal proceedings to criminologists. The knowledge of what economic, social, and cultural rights means is something different from the knowledge of economics, social services, or culture. It is a knowledge of what rights mean. That is essentially a legal task, properly the domain of human rights institutions and the courts.

Myth Number Fifteen: Judges are ideologically opposed to economic, social, and cultural rights. Putting economic, social, and cultural rights in the constitution will mean nothing because judges will just restrict them or ignore them.

The Reality: There is a long-standing jurisprudential debate on what judges do, and why they do it. It is well out of the scope of this book to go through that debate here. In brief, my own position is that judges take rights seriously. Their decisions are based on the law in front of them and a desire to achieve justice, rather than by what they ate for breakfast or a knee-jerk self-defence of their class interest.[29]

Perhaps the best answer to this argument is the Charter as it stands. The Charter has had a substantial impact on Canadian law, an impact in many ways that was not anticipated when the Charter was introduced. The judges have not ignored or restricted the Charter's civil and political rights, although there was concern that they might. There is no reason to believe that Charter-entrenched economic, social, and cultural rights would be treated with any less respect.

Myth Number Sixteen: Judges will do too much to promote economic, social and cultural rights. They will use the power given to them by entrenched economic, social, and cultural rights to usurp the role of legislators.

The Reality: Courts and legislatures, even when dealing with the same subject matter, do two very different things. Legislatures enact policies, reflecting the will of the majority or the powerful. Courts, when interpreting human rights instruments, elaborate the meaning of rights protecting the position of the minority or the powerless.

Economic, social, and cultural rights cannot be left to legislatures any more than political and civil rights can. If rights are left to legislatures, then the majority or the powerful decide what rights the minority or the powerless will have. The realization of economic, social, and cultural rights becomes a matter of convenience for the majority or the powerful. The notion that rights are inherent in the individual is denied.

Giving courts the power to interpret economic, social, and cultural rights does not mean that courts can do whatever they please. They are limited to enforcing respect for entrenched rights. It does mean that legislatures can no longer do, or neglect to do, whatever the please. But that is what the entrenchment of rights is all about.

Myth Number Seventeen: Putting economic, social, and cultural rights in the constitution will only create an illusion of protection of these rights. The reality will be that those who are denied economic, social, and cultural rights will be financially unable to go to court to assert them. Entrenchment of the rights will be entrenchment of a mirage.

The Reality: The problem with this objection is it makes an obstacle seem insuperable when it can, in a number of different ways, be overcome. It is, of course, true that the disadvantaged have less money for lawyers than the advantaged and therefore less ability to litigate to assert Charter rights of any sort.

However, to compensate, there are legal aid funds across Canada that have funded Charter litigation on behalf of the indigent, and presumably would continue to do so with an expanded Charter. Indeed, many of the claims now asserted by legal aid litigants would be buttressed by Charter economic, social, and cultural rights.

Litigants are now in court or have been in court asserting economic, social, and cultural rights without the benefit of Charter entrenchment of these rights. These litigants would not disappear once we entrenched these rights.

Secondly, there has been, and according to the Government of Canada, there will be, a Charter Challenges Fund, funded by the government, to fund legal challenges based on the Canadian Charter of Rights and Freedoms. The fund, when it was in existence, allowed for challenges based on equality rights as well as language rights. The fund was limited to challenges against federal law, policy, and practice. However, there is no reason, in principle, why we could not have in Canada provincial Charter challenges funds as well as a federal Charter Challenges Fund.

Thirdly, there are a host of nongovernmental organizations that fund the cases of those who wish to assert Charter rights. According to the common law, maintenance, providing financial support for another to bring or defend an action, is a tort, a legal wrong. Maintenance is considered wrongful unless privileged on some ground.[30]

It is clear now that one of the grounds of privilege is funding of Charter litigation. One Canadian High Court judge has said:

> In my view, it is desirable that Charter litigation not be beyond the reach of citizens of ordinary means. The citizen of ordinary means is a term that covers, of course, the vast bulk of Canadians. There are few individuals, regardless of their walk of life, who could afford Charter litigation of the type experienced in this application. I accept the validity of the applicants' proposition that, of necessity, the individual must seek assistance from third-party organizations at times to assist in asserting his or her constitutional rights. Otherwise, the individual unaided by a third-party organization, such as the N.C.C. [National Citizens' Coalition], would be a David pitted against Goliath.[31]

Fourthly, nongovernmental organizations are themselves, in many cases, willing to undertake Charter litigation as principal litigants. However, the Supreme Court of Canada has put a damper on such litigation by holding that there must be no other reasonable and effective manner in which the issue may be brought before the court. As long as an individual directly affected by the challenged law could, in theory, bring the issue before the court, a nongovernmental organization has no standing to bring the issue to court on its own.[32]

Myth Number Eighteen: Entrenching economic, social, and cultural rights in the constitution will generate false expectations and divert energies into unproductive channels. The realization of economic, social, and cultural rights will come through political struggle, not legal interpretation. Entrenching economic, social, and cultural rights in the constitution will lead their advocates to charge off in the wrong direction, into the courts, instead of into the political arena where they need to be.

The Reality: It is never a wise strategy in assertion of rights to rely on litigation alone. Litigation is a dispute resolution mechanism that is available when other recourses fail. But the availability of a legal recourse does not cut off other avenues of recourse. Economic, social, and cultural rights advocates cannot possibly be worse off by having an additional recourse for assertion of those rights.

Litigation is more than just an add on, an extra option. It reinforces the assertion in the political arena of economic, social, and cultural rights. The political assertion of a right that has a sound legal foundation is going to be a good deal easier than the assertion of the same right without legal basis.[33] As long as economic, social, and cultural rights advocates do not abandon political recourses for legal recourses alone, they will be far better off with economic, social, and cultural rights in the Charter than without them.

Conclusion: There are no good reasons why we should keep economic, social, and cultural rights out of the constitution. And there is every reason why those rights should be in the constitution. If and when there is a new round of constitutional reform in Canada, we should take advantage of that round to entrench economic, social, and cultural rights.

PART VI

THE UNITED NATIONS

CHAPTER FIFTEEN

HUMAN RIGHTS AT THE UNITED NATIONS

Is the United Nations an appropriate institution for the promotion of human rights? In light of the history and Charter of the United Nations, this question may seem strange. The preamble to the Charter states: "We the people of the United Nations, determined to reaffirm faith in fundamental human rights, in the dignity and worth of the human person, in the equal rights of men and women, and for these ends, to practice tolerance, have resolved to combine our efforts to accomplish these aims." The first article of the Charter states: "The purposes of the United Nations are: ... to achieve international cooperation in promoting and encouraging respect for human rights and for fundamental freedoms for all without distinction as to race, sex, language or religion."

One of the principle organs of the United Nations established by the Charter is the Economic and Social Council. The Charter requires the Council to set up a commission for the promotion of human rights. The Charter gives the council power to make recommendations for the purpose of promoting respect for and observance of human rights and fundamental freedoms for all.

Historically, the United Nations was the result of and a reaction to the Nazi atrocities of World War II. The founders of the United Nations saw a direct link between peace and respect for human rights. The linkage is implied even in the present Charter. In earlier drafts it was a good deal more explicit. The United Nations was established primarily as an institution to maintain international peace and security. The promotion of human rights was seen as an integral part of the work towards peace.

The question whether the United Nations is an appropriate institution for the promotion of human rights, nonetheless, has to be asked in light of the record that has accumulated over the years. The record has been a troubled one.

The reality is that many members of the United Nations consists of countries which pay little respect for human rights. The United Nations is, to quote the words of Daniel Patrick Moynihan, former U.S. ambassador to the United Nations, packed with dictatorships whose jails are filled with their own people.[1]

A report submitted to the United Nations Commission on Human Rights in 1983 Geneva said that at least two million people had been put to death during the past fifteen years without a fair trial, their own lawyer, or a right to appeal.[2] Officially inspired executions were reported in thirty-seven countries – that was about one-quarter of the then United Nations membership, about one-quarter of the body we are here considering as a vehicle for the promotion of human rights.

A distinction is sometimes made between authoritarian and totalitarian governments. Authoritarian systems have within them alternative power bases. Totalitarian governments have a monopoly of power.[3]

In terms of voting patterns at the United Nations, this distinction has meant nothing. Governments vote against human rights initiatives, governments set up obstacles to human rights initiatives undertaken, whether they are authoritarian or totalitarian.

It is a fitting, if unwelcome, tribute to George Orwell, that we saw, in 1984 and since, at the United Nations, a world of newspeak and double think. Orwell defined double think as "the power of holding two contradictory beliefs in one's mind simultaneously, and accepting both of them." It is "to use conscious deception while retaining the firmness of purpose that goes with complete honesty. To tell deliberate lies while genuinely believing in them, to forget any fact that has become inconvenient, and, then, when it becomes necessary again, to draw it back from oblivion for just so long as it is needed, to deny the existence of objective reality and all the while to take account of the reality which one denies – all this is indispensably necessary."[4] That, to my mind, is a fair description of human rights debates at the United Nations.

Jerome Shestack, a former U.S. representative to the United Nations Commission on Human Rights, at its 1981 meeting, said we have to take a perspective of time. When the Commission on Human Rights began in 1946, there was not, really, any international law of human rights. The commission developed norms of international law. Today, through United Nations resolutions, declarations, conventions, and covenants, we have a body of international law of human rights. There are protocols or optional provisions that recognize the status of individuals. The instruments that have developed have served to chop away at the doctrine that protecting human rights is an intervention in domestic affairs.

That is one perspective. Another is that the proliferation of international instruments with no enforcement mechanisms or with only optional enforcement mechanisms is just Orwellian double think. It is just telling "deliberate lies while genuinely believing in them."

It is easy enough to have the illusion of progress, when faced with governments holding "two contradictory beliefs," if you look only at the belief that indicates progress. However, to see only the positive parts of the contradictions asserted by authoritarian/totalitarian members of the UN is blindness.

States can promote, and have promoted, the human rights of their own citizens through the Human Rights Committee established under the International Covenant on Civil and Political Rights. As of October 1994, seventy-eight countries had ratified the first optional protocol allowing for individual complaints by citizens that their own government had violated the Covenant.[5]

There is little states can do to promote the human rights of citizens of other states through the Human Rights Committee. A state may recognize the competence of the committee to consider communications from a state party to the Covenant that the state is not fulfilling its obligations under the Covenant.[6] Once it has declared that recognition, the state is entitled to bring before the committee any other state party that has, itself, made such a declaration, for violation of the Covenant. As of October 1, 1994, only forty-four states had made such declarations.[7] No state has yet, to my knowledge, ever brought an inter-state complaint before the committee.

When the committee considers compliance reports from states parties, or individual communications from citizens of countries that have signed the optional protocol, there is nothing other governments can say or do. Other governments have no status to appear before the committee to argue that the reporting state is not meeting its obligations under the Covenant.

The Commission on Human Rights is a body of fifty-three member states of the United Nations. The members are selected by the Economic and Social Council, each for a term of three years. The commission deals with human rights violations both in public, and under a confidential procedure, discussed in Chapter Eighteen.

The commission can and does appoint special envoys, special rapporteurs, and ad hoc working groups to examine the human rights situations in particular countries. These examinations are made public. Initially, the commission focused on three countries only – Chile, South Africa, and Israel. More recently, the commission has undertaken initiatives with respect to several other countries.

Human rights fact-finding is best conducted with the co-operation of the state concerned. A consistent theme that runs through the reports of all these rapporteurs, envoys, and working groups is the lack of co-operation of the country concerned. To a certain extent, this lack of co-operation could be expected from human rights violators.

However, the United Nations is, itself, in part, responsible for this lack of co-operation, because of its lack of regularized procedures. Chile, for instance, after some measure of co-operation with the Ad Hoc Working Group of Study on Chile, refused to co-operate with the Special Rapporteur on Chile, appointed after the Working Group disbanded, on the ground that it would not accept ad hoc procedures, but would accept any procedure applied in a nondiscriminatory manner.[8]

A nondiscriminatory procedure is necessary not only to induce state cooperation. It is necessary as well to give persuasiveness and credibility to the results obtained. Ad hoc reports are going to be unpersuasive both to the country concerned and the international community at large, as long as their origin is the political configuration at the commission at the time the studies are undertaken.

A problem that pervades the United Nations, in the human rights field, as well as in others, is politicization.[9] It was thought, in the early years of the United Nations, that specialized agencies, like the Commission on Human Rights, would be insulated from the members' high politics, and that agreements would be reached in these agencies. It was hoped that habits of cooperation in the specialized agencies would spill over into politically sensitive areas, such as security.

In fact, the opposite has occurred. The politics of the General Assembly and the Security Council have been replicated in the specialized agencies. The efforts of the Commission on Human Rights, amongst others, have been threatened by the injection of extraneous political issues that provoke friction and confrontation, and hinder cooperation.

There are two patterns involved in this development. The Commission on Human Rights will take action on matters outside its functional domain. It will reach decisions on matters within its competence on the basis of political considerations irrelevant to the problems at issue.

The politicization not only distorts debate, it creates disputes where there were none and worsens disputes that are there. In the opinion of Kenneth Adelman, former U.S. deputy-chief delegate to the United Nations, the United Nations defies the principles of its Charter regularly, by exacerbating conflicts, rather than resolving them. A United Nations commentator has said that the "very act of airing tensions at the United Nations becomes an attempt to sharpen rather than conciliate conflict. ... The United Nations increases the number of states which are party to a conflict, making it harder to resolve. States which are peripheral to a dispute offer their votes to those directly implicated in return for future considerations."[10]

The Commission on Human Rights has become a highly political place. Instead of promotion of respect for human rights being used as a tool or a precondition for developing friendly relations between states, unfounded or exaggerated accusations of human rights violations have become weapons in hostile exchanges between states.

States on decidedly unfriendly terms exchange accusations of human rights violations back and forth. These exchanges lead to an envenoming of relations rather than to an improving of relations. Because the United Nations assembles the nations of the world and votes regularly on resolutions, states which might otherwise not have been involved are drawn into these verbal hostilities and end up taking sides.

The United Nations is too often a forum for unfriendly relations. It more than just mirrors these unfriendly relations. It magnifies them. And human rights violations accusations assist in the magnification.

The human rights vocabulary, at the United Nations, has become distorted and degraded. Perhaps the most egregious example, but not an isolated one, is the United Nations resolution equating Zionism with racism, passed in 1975 and repealed only in 1991. Zionism is the expression of the right to self-determination of the Jewish people. The Charter states as one of its purposes, "To develop friendly relations among nations based on respect for the principle of equal rights and self determination of peoples." Yet an attempt to assert the right to self-determination of one of the people of the United Nations was called, by the United Nations, racism. This resolution sat, unrepealed, on the United Nations books until December 1991, as a continuing condemnation not so much of Zionism, as of the ability of the United Nations to deal meaningfully with human rights.

Because the United Nations is so politicized, it often ignores violations of the politically popular, those who can line up voting blocs behind them. Those who are politically unpopular, who cannot call on large voting blocs to silence their critics, find it easy to dismiss United Nations criticism because of its political nature.

The problem is not only that some countries get mentioned and that others are passed over in silence. The problem, as well, is what is said and not said about the countries that are mentioned. Israel, for instance, was the subject of a resolution in 1989 before the Commission on Human Rights, which used such language as "noting with severe disapproval," "strongly condemns," and "deplores." It referred to Israeli practices as "inhuman treatment," "terror," and "flagrant violations of human rights."

The language the commission used, for instance, about Guatemala was, in 1989, a good deal more mild. The resolution stated only that the commission was "seriously concerned" about the climate of violence and the human rights situation. The resolution "recognizes that the Government of Guatemala is committed to promoting the protection of human rights" and "urges the Government to intensify its efforts."

Even Iran was handled a good deal more kindly then Israel. The commission "expresses its deep concern" to Iran at reports and allegations of human rights violations and "urges" the Government of Iran to respect human rights.

The politicization in the choice of countries is not completely dissipated as the list of countries chosen expands. The politicizations remains in the language used for the countries that are chosen.

I do not suggest governments refrain from naming and criticizing human rights violators, even where the criticism will be, and will be seen as, political. But where political denunciations are the only mechanism for dealing with violations, the system is not functional. Political intervention can be effective. But it needs to be launched from a base of facts and analysis that are independently, unpolitically generated.

The General Assembly, the Economic and Social Council, and the Commission on Human Rights are all intergovernmental bodies. It is hardly surprising that intergovernmental bodies will be political. Parliaments of countries which have solid records for respect for human rights are themselves highly political. There is no inherent incompatibility between a politicized governing body and an institutional respect for human rights. The secret of success is independence of those administering respect for human rights from their political masters. But again, here, the United Nations is sadly failing.

Domestically, in many countries, we see human rights mechanisms that do function free from political considerations. What makes these institutions function effectively, above all, is independence from government. Independence from government is a principle that is accepted domestically for the judiciary and for all effective domestic human rights implementation mechanisms.

Independence from governments is, however, nowhere accepted in the intergovernmental sphere. It may be accepted in theory. But it is not accepted in practice.

The administration of the United Nations is under the secretariat. The UN Charter states the principle that the secretary-general and his staff shall not seek or receive instructions from any government.[11] The staff are stated to be international officials responsible only to the organization. According to the Charter, the paramount consideration in the employment of staff is the necessity of securing the highest standards of efficiency, competence, and integrity.

Each member state undertakes not to seek to influence the secretary-general and the staff in the discharge of their responsibilities. But, in fact, positions at the UN, particularly at the higher levels, are filled by candidates of member states. Governments have lobbied on behalf of candidates to obtain the posts.

UN officials have, in the past, been summarily dismissed by the secretariat at the request of their home governments, when their loyalty to those governments have been put in question. Dozens of UN officials have even been arrested and detained by their home governments for disloyalty to their states in the service of the UN, with the UN doing little or nothing about these detentions.

There are committees of so-called independent experts within various UN institutions and under various UN human rights instruments to assess human rights compliance. Examples are the Subcommission on Prevention of Discrimination and Protection of Minorities, a Subcommission of the UN Commission on Human Rights, or the Human Rights Committee established under the International Covenant on Civil and Political Rights. But an "independent" expert is truly independent only when the government of the country of the expert lets the expert be independent.

Governments that have a tradition of an independent judiciary tend to let their nationals in these expert bodies function independently. Governments without such a tradition send nationals to those expert bodies that are anything but independent.

Regrettably and all too often, standards have been violated. To take an egregious, but not unique, example, there was the selection of Kurt Waldheim as secretary-general of the United Nations, a former Nazi S.S. officer, a person on the list of the United Nations War Crimes Commission as a major suspected war criminal. Those who chose Waldheim either knew of his past, the accusations against him, and pushed them aside, or did not bother to make the enquiries that would have alerted them to his past. The selection of Waldheim was politically convenient at the time. And that was all that mattered.

The UN staff regulations prohibited the employment of persons discreditably associated with Nazism and Fascism. The General Assembly repealed the prohibition in 1952. And twenty years later such a person was Secretary-General.

His election spoke volumes about the failure of the intergovernmental system to put in place independent, depoliticized personnel committed to the promotion of human rights. Shirley Hazzard has written, "The UN Secretariat itself suffers drastically from a denial of experience that, now strangely exemplified in Waldheim's own story, has debilitated the organization from its earliest years."[12]

The secretariat has many fine international civil servants dedicated to promoting the ideals of the organization. The United Nations has within its membership many principled governments that refrain from attempting to instruct or influence their nationals within the secretariat. However, what should be continuous and universal is only erratic happenstance. The ideals of the United Nations may be respected. One cannot say with confidence that they always and everywhere are.

The problem is not just a problem with the current institutions. It is a problem, as well, with establishing new institutions free from the problems the secretariat poses. Establishing effective, independent human rights mechanisms at the United Nations has been an extremely difficult task. Governments have been reluctant to establish institutions that might end up criticizing them.

There is a Human Rights Centre within the United Nations Secretariat. The Centre does not do general human rights fact-finding. In 1982, when the Centre was still called a "Division," the United Nations refused to renew the contract of its director, Theo Van Boven, because of what he claimed to be major policy differences with his superiors.

The major policy difference was that Van Boven wanted a stronger United Nations involvement in the human rights field. His superiors did not. Or rather, the coalition of authoritarian and totalitarian countries that formed the United Nations majority, did not, and made sure the secretariat acted on their wishes.

The Sub-Commission on the Prevention of Discrimination and Protection of Minorities is, in theory, a body of independent experts. It consists of twenty-six persons, serving in a personal capacity, each elected for a three-year term by the Commission on Human Rights. In practice, many of the working members of the sub-commission are alternates to those elected, named by and in the service of member governments. In 1981, the Commission on Human Rights passed a resolution noting that the use of alternates to represent expert members on the sub-commission "might not on occasion be in keeping with the character of that body."[13]

In spite of that resolution, in 1981, the sub-commission had some fourteen alternates, i.e., more than half of the membership, most of them being part of the permanent missions in Geneva where the sub-commission sits.[14] Again, in 1982, the Commission on Human Rights passed a resolution, this time saying, "It must be kept in mind that the appointment of a government official as an alternate may sometimes not be in keeping with the character of the Sub-Commission, as a body composed of experts."[15]

One of the many gaps in the United Nations human rights system is that the United Nations has no general human rights fact-finding capacity. Except in special cases, the United Nations relies on information supplied by nongovernmental organizations. The sub-commission, in 1980, passed two resolutions in an attempt to remedy this defect.

In one resolution, the sub-commission recommended the establishment of an information-gathering service within the United Nations Division of Human Rights.[16] In another resolution, the sub-commission asked the Commission on Human Rights for authorization to send members of the sub-commission on independent fact-finding visits to countries the subject of allegations of gross and flagrant violations of human rights.[17]

All these resolutions did was lead to a scolding by the commission. In 1981, when the report of the sub-commission came up for consideration by the commission, the commission discussion centred, for the first time, on the report as a whole, rather than on particular recommendations.[18]

Several members of the commission strongly criticized the sub-commission for exceeding its terms of reference.[19] A resolution was passed asking the sub-commission "to bear in mind the tasks assigned to it by the Commission" as well as "to take note of the comments and suggestions made in the course of discussion" of the commission.[20]

The sub-commission did take note. In 1981, the request for general authorization to conduct on-site investigations was not re-submitted to the commission. The request for an impartial information-gathering service was also dropped.

No government is free from human rights violations. Many government members of the United Nations do not have internal functioning independent human rights mechanisms, or even court systems that are independent from government. These governments are unlikely to want to establish institutions outside of their borders that have greater scope for promoting human rights than those inside their borders do.

Given the spotted record, the political nature of the United Nations, the problems with the secretariat, the hostilities amongst member states, the distortion of the human rights vocabulary, should the United Nations remain in the human rights business? Or would the world and the United Nations itself be better off out of it?

My answer to that question is that, in spite of all of its faults, the United Nations should remain concerned with human rights. One obvious reason is that just because an ideal has not been attained, or is difficult to attain, does not mean any attempt to realize the ideal should be abandoned. If an ideal is worth achieving, it continues to be worth pursuing even if initial attempts to fail. And it would be worthwhile to have a functioning effective human rights mechanism within the United Nations.

The second reason is that, in spite of its drawbacks, the United Nations has helped in the promotion of respect for human rights. The random nature of the mobilization of shame generated through the United Nations dilutes its impact, but does not destroy it altogether. Even though United Nations condemnation may be easy to avoid, and, if not avoided, easy to dismiss, nonetheless, condemnation will have an effect. Given the choice, any state would rather avoid criticism for human rights violations than incur it. The mere fact that the criticism can occur will have a salutary effect on respect for human rights.

When it comes to dealing with violations, the United Nations, for many years, was not in the human rights business. The Commission on Human Rights started off solely as a drafting body. It was not until 1967 that the Commission began to look at violations – in South Africa alone. It began to look at the "occupied territories" of Israel in 1969, and at Chile in 1975.

The initial efforts to look at violations were roundly criticized by many committed to human rights as inevitably political, as diverting the commission from its true task of drafting. While those criticisms rang true then, and have an echo of truth even today, one cannot say doing nothing about violations is the ideal. As the scope of the concerns of the commission expands, the politicization is lessened. The faults of politicization lead to their own cure.

The thematic mechanisms, discussed in greater detail in the next chapter – such as the Working Group on Disappearances, the working group on arbitrary detention, and the special rapporteurs on torture, arbitrary executions, mercenaries and religious intolerance – are unpolitical in nature, but have a political history. The first thematic mechanism, the Working Group on Disappearances, was established in 1980 as a political compromise. At the commission in 1980 there was an initiative to have a resolution on the situation of disappearances in Argentina. But Argentina was on the commission and lobbied heavily against the resolution. The Working Group on Disappearances was the compromise result.

There is hope, as revulsion against politicization of the commission grows, that the result will be a further development of depoliticized human rights institutions, rather than an ending of the work of dealing by the commission with violations. Certainly, if the commission were to stop dealing with human rights violations, that dynamic of institution building would disappear.

There are aspects of United Nations human rights work that are immune from the criticisms I have mentioned. United Nations human rights education and training, advisory services on human rights, human rights publications, publicity about human rights standards, the development of human rights norms are all work of the United Nations important to human rights and untainted by United Nations politicization. The real problem is coming to grips with violations that occur.

Indeed, one wonders how the advisory services program of the Centre for Human Rights in the United Nations Secretariat would deal with the

Commission on Human Rights. The Centre provides the advisory service of experts to requesting governments to assist governments in establishing and strengthening national human rights institutions. It is hard to imagine that any such expert would advise establishing at a national level an institution that resembles the Commission on Human Rights. In fact, there is no record of their having done so.

CHAPTER SIXTEEN

NONGOVERNMENTAL ORGANIZATIONS AT THE UNITED NATIONS

Given the real difficulties that exist at the United Nations, should nongovernmental organizations dedicated to the promotion of human rights have anything to do with the United Nations? Nongovernmental organizations do not have to play the United Nations game in order to combat human rights violations. They can address themselves to governments directly. The United Nations needs nongovernmental organizations, but do nongovernmental organizations need the United Nations?

The United Nations may be more than just an unnecessary intermediary. Use of the United Nations can taint the nongovernmental organizations with the very distortions from which the United Nations itself suffers. The United Nations Commission on Human Rights has a highly selective list of countries with which it is concerned. All others pass unmentioned. There is a danger that nongovernmental organizations come to these commission meetings prepared to discuss only those countries on the commission agenda, thereby mirroring and internalizing the United Nations political imbalance.

There is an inevitable tendency for nongovernmental organizations addressing themselves to the Commission on Human Rights to focus on those countries on the commission's agenda, and to leave the rest of the world aside. Discussing others, in the context of the commission, may be considered an irrelevancy. Yet discussing these countries alone is obviously imbalanced.

Agenda item 12 at the commission, titled "Questions of the Violations of Human Rights and Fundamental Freedoms in Any Part of the World," has become a dumping ground for nongovernmental country concerns. During debate on this item, one nongovernmental organization after another, in the ten minutes alloted to it, lists a few of the country situations of concern. Many countries not otherwise on the United Nations agenda do get introduced by nongovernmental organizations into this item. But this exercise is not, in itself, a redressing of the imbalance the United Nations imposes.

Nongovernmental organizations have status at the United Nations to speak, to circulate documents, and to lobby. But they cannot vote. They cannot sponsor or co-sponsor resolutions. What is decided at the United Nations is decided by governments, not by nongovernmental organizations. Nongovernmental organizations doing human rights work at the United Nations are working through a governmental filter. They rely on sympathetic governments to adopt the positions and information the nongovernmental organizations wish to promote. Would it not be better to work without the filter, without the result that some of what the nongovernmental organizations wish to say and do will inevitably get filtered out?

My answer is that nongovernmental organizations should stay, and should continue to work for human rights through the United Nations system. The reason are both idealistic and practical. Nongovernmental organizations can help the United Nations do the human rights work it should be doing. They can provide the information the United Nations system lacks, the analyses United Nations institutions are too timid or discreet to do. As ineffective a place as the United Nations is now for the promotion of human rights, it would be a good deal more ineffective if the nongovernmental organizations were to withdraw.

As well, if a functioning United Nations human rights mechanism is an ideal, it is a nongovernmental ideal as well as a governmental ideal. An effective United Nations human rights system would be an advantage to more than just the United Nations. It would be to the advantage of the cause of human rights. Nongovernmental organizations, by working with the UN, can work to improve it. If nongovernmental organizations abandon the United Nations to its problems, these problems are less likely to be overcome.

On a practical level, the United Nations represents an opportunity, a forum. When a nongovernmental organization has a concern it wishes to pursue, it is unrealistic to suggest it should turn down an opportunity offered to it, on the world stage, to express that concern. The forum may not be designed in exactly the fashion it would have been if left to nongovernmental organizations. Nongovernmental organizations may have an opportunity to express only some of their concerns and not others. All the same, their work is more likely to be advanced by taking advantage of the opportunity offered by ignoring it.

What can and should nongovernmental organizations do to promote human rights through the United Nations? The answer is two-fold. Nongovernmental organizations must work to build human rights institutions within the United Nations system that are effective, generalized, independent, and depoliticized. Second, nongovernmental organizations must use existing institutions in such a way so as not to distort their own work, and so as to correct the distortions the United Nations imposes.

United Nations human rights institutions, aside from the problems of weakness and politicization, suffer from the same vice as United Nations human rights standards – proliferation. There are treaty-based bodies such as the Human Rights Committee established under the International Covenant on Civil and Political Rights, theme mechanisms such as the Special Rapporteur on Torture, and country mechanisms such as the Special Rapporteur on Iran, and a number of each of these.[1]

Nongovernmental organizations facing this wealth of institutions must first of all decide – do they want more, or do they want less? Is the proliferation a duplication, a waste of scarce United Nations resources? Or is it a positive development.

These questions are answered with the greatest difficulty when examining the country mechanisms. For the choice of countries is arbitrary and political. In the words of Ian Martin, former secretary-general of Amnesty International, no student of human rights or reader of human rights reports would consider the situations studied by the country rapporteurs, representatives, and working groups a comprehensive list of grave situations meriting such consideration.[2]

The United Nations, like every political body where power is dispersed, tends to function by inertia. It is difficult to mobilize the United Nations to focus on any country. In the history of the commission only a few countries have been the subject of special investigative procedures.

Once the United Nations turns its attention to a country, it tends to stay turned. Countries that are removed from the agenda item on human rights violations in any part of the world, such as Equatorial Guinea and Guatemala, remain on the commission agenda, under the heading "Advisory Services." Only a handful of the countries considered in United Nations history have disappeared from the agenda.

A problem with the country mechanisms is the quality of the reports. The reports on Guatemala, in particular, generated a good deal of criticism as being more an apology for the government than a true picture of the human rights situation in the country.

Nongovernmental organizations should not be calling for an end to the country mechanisms. They should instead try to add to the mechanisms, so that the sample of countries is more balanced and representative, geographically and ideologically. Nongovernmental organizations should not allow the United Nations list to distract their own work. Country-specific work should cover every country that is the subject matter of legitimate concern.

That coverage should be attempted both outside and within the United Nations. If country mechanisms do not allow for comprehensive coverage, theme mechanisms and thematic commission debates do. Nongovernmental organizations should not hesitate to be country specific and to encourage participating states to be country specific when taking part in the commission thematic debates.

Ideally, the countries chosen for investigative procedures should be chosen not on the basis of their political unpopularity but on their degree of violation of human rights. So long as the choice of countries for special investigative mechanisms is going to be limited, those chosen should be the most gross and flagrant violators of human rights.

To a certain extent, that is happening already. One cause of political unpopularity is being a gross and flagrant violator of human rights. Grotesque human rights violations are not just an attack on the population living in the territory controlled by the perpetrating government. They are an attack on all humanity. And all humanity takes offence.

One reason Iran or Romania, to take two examples, were so friendless, were so unable to fend off a United Nations investigation, was their violations of human rights themselves. However, that was not the only reason. Iran and Romania, by their political actions, had isolated themselves from large voting blocs that might have otherwise come to their defence.

Nongovernmental organizations have to work to have the United Nations establish a depoliticized mechanism to identify countries appropriately the subject of investigative initiatives. In the absence of such a mechanism, nongovernmental organizations should, themselves, supply one. They should make their own decisions about which countries would be most appropriately the target of investigative procedures and attempt to persuade the governments of the United Nations to establish country mechanisms for these countries.

For theme mechanisms and treaty based-bodies, dealing with proliferation is easier. The proliferation serves a purpose, in the same way that the proliferation of standards serves a purpose.[3] States sign some instruments and not others. States may be party to no instruments at all, but yet be subject to the theme mechanisms.

The variety of mechanisms and bodies allows for a variety of operating techniques to develop. A rapporteur given one mandate may be timid. A rapporteur with another mandate may be bold. The multiplicity of mechanisms and bodies mean there is scope for initiative and experimentation.

Ideally, it would be useful to have one covenant, one treaty-based body, with a sequence of optional protocols dealing with specific rights and remedies into or out of which states could opt. Within the United Nations system, it would be useful to have the High Commissioner on Human Rights accumulate the work of all the theme mechanisms and country mechanisms.

The example of the International Labour Office and its Committee of Experts is instructive. The International Labour Organization has one implementation body, the Committee of Experts on the Application of Conventions and Recommendations, for 169 different Conventions. The Committee of Experts considers and comments on, in an unpolitical way, compliance reports of the signatory states to the various International Labour Organization conventions. The report of the Committee of Experts is sent to a committee on the application of standards of the International Labour Conference. The Conference is the International Labour Organization equivalent of the United Nations General Assembly.

While the observations of the Conference Committee are politically tinged, their politicization is muted by the tripartite nature of the International Labour Organization. The International Labour Organization is not restricted to representatives of governments. It includes, in equal measure, representatives of governments, and representatives of labour and employers. In situations where governments are reluctant to criticize, workers and employers keep the system honest.

The proliferation in the human rights system can be seen as tentative steps towards the goal of unified procedures. When enough of the field with which unified procedures would deal is covered by theme and country mechanisms, the creation of unified procedures with comprehensive coverage will not seem like such a major change.

It is, however, too early to start standardizing, harmonizing, and removing overlap. The danger is that if standardization and harmonization are attempted now, we could be left with the lowest common denominator. Theme and country mechanisms would end up becoming mere conduits, or messengers, instead of taking an active role.

There is a gap between what human rights mechanisms do, and what they are mandated to do. With standardization, the mechanisms may end up being reined in, restricted to what they were told to do. Initiative would be squelched.

The problem with the theme mechanisms is not so much duplication or overlapping as gaps in the system. When allegations are received that contain a combination of human rights violations covered by more than one special mandate, the dominant element determines which mechanism is used. If, for instance, a corpse is found with gunshot wounds and marks of torture, the killing is considered the dominant element. So the case is referred to the Special Rapporteur on Summary or Arbitrary Executions. If torture wounds alone are found, the Special Rapporteur on Torture deals with the case.

There are, on the other hand, human rights violations for which no theme mechanism is appropriate. One example is the right to a fair trial. The Commission on Human Rights in 1991 passed a resolution endorsing a decision of the Subcommission on Prevention of Discrimination and Protection of

Minorities to entrust Stanislaw Chernichenko and William Treat with the preparation of a study on the right to a fair trial. The study may one day lead to a fair trial theme mechanism. But there is not one now.

Both country and theme mechanisms make their own contribution to the UN human rights operation. There is value in keeping both even where the theme mechanisms make country visits.

The theme mechanisms, when they do visit a particular country and report, have the advantage of not having to pass through the political filter of the commission before acting. They also, for each country, can and do "respond effectively," take up cases before a country report of a visit comes out. Country mechanisms are, on the other hand, more comprehensive, dealing with all human rights violations in the country rather than just with a few forms of violations.

The existence of treaty-based bodies does not justify termination of the work of theme and country mechanisms, even where states have signed optional individual complaints procedures. Nor do the existence of the theme mechanisms render superfluous the treaty-based bodies.

The treaty-based bodies are a good deal more comprehensive thematically than the theme mechanisms. The Human Rights Committee, for instance, covers the whole range of civil and political rights under the International Covenant on Civil and Political Rights.

The treaty-based bodies are, as well, judgmental, at least under the individual complaints mechanisms. Even for the reporting requirements, the requirements that states report to the treaty-based bodies on their implementation of the instruments, probing questions are asked at the presentation of the reports.

The theme mechanisms, on the other hand, make no judgments about whether violations in the mandate of the mechanism actually occurred. The Special Rapporteur on Religious Intolerance, Angelo Vidal d'Almeida Ribeiro of Portugal, says quite explicitly in his 1990 report, "There is no question of the Special Rapporteur making any judgment on the allegations." Allegations of torture or executions and the replies of the governments to these allegations are presented without any comment by the rapporteurs.

The Working Group on Disappearances is restricted to screening information from reliable sources. The Special Rapporteur on Torture is asked to respond to accessible and reliable information. These mandates allow the mechanisms to do a certain amount of filtering. Whenever an allegation is not sufficiently detailed or patently fabricated, the Special Rapporteur on Torture will, for instance, not transmit it to the government concerned for a response. The mere fact, however, that an allegation is transmitted is not a finding by the rapporteur that the allegation is apparently well founded.

The treaty-based bodies are, on the other hand, a good deal less comprehensive geographically then the theme mechanisms. For instance, as of October 1994, 127 states had ratified or acceded to the International Covenant on Civil and Political Rights. Seventy-eight states had acceded to the optional individual complaints mechanism. The theme mechanisms cover the whole globe, and are not limited only to countries that agree to accept the mechanisms.

The theme mechanisms also operate more quickly. The Working Group on Disappearances, the Special Rapporteur on Torture, and the Special Rapporteur on Executions all have urgent action procedures. For the treaties, where individual complaints procedures are in place, the procedures have strict admissibility requirements. It can be years before a treaty-based body decides on the merits of an individual case before it.

There is an urgent action procedure under the Torture Convention, but signatory states can opt out of it. The Human Rights Committee, under the International Covenant on Civil and Political Rights, and the Committee on Elimination of Racial Discrimination, under the Convention on the Elimination of All Forms of Discrimination, have the power to take interim measures to avoid irreparable damage. But these last two mechanisms are available only when an individual complaint is being considered under the optional complaints mechanisms.

Because there is both a Special Rapporteur on Torture and a Convention against Torture, with a Committee Against Torture to oversee implementation, there has been some suggestions that the Special Rapporteur on Torture should have his mandate restricted to those countries that have not ratified the Convention, or, at least, to those countries which have not signed on to the individual complaints mechanism. One disadvantage of that proposal is that it weakens the thematic powers of the theme mechanism.

The Special Rapporteur on Torture is supposed to examine and report on questions relevant to torture around the world. If the rapporteur cannot look at the situation of torture in some countries, because of a technical limitation on his mandate, then his power to deal with general questions about torture in a comprehensive way is diminished.

There is a contrary consideration. If the United Nations allows the special rapporteur to function where states sign on to the individual complaints mechanism under the Torture Convention, then that may discourage states from signing on to the mechanism. That, however, is a practical, speculative consideration, rather than a question of what should happen ideally. From the point of view of principle, it makes sense to keep the mandate of the special rapporteur entire, rather than to cut pieces out of it.

The treaty-based bodies, amongst themselves, also each serve useful functions. There are states, as I mentioned, which have signed one human rights treaty, and become subject to the jurisdiction of one treaty-based mechanism, but not another. Greece, for instance, has ratified the Convention against Torture and acceded to the individual complaints mechanism. But Greece has not signed the International Covenant on Civil and Political Rights.

There are admissibility requirements imposed by the treaty-based bodies to prevent an individual from invoking several of these bodies simultaneously. For instance, the Human Rights Committee has as an admissibility requirement that the same matter is not being examined under another procedure of international investigation. The Human Rights Committee has observed that study of a human rights problem of a global character, such as that of the special rapporteur of the Commission on Human Rights on Summary or Arbitrary Executions, although such a study might refer to or draw on information concerning individuals, cannot be seen as being the same matter as an examination of individual cases within the Optional Protocol of the Covenant.

As well, the specialized treaty-based bodies, like the Committee Against Torture, and the Committee on Racial Discrimination, allow for specialized consideration on matters before them. The more specific the mandate of a supervisory body, the greater the expertise and experience that can be brought to bear on complaints and reports before it.

There are practical, administrative difficulties in the proliferation of human rights remedies. The costs multiply with each new body that has to be financed. Financing has been a particular problem for the Committee on Racial Discrimination, which, in the past, has not been able to meet regularly for lack of funds. But it affects, generally, the whole United Nations system.

Reporting becomes more burdensome for signatory states the more reports that have to be filed. There is substantial delay for treaty-based bodies both in receiving reports, and in considering reports. A simplified system might mean shorter delays.

There is, as well, a conceptual danger that follows upon the fragmentation of human rights remedies. Human rights are, in a sense, just one right, the right to human dignity and self-realization. The overall sense of human rights as a unified concept is lost when rights are articulated and remedies established in a piecemeal fashion. Losing sight of the overall concept of human rights, in turn, weakens the effort to promote any one component of human rights. For the promotion of any one human right to be effective, the overall notion of what human rights is must imbue the effort.

England, in 1873, unified a system of eight separate courts that traced jurisdiction, in some cases to the reign of Edward I (1272-1307). It will not take the United Nations, it is to be hoped, six hundred years to unify its human rights procedures. Yet, to do it now would be destructive. When the institutions are still fledgling, and when there is so such hostility to the effective promotion of human rights, any attempt at simplification runs the risk of weakening the overall human rights effort.

For nongovernmental organizations, the task at the United Nations has to be institution building so that unification of procedures, when and if it does occur, comes from a strong and widely accepted base of procedures. Just as the urgent action procedure spread from the Working Group on Disappearances to the Special Rapporteur on Summary and Arbitrary Executions and then to the Special Rapporteur on Torture, so too must each innovation in the promotion of human rights initiated by any one country, theme, or treaty-based mechanism spread to other mechanisms. It is only when these innovations have become widely accepted and established that examination of unification of procedures will make sense.

The thaw in East-West relations and the collapse of the Soviet Union represent both an opportunity and a danger for the promotion of human rights. Opportunities are greater because politicization at least along East-West lines has decreased. The danger is two-fold. One is that, as discussed in Chapter Seven, along with the disappearance of interest in the East in criticizing the West and the interest of the West in criticizing the East, the interest in promotion of human rights itself will weaken.

A converse danger is that human rights assume a different political dimension, more of a North-South than an East-West one. The developing community of interest between East and West creates an increasing potential for North-South division. The Commission on Human Rights was expanded from forty-three to fifty-three members as a result of a decision of the General Assembly. The additional number comes, almost entirely, from the Third World. Bloc voting, and North-South divisions, will increase.

In this context, nongovernmental organizations can bring a balanced and nonpolitical approach to what has every appearance of continuing to be a highly political debate on human rights. Nongovernmental organizations are an antidote to the disease of politicization from which the United Nations suffers. It is a disease from which the United Nations will never be cured. But, at least, if institutions can be established that seal off human rights from the political virus, the effort to use the United Nations to promote human rights will have been worthwhile.

PART VII

NONGOVERNMENTAL ORGANIZATIONS

CHAPTER SEVENTEEN

THE STRATEGY OF AMNESTY INTERNATIONAL

Amnesty International is a mass-movement human rights organization. Its focus has been limited, clear, and specific. When it began, in 1961, its concerns were only imprisonment of prisoners of conscience who neither use nor advocate violence, and torture. Amnesty International has a membership around the world which it mobilizes in letter-writing campaigns to seek the release of prisoners of conscience and an end to torture.

Torture and imprisonment of prisoners of conscience are universally abhorred. They are not only rejected by governments in international declarations and covenants; they are repugnant to individuals everywhere. It is relatively easy to mobilize mass concern over torture and imprisonment of prisoners of conscience. The notion of rejecting these abuses is easily accessible to all. As well, a world-wide expression of concern over these violations is an effective technique for removing them.

Their very unacceptability makes publicity and mobilization of concern about these practices means in themselves for ending them. No government argues for torture in principle, even though many perpetrate it in practice. No government promotes imprisonment of prisoners of conscience in principle, even though in practice it is all too common. Every government wishes to maintain respectability and credit in the eyes of its citizens and of the world. Calling governments to account on these basic principles they accept in theory and violate in practice brings governments closer to applying these principles.

The idea of Amnesty International was simple. But as the organization grew, it became apparent that the simplicity was deceptive. There is an inherent tension between the logic of the movement and logic of human rights. The logic of the movement is specificity. The logic of human rights is universality and indivisibility.

Human rights are rights of individuals against governments, the rights of individuals to promote their human dignity, to realize their humanity. Aside from the right to life, which is the foundation for the enjoyment of all the other human rights, and the nonderogable rights, which cannot be removed even in an emergency, it is impossible to rank human rights. Civil and political rights are no more important than economic and social rights. While torture and imprisonment of prisoners of conscience may be universally abhorred, one cannot say that they are the most important violations of human rights in the world or, indeed, that any violation of human rights is more or less important than any other. Whatever form the attack on human dignity and individuality takes, a consistent human rights policy would reject and condemn the attack.

Amnesty International could not become a general human rights organization, promoting all human rights equally, without destroying its identity, losing its membership and abandoning its techniques. While in theory all human rights rank equally, in reality, it is easier to spread concern about torture and imprisonment of prisoners of conscience than alleviate many other violations of human rights. While mass letter-writing campaigns are particularly effective to assist in the removal of torture and the release of prisoners of conscience, for violations of other human rights, mass letter-writing campaigns are simply inappropriate.

Amnesty International could not, however, simply remain as it was, combatting only torture and imprisonment of prisoners of conscience without losing its human rights soul. When two human rights are arbitrarily selected out of a whole panorama, inconsistencies and contradictions inevitably emerge.

What has developed within Amnesty is an ongoing, a perennial, debate about the nature of the mandate. The governing body of Amnesty International is the International Council Meeting, a country delegation meeting that takes place every two years. At these meetings, there are those who argue for extension of the mandate, that consistency requires it. There are others who argue that the present mandate should be maintained, that otherwise the unique character of the movement would be destroyed.

The most significant expansion of the mandate was at the Vienna International Council Meeting of 1973. At that meeting the mandate was expanded to include opposition to the death penalty. Since the right to life is necessary for the enjoyment of all human rights, it is impossible to defend other human rights and ignore the death penalty. Whatever the technique of execution, if the technique fails, the person has been subjected to torture. It made little sense for Amnesty International to be concerned if the attempt at execution failed, and not to be concerned if the attempt succeeded and the person died.

The expansion of the mandate had an inherent, an inescapable logic. But it caused problems for the movement. The death penalty does not meet with the same universal disapproval as torture and imprisonment of prisoners of conscience. Indeed, in every country of the world, there is either a majority or a significant minority in favour of the death penalty. People who might otherwise join Amnesty now will not join because they support the death penalty.

Another mandate debate revolved around nongovernmental entities, terrorist groups, revolutionary forces, liberation movements. For Amnesty International to be credible, for human rights promotion to be credible, it must be balanced. Amnesty International could not credibly call on governments to end torture, the death penalty, and the imprisonment of prisoners of conscience, and yet say nothing when nongovernmental entities engaged in the same practices in opposition to governments. The International Council Meeting of 1983 at Jouy-en-Josas near Paris, France, called on Amnesty International to condemn the torture and/or killing of prisoners by nongovernmental entities.

That step was perfectly logical and indeed necessary. Yet, it too caused problems for Amnesty International. Nongovernmental entities are not signatories to international human rights instruments. Amnesty International calls wrongful acts of nongovernmental entities "abuses" instead of human rights violations.

At the level of techniques, there is a problem. Terrorist organizations often have no fixed address. A letter-writing campaign by the membership in these cases becomes impossible. Amnesty International is a membership organization. In combatting nongovernmental entities abuses, it becomes more difficult to get the membership involved.

At the 1987 International Council Meeting in Brazil, the Amnesty International French section proposed that the movement go one step further and decide that the taking of hostages for political motives by nongovernmental entities should be condemned by Amnesty International in the same way as the torture or execution of prisoners. The French proposal passed the strategy working party with an amendment that the taking of hostages had to be with the threat that the hostages would be tortured or executed.

When it came to the plenary, this further step, this French proposal, though perfectly logical, was one more than the movement was willing to take. Instead, the whole issue was referred to a mandate review committee that the plenary had just voted to establish.

The Mandate Review Committee at the International Council Meeting in Yokohama Japan in 1991 recommended only small changes in what Amnesty did about nongovernmental entities. The view of the Mandate Review Committee was that the role of Amnesty lies in relations between governments and the people they govern. To them it did not seem logical to extend this role to the activities of political opposition groups. The only opening the committee was willing to contemplate was that it believed Amnesty should leave itself with some flexibility to do more than merely condemn acts when they are committed by those entities which have effective control over the population concerned.

The committee proposal was an advance over the then current Amnesty policy, which addressed quasi-governmental entities but not nongovernmental entities. A quasi-governmental entity is an entity which exercises effective authority over the population in the territory which it controls. The committee proposed that an entity which controlled population but not territory could also be addressed. As well, for the committee, the condemnation policy should be extended beyond torture and killing of prisoners, Amnesty's then current limits, to hostage taking and deliberate targeted killings of noncombatants.

A suggestion of principle put before the Yokohama International Council Meeting was to use the same vocabulary for acts of governments and nongovernmental entities. The techniques used to oppose the violations would be whatever techniques would be appropriate and practical. There would be no list of specific techniques that Amnesty would and would not use. The only limitation on the entities that would be the subject of Amnesty concern would be that they be political and not criminal. And there would be no limit on the violations within the Amnesty mandate that Amnesty would bring into the scope of concern for such activities. All violations within the Amnesty government mandate would be within the Amnesty nongovernmental mandate.

That solution would have been clear, simple, and straightforward. It would also have meant a quantum leap in Amnesty activity. But it was just too much of a leap for Amnesty to make at once.

Members decided to push forward in the nongovernmental area, and push further than the Mandate Review Committee had proposed. But the result was still a compromise. The boundaries changed, but they did not disappear.

The language difference remained. The meeting refused to apply the language of human rights violations to nongovernmental entities. Although, in a sense a change in language is purely formal, a change would have signalled a radical shift in the philosophical underpinnings of the Amnesty approach. With the language shift, all the other proposed changes would have followed, to equate Amnesty nongovernmental work with Amnesty governmental work. Before the Amnesty philosophy could change, Amnesty practice would have to change. Once the work on nongovernmental entities caught up with the work on governments, changing the verbal formulation to equate the two linguistically would be easy. In advance of that catch up, members were not prepared to dictate equality by a language shift alone.

In terms of the entities, the subject matter of Amnesty concern, the only limitation was that the entities be political. The International Executive

Committee was asked to develop criteria to distinguish political nongovernmental entities from criminal nongovernmental entities. Members decided to have Amnesty concentrate its resources on those entities with greater control over people, territory, and the use of force. But that is a matter of concentration, not a fixed limitation.

Again, when it came to actions, the Council went virtually the whole way. The Yokohama meeting decided Amnesty would oppose abuses by nongovernmental entities whenever the opposition is practical. Amnesty would use any appropriate technique, including directly addressing the entity. The only distinction was the type of entity to which this comprehensive approach applied. The type of entity to whom the full range of techniques now applies is an entity either that has effective control over a population, or is recognized internationally, or is otherwise accessible to approach.

That sort of limitation is more practical than technical. There would be no point in asking Amnesty to approach an entity which is not accessible to approach. With this policy, there remains very little that Amnesty can not to do to oppose abuses by nongovernmental entities.

For the acts by nongovernmental entities, the subject of Amnesty concern, again the decision went practically as far as it could. There was no question that hostage taking would be opposed. Opposition to torture and killing of prisoners had already been part of the Amnesty mandate. The main debate was over what other killings besides killings of prisoners Amnesty should oppose.

The choice was between all deliberate killings in violation of international law or just some killings. The eventual decision was flexible in form. It said Amnesty would bring within the scope of its concerns other deliberate killings besides killing of prisoners. Two examples were listed. One was the killing of people under the entity's immediate control. The other was killings carried out solely by reason of the victim's own beliefs, ethnic origin, sex, colour, or language.

The debate made clear, given the option that prevailed, that there was a whole set of killings about which Amnesty has decided to say nothing. In the debate on this issue, Peter Duffy, the outgoing chair of the International Executive Committee, said that Amnesty does not take a position on political violence. To oppose all deliberate killings in violation of international law would mean supporting governments against opposition groups. Governments create international standards. These standards can be used to preserve the status quo. There may be situations that call for recourse to violence to change the status quo. Amnesty should take no position in these situations where violence is used.

Until 1993, Amnesty opposed hostage taking by nongovernmental entities, but not nonhostage imprisonment. In 1993, the International Council

Meeting held in Boston decided that Amnesty's concerns with respect to prisoners of conscience should be the same, irrespective of the perpetrator. Members resolved that Amnesty should oppose imprisonment by nongovernmental entities of prisoners of conscience.

The most persistent, the most vexed debate in which Amnesty International has engaged, is the debate over homosexuality. At the level of principle, imprisonment of persons for their homosexuality is a violation of their fundamental human rights. There is a clear proximity between imprisonment of prisoners of conscience who neither use nor advocate violence, an originating component of the Amnesty International mandate, and the imprisonment of prisoners because of their sexual orientation, who also neither use nor advocate violence.

Yet, no single extension of the mandate was more likely to be controversial than this proposal. Homosexuality meets with elements of moral disapproval everywhere. Promoting human rights for homosexuals does not mean promoting homosexuality. But many people do not make that distinction. In meeting after meeting, the proponents of extension have argued rights. The opponents of extension have argued effectiveness.

In International Council Meeting working parties, each country has one vote. The small Third-World sections predominate. In Brazil, in 1987, at the working party where mandate issues were discussed, the proposal for extension was defeated. In the plenary, voting is weighted according to the size of the Amnesty International section in the country. In the plenary, the large Western sections predominate. The Dutch and Danish sections, who had lost their proposal at the working party on extending the mandate to cover imprisonment because of homosexual orientation, could have reintroduced their proposition in the plenary and could have probably won. But they chose not to do so in order to avoid splitting the movement on the issue. Instead, the plenary passed just a compromise resolution asking that the mandate review committee consider and report on the implications for Amnesty International of including persons imprisoned because of their homosexual orientation.

The Mandate Review Committee, at the International Council Meeting at Yokohama, Japan, in 1991, recommended that Amnesty should oppose only imprisonment for advocacy of homosexual equality including expression of homosexual orientation. In other words, if you are imprisoned for *saying* you are a homosexual, Amnesty would intervene. If you are imprisoned for *being* a homosexual, Amnesty would not intervene.

The result was a compromise. The most bold way of dealing with the issue would have been by changing the statute to actually put the "h" word in it, so that the statute would say that persons imprisoned because of homosexual acts or homosexual orientation would be considered prisoners of conscience. But that turned out to be the least favoured option.

The second alternative was to change the statute in a neutral way. The Luxembourg section proposed, and eventually the International Executive Committee and the Mandate Review Committee accepted, a statutory change to have Amnesty oppose the imprisonment of anyone because of their personal attributes. It was understood that sexual orientation would be one of those attributes.

That option, though more popular than an explicit statute amendment, also did not carry the day. Instead, the meeting decided to adopt people imprisoned because of homosexual acts or homosexual orientation without changing the statute. The new Amnesty activity would be done by way of interpretation of the existing statute.

Amnesty International's adopting prisoners of conscience who neither use nor advocate violence led inexorably to a debate about the meaning of violence. In Brazil, the Belgium Amnesty International section proposed that violence not include self-defence. Amnesty must not exclude from the category of prisoners of conscience any person who has availed himself of his right to self-defence. Again the two protagonists stood face to face – the logic of the movement and the logic of human rights.

How can a human rights organization ignore the concept of self-defence? A person who defends himself against lethal attack, who is imprisoned for political reasons and not for his self-defence, has to be of concern to an organization standing up for political prisoners.

Yet, a person may kill in self-defence. Adopting a prisoner of conscience who kills in self-defence is hardly adopting someone who has not used violence. As well, simplicity is lost. The legal definition of self-defence varies from country to country. Self-defence is often a complex question of fact, difficult to prove.

The Belgian resolution carried in the working party. It was, in turn, defeated in the plenary.

At Yokohama in 1991, the International Executive Committee and the Mandate Review Committee proposed that the mandate be changed to allow Amnesty to take up as prisoners of conscience persons who have used violence in clear and unambiguous instances of self-defence. That proposal passed the Council Meeting nearly unanimously.

The change takes Amnesty out of the victim perpetrator framework. Before one could say that Amnesty took the side of the victim against the perpetrator. With the changed violence position that would no longer be so.

Part of the law of self-defence in many countries is reasonable mistake of fact. A person can be acquitted if the person thought, reasonably, that it was necessary to use violence to protect himself or herself even if in fact it was not necessary. With the new Amnesty policy, Amnesty could potentially adopt as prisoners of conscience people who killed when the killing objectively was unnecessary for self-protection, as long as it was reasonable for the prisoner to have thought that it was necessary to have killed for self-protection. The person killed by the prisoner cannot be considered to be a perpetrator or wrongdoer.

There is in this context a wrongdoer, the state that imprisons the accused for political reasons in spite of the fact the person used violence in self-defence. But where the attack that generated the reliance on self-defence was not itself a wrongful act, the moral imperative for Amnesty intervention is not so clear-cut.

Freedom of movement was yet another cause for discussion. The Chileans and the Italians proposed in Brazil that Amnesty International concern itself with those who, for reasons of conscience, are prevented from leaving any country or re-entering their own. The Amnesty International mandate covers persons in detention and persons otherwise physically restricted. The words "otherwise physically restricted" had historically been interpreted to mean restrictions akin to detention. The Chileans and the Italians wanted to give the phrase a good deal broader scope.

From a human rights perspective, the Chilean/Italian proposal was convincing. It is a human right recognized in all the basic human rights instruments that everyone should be free to leave any country, including his own. These same instruments state that every person has a right to enter his own country.

From an Amnesty International perspective, the Chilean/Italian proposal was not so obvious. Intervening in cases where persons, for reasons of conscience, are denied freedom of movement is taking Amnesty International away from its prisoner orientation. People who can go everywhere in the world except their own country, people who can go anywhere in their own country, even if they cannot leave, are not prisoners in the normal sense.

Those in favour argued that the prisoner orientation of the Amnesty International is not sacrosanct. What is important is working for human rights. Now people are being expelled rather than being put in prison. If Amnesty International is concerned about people who are victimized by reason of their opinions, it should combat the victimization no matter the form it takes.

Those opposed argued that the resolution would turn Amnesty International from a prisoner organization into a general human rights organization. Amnesty International draws its strength from a concentrated effort. The prisoner emphasis is a safeguard against Amnesty's becoming a general human rights organization. Amnesty International would lose its identity and its power to influence.

The Chilean/Italian resolution suffered the fate of the Belgian resolution on self-defence. It was won in the working party, but lost in the plenary.

At Yokohama in 1991, for forcible exile there was movement as well. This was an area where the Mandate Review Committee was prepared to contemplate action, in general policy, but not in individual cases. Members went beyond the recommendation of the committee and decided that Amnesty should oppose forcible exile in individual cases, as well as a matter of policy.

Fair trial within a reasonable time for political prisoners became part of the Amnesty International mandate as the result of an International Council Meeting in Denmark in 1974. At the time, it was a logical extension of the mandate. For some political prisoners, it was a matter of doubt whether or not they used or advocated violence. Only a fair trial within a reasonable time could resolve the doubt. When allegations of violence or advocacy of violence were made against political prisoners, they had to be resolved quickly and fairly.

But that, of course, raised the question, why should Amnesty International not be concerned about the fair trial of all prisoners, nonpolitical as well as political? In Brazil, the Danes suggested Amnesty International study the consequences of expanding the mandate to cover fair trial for all prisoners. So did the Italians.

For the movement as a whole, that was too big a leap to take. Assessing the fairness of trial for all prisoners would make Amnesty International much less a mass movement and much more a legalistic, indeed, a lawyers' organization. The proposal just to make a study of the possible extension was defeated.

At Yokohama in 1991, the Italian section proposed to extend fair trial from political prisoners to all prisoners was defeated overwhelmingly. The Danish proposal was to extend fair trial to prevent people being tortured or subjected to the death penalty. Although, in principle, Amnesty opposes the death penalty and torture by all appropriate means, it has not in the past used, as one of those means, urging that standards for a fair trial are applied when torture or the death penalty may result.

When a person is convicted and sentenced to death after an unfair trial, what Amnesty in the past has done is call for clemency on the basis of the unfair trial. It has not asked for a new fair trial. The Danish proposal, which passed the Meeting, would allow Amnesty to do that. It would also allow Amnesty to intervene, even before sentence was imposed, during the course of the trial or appeals to ask for a fair trial, where it could reasonably be expected that the death penalty would be imposed after a final conviction.

A similar quantum leap, to discrimination, was proposed by the Italians in Brazil. The Italians noted that ethnic/racial discrimination constitutes an affront to human dignity. The reason Amnesty International opposes torture or the death penalty is its commitment to ensure respect for the dignity of the person. The basis for opposition to torture, and the death penalty would equally justify opposition to ethnic/racial discrimination. Again, only a study on the matter was proposed, to determine what activity in the field Amnesty International could undertake.

That proposal, too, was defeated. Those opposed argued that Amnesty International would be moving away from its prisoner oriented basis. Moving into racial and ethnic equality would weaken the understanding in the general public of what Amnesty International is about.

After Amnesty International had moved into opposition to the death penalty, in 1973, the issue of extra-judicial executions arose. How could Amnesty International oppose the death penalty after a fair trial, and not oppose vigilante killings, by the authorities, of political enemies, without any trial at all? The mandate was extended, by way of guidelines, in 1979, to cover extra-judicial executions, where the executions were politically motivated. In 1979, the addition of the death penalty to the mandate was still relatively new. The further extension to extra-judicial execution was done in a manner to conform to the original prisoner orientation of Amnesty International. Just as Amnesty International opposes imprisonment imposed for political reasons, and not all imprisonment, it was thought appropriate to oppose extra-judicial executions perpetrated for political reasons, and not all extra-judicial executions.

By 1987, the logic of this position had worn thin. The acceptance of opposition to the death penalty as part of the Amnesty International mandate had matured. It was considered as basic to Amnesty International as opposing the imprisonment of prisoners of conscience. How could Amnesty International condemn death squads killing political opponents and say nothing about death squads killing petty criminals?

The answer was it could not. The 1987 Brazil International Council Meeting passed a resolution extending the guidelines on extra-judicial executions to cover all intentional killings of persons by governments whether the killings had a political or nonpolitical character.

For extra-judicial executions, at Yokohama in 1991, there was a small step forward. Opposition to extra-judicial executions was put in the statute. Before it had simply been a policy.

Putting opposition to extra-judicial executions in the statute was simply a matter of honesty and clarity. There was, as well, a small policy step forward. The 1987 International Council Meeting referred to the International Executive Committee the question whether the extra-judicial execution policy should cover the killing of people trying to leave their own country. The

Mandate Review Committee recommended it should. The International Executive Committee at Yokohama presented a resolution to the International Council Meeting putting forward that resolution. That resolution passed with a large majority.

The original Amnesty International mandate said nothing about refugees. Yet it makes little sense to oppose torture, the death penalty, or political imprisonment but do nothing for refugees. Refugees flee those very violations Amnesty International was established to combat. That was a conclusion Amnesty International itself came to in 1979. In that year, the executive body of Amnesty International approved recommendations that Amnesty International oppose the sending of persons from one country to another where they can reasonably be expected to be prisoners of conscience, victims of torture, disappear, be subject to politically motivated extra-judicial execution, or subject to the death penalty.

Doing refugee work, though it may be theoretically related to prisoner work, practically, launched Amnesty International into a vast new field. The continuing, expanding outflow of refugees around the world has been absorbing more and more of Amnesty's attention. In many Amnesty International sections, the section employs a staff person to do nothing but refugee work.

By 1987, practicality was starting to get the upper hand. The increasing emphasis on refugee work had taken place without an examination of the place of refugee work in Amnesty International's overall work. The Amnesty International Italian section in Brazil proposed a resolution that stressed the need for an intensifying of Amnesty International's refugee work. That proposal was defeated. Instead an Australian proposal to initiate discussions on the future of Amnesty International's involvement in refugee work passed.

The tension between the logic of human rights and the logic of the movement has been a creative tension. Whether, after each of the debates, the mandate was extended or not, the movement achieved a greater appreciation of the linkages in human rights. The membership has learned that torture and imprisonment of prisoners of conscience who neither use nor advocate violence cannot be viewed in isolation from the whole panorama of human rights violations.

The tension has been creative not only because of what has been learned. It has been creative as well because of what has been achieved. There is a parallel between the development of human rights generally and the development of Amnesty International. Both human rights standards and human rights mechanisms have proliferated internationally since the war. We are in a human rights era. Human rights has become the secular religion of our time.

Amnesty International has been part of this development. Not only has it helped the development happen in areas of Amnesty concern, but the organization itself has internally developed, forging the human rights linkages as much as appreciating them, expanding human consciousness in the arena of human rights as it expands its own consciousness.

There has been an internal dialectic at work within the Amnesty International movement. It is not just that the concepts of rights are evolving. The techniques of wrongdoing themselves are evolving. New forms of violations require new responses. For instance, death squads and disappearances are a relatively recent and widespread phenomena. One reason they have become more common is to circumvent the political mobilization that follows upon arbitrary detention for political reasons. Amnesty International had to react to disappearances and extra-judicial executions if it was to continue to come to the aid of people victimized solely for their beliefs.

The expanding consciousness of human rights poses its own problems. There is an uneven development of rights appreciation. The less developed sections of Amnesty International start from the point where Amnesty International began – focussing on prisoners of conscience and torture. These sections tend to be conservative about mandate extension. They were, for instance, the most opposed to asserting the rights of persons not to be imprisoned for their homosexuality. The larger, the more developed sections of Amnesty International, are also the ones most impatient to extend the mandate, to move on to new human rights violations.

As the movement expands, its capacity for work increases, not only in traditional areas, but, as well, in new areas. But if the mandate expands, the original formula for success is diluted.

The Statute of Amnesty International states that its object is to contribute to the observance of the Universal Declaration of Human Rights. Opposing imprisonment of prisoners of conscience, the death penalty, and torture, and advocating fair trial with a reasonable time for all political prisoners are means, not ends, in themselves. The end is the observance of all the provisions of the Universal Declaration of Human Rights, not just those dealing with torture, the death penalty, fair trial, and political imprisonment.

Prisoner work is not the essence of Amnesty. It is a strategy or a tactic. Indeed, the working party at International Council Meetings that discusses mandate issues is called the strategy working party. The essence is securing observance of the Universal Declaration of Human Rights.

Working for prisoners of conscience, for fair trial, and working against the death penalty and torture are not the only means to secure observance of the Universal Declaration of Human Rights. But are they the best means?

The tensions in the movement can be expressed in another form. Does the movement stay as limited and clear as possible in order to reach outward to new people with just a beginning of human rights awareness? Or does the movement increase the sophistication and involvement of its present membership? Should the movement broaden, or should it deepen?

These questions are not just questions pertinent to Amnesty International as an organization. They are basic to the promotion of human rights itself. Human rights belong to individuals, not governments. Unless they are asserted by individuals worldwide, they will mean little. How can we mobilize humanity to assert human rights? Do we stick to a few clear, simple, isolated rights, a few flagrant and egregious wrongs, to marshall the greatest possible concern? Or do we move beyond that to defend against other attacks on human dignity, that are inextricably linked to the wrongs we have chosen to oppose? Answering these questions is a perpetual task Amnesty International has given itself.

CHAPTER EIGHTEEN

HUMAN RIGHTS THROUGH NONGOVERNMENTAL ORGANIZATIONS

How do nongovernmental organizations contribute to the promotion of human rights? Nongovernmental organizations are the implementation arm of international human rights instruments. They provide the remedy for violations of human rights standards.

International human rights instruments tend to be viewed in isolation. Ever since World War II, there has been an explosive growth in these instruments. Covenants, conventions, declarations, treaties, principles, resolutions, and accords have followed quickly on the heels of each other. The drafting of any one instrument is never quick. But the total output has been voluminous.

The instruments have been general, such as the International Covenant on Civil and Political Rights or the International Covenant on Economic, Social and Cultural Rights; and they have been specific, such as the Convention against Torture or the Refugee Convention. The instruments have been regional, such as the Helsinki Accord or the Organization of African Unity Human Rights Convention; and they have been global.

The drafting of international human rights instruments has been an industry, keeping diplomats busy at meetings around the world. The instruments overlap and compete with each other for high-sounding phrases.

For many, both inside and outside of government, the burgeoning of these instruments has met with a good deal of skepticism. The enforcement mechanisms in these instruments are either weak or nonexistent. What enforcement mechanisms there are, are, for many mechanisms, rarely used. Human rights violations continue in the face of these instruments. The proliferation of these instruments seems nothing more than a proliferation of futility, of hypocrisy.

Some governments, which are serious in their pursuit of respect for human rights, are reluctant to continue with the drafting game. They hesitate to propose new conventions. They think twice about joining the efforts of those campaigning for yet another instrument. They argue: better that efforts be directed to ensuring the instruments in place be respected than that they be spent in drafting one more instrument restating what is already in slightly different form in the existing instruments. They suggest that time spent on drafting is a diversion from the time that should be spent on compliance assessment and dealing with violations of existing instruments.

A proposed convention on religious intolerance was one victim of this hesitancy. Instruments develop by escalation. The first step up the escalator is a simple resolution of the relevant international body. Resolutions are political and transient statements of inclination. They usually have no legal force. They may be passed by a simple majority.

Next comes declarations. Declarations themselves are passed by way of resolution. But they are more than just resolutions. They involve a good deal of thought and work. They take years to develop. They represent a consensus of the international community. Declarations have a moral, if not legal force, in the international arena.

Treaties are at the top of the escalator. Treaties, or conventions, or covenants, are legally binding instruments. Their drafting is done by the world community as a whole. Then, each state decides if it wishes to be bound by the instruments.

Religious intolerance has gone through the stages of resolution and a declaration. But it has stalled at the convention stage. Prohibitions against religious intolerance are, after all, already in several international instruments. Some governments have viewed the push to draft a convention as a ploy by those responsible for religious intolerance to turn attention away from the actual violations taking place.

My own view is that this overgrowth of human rights instruments covering the international scene is a positive development. I do not share the hesitancy that I have heard governments express about the continuous, the endless drafting. To my mind, the skepticism comes from a blinkered approach, from looking at governments in isolation.

There are real problems of implementation in the intergovernmental arena. The implementation mechanisms in the instruments are nowhere near adequate. But implementation in the intergovernmental arena is not the whole implementation picture. It ignores the contribution that nongovernmental organizations bring to implementation. When that contribution is taken into account, the implementation picture is nowhere near as bleak.

We should look for seven basic characteristics when there is to be implementation of human rights standards. There should be a right of petition, confidentiality for those who provide the information, an independent fact-finding capacity, an impartial judgment on the facts, direct contact with the violators, publicity about the final result, and, finally, speed in performing all of these tasks.

If we assess the international instruments and the intergovernmental organizations alone, the report would be abysmal. It would be sufficient to make us wonder about the value of the instruments themselves. But if we assess the nongovernmental organizations and their ability to perform these seven basic tasks using the instruments as a starting point, the result would be totally different.

For example, let us look at the Universal Declaration of Human Rights. And let us see how the United Nations implements that Declaration on its own, and how Amnesty International contributes to implementing that Declaration.

First, the right of petition. Forwarding is a small point, but it can be a crucial one. If you contact a local office of Amnesty International about a violation within the Amnesty mandate, your complaint or petition will be forwarded to the headquarters in London for investigation and action. If you contact a local office of the United Nations, your complaint will not be forwarded to the United Nations secretariat in Geneva that handles these complaints. You must contact the Geneva headquarters of the United Nations yourself directly.

The United Nations information centres abroad used to forward human rights complaints received to the United Nations in Geneva. The secretary-general of the United Nations directed, on October 28, 1969, that the practice of forwarding be discontinued. For the secretary-general, to accept and transmit petitions alleging violations of human rights in host countries would generate a tremendous protest from all host governments.[1]

Then there is the question of the admissibility of the complaint. Amnesty International restricts itself to a limited range of gross violations of human rights. It has traditionally focussed on imprisonment of prisoners of conscience, torture, and the death penalty. It will not take up cases of, say, sexual discrimination, where the discrimination does not lead to imprisonment. Nor, to take another example, will Amnesty protest persecution that consists, not of imprisonment, but of systematic denial of work commensurate with skill and experience.

The United Nations is even more restrictive than Amnesty when it comes to admissibility of complaints. The mandating resolution of the United Nations that gives it authority to consider human rights violations is Economic and Social Council resolution 1503.[2] The United Nations has a vast array of human rights mechanisms, each with its own jurisdiction and procedures. The 1503 procedure has limitations which other mechanisms do not. It, nonetheless, remains the most general human rights procedure in the

UN system, embracing, in principle all countries and all categories of human rights violations.

Resolution 1503 requires that the human rights violations be reliably attested, gross, and part of a consistent pattern. For the United Nations, a gross violation of human rights means an atrocity – either murder or extreme torture. Psychiatric imprisonment for political prisoners in the USSR, for instance, fell within the mandate of Amnesty, but not within the mandate of the United Nations human rights complaints procedure.[3]

For the United Nations, human rights violations must be part of a consistent pattern. What that means is that a complaint about an isolated human rights violation is inadmissible. If you have been tortured but your government has not consistently tortured others, the 1503 procedure will not allow consideration of your complaint of torture. Amnesty has no such restriction.

For a complaint to the United Nations to be admissible, it must be reliably attested. The United Nations expects the complainant to provide his/her own corroboration. It makes no independent effort to collect reliable evidence itself to determine if the complaint is a valid one. Again, Amnesty has no such admissibility requirement.

This last United Nations admissibility requirement, about reliable evidence, stems from an even more basic difference between the United Nations and Amnesty procedures. Amnesty does human rights fact finding. The United Nations does not. Once a complaint is received and admitted by Amnesty, it will be investigated. If it is received and admitted by the United Nations, it will not be investigated. Amnesty collects and assesses information about human rights violations around the world. It produces studies, books, press releases. It sends out missions of investigation to countries where alleged violations of human rights take place. It has a staff of over 250 in its London office doing, in large part, this investigative and research work. Every complaint Amnesty receives within its mandate is assessed for accuracy. The Amnesty research bureau attempts to see, for every complaint within its mandate, whether the complaint is verifiable from other sources.

Aside from working groups or rapporteurs directed towards particular countries, or particular subjects, the United Nations does no human rights research. It does not attempt to verify complaints. It does not investigate, independently, allegations of human rights violations. It produces no general publications of human rights violations. It does not, outside of the specific focus mechanisms, send out investigation missions.

An alternative to an independent fact-finding capacity is a right of response. When the complainant has a right of response, any self-serving obfuscations or falsifications the government alleged to be violating human rights produces can be rebutted. In many countries whose tribunals have no independent fact-finding capacity, a right of response is considered part of natural justice or due process or fairness.

In the 1503 procedure, there is no right of response. Governments can respond to the allegations against them. But petitioners never get to see the government response. The most elementary errors of fact in a government justification may stand uncorrected.

Treaty-based mechanisms, such as the individual complaints system recognized by the Human Rights Committee under the International Covenant on Civil and Political Rights, do provide a right of response. But the right is carried to ridiculous extremes. The complainant can respond to the government. But so can the government respond to what the complainant says. The right of response is never-ending. The result is that cases take years to resolve. As well, these treaty-based individual complaints mechanisms have strict admissibility requirements, and are limited to those few countries which have consented to their applicability. The result is that few of the many human rights violations around the world can be considered by the treaty-based bodies.

Confidentiality is another point of contrast between the United Nations and Amnesty. When an individual complains to Amnesty about a human rights violations, the violation itself may be publicized, but the source is never revealed. Amnesty does not put a source who provides information of violations at risk.

Complaining to the United Nations can, however, be very risky indeed. When complaints are presented to the government, the target of complaint, for their response, not only is the substance of the complaint presented, the source of the information is made known as well.

In theory, if a source specifically requests anonymity, that request will be respected. But even that request, in practice, may be ignored. *Newsweek*, for instance reported in May 1979, that Yuri Reshetov, then a senior officer at the United Nations Human Rights Division in Geneva and a Soviet national, as a matter of practice sent to the authorities in Moscow the names of Soviet citizens who wrote to the United Nations to inform the institution of Soviet human rights violations. Reshetov went on to become secretary to the United Nations Subcommission on Prevention of Discrimination and Protection of Minorities. He later became part of the United Nations Committee on the Elimination of all Forms of Racial Discrimination.

Lack of confidentiality is different from publicity. The United Nations may not respect confidentiality. But it is anything but public.

A major difference between Amnesty and the United Nations is publicity. As one of the methods set out in its statute, Amnesty publicizes the cases of prisoners of conscience.

Although Amnesty does have internal documents confidential to its members, its requests, studies, appeals for prisoners, and its examinations of human rights situations in different countries are all public documents.

The United Nations complaint system is entirely hidden from public view. It does allow for publicity at the end of the day, when the Commission on Human Rights makes recommendations to the Economic and Social Council about action to be undertaken. However, that stage has never, at the United Nations, been reached.

The United Nations ad hoc working groups or rapporteurs examining human rights violations in particular countries, or examining particular human rights, do make public reports. For most countries, the governments of which perpetrate human rights violations, the complaints the United Nations receives are not made public. The regime of Idi Amin, in Uganda, a perpetrator of a consistent pattern of gross and reliably attested human rights violations, was never subject to public scrutiny in the United Nations. The silence of the United Nations about Uganda prompted President Binaisa of Uganda, the head of a successor regime to the regime of Idi Amin, to say at the United Nations, at its 1979 General Assembly:

> The United Nations looked on with embarrassed silence as the Uganda tragedy unfolded ... somehow it is thought to be in bad taste or contrary to diplomatic etiquette to raise matters of violations of human rights by member states within the forum of the United Nations. For how long will the United Nations remain silent while governments represented within this organization continue to perpetrate atrocities against their own people?[4]

It used to be that not even the names of countries subject to 1503 procedures was made public. Now names of countries are publicized, but not the substance of the complaints.

There is a comparison to be made on the point of direct contacts. The United Nations will contact governments, the target of complaints, to give them the opportunity of replying to the complaints. The United Nations does not, as a rule, contact governments, the target of complaints, in order to assist in the removal of human rights violations.

At the 35th General Assembly of the United Nations in 1980, Canada proposed that the General Assembly of the United Nations request the secretary-general, when urgent situations of mass and flagrant violations of human rights arise, consider establishing direct contacts with the government concerned, with the view to assisting the government concerned, with its consent, in the full restoration of respect for human rights and fundamental freedoms, as quickly as possible.

When Canada put forward this proposal, as a resolution, India proposed an amendment that, instead of assistance being given to the government concerned "with its consent," assistance be given to the government concerned "at its request." In other words, an attempt could be made to remove human rights violations only at the request of the government violating human rights. That amendment passed. Once it had passed, Canada and others who supported the original resolution, in effect, withdrew the resolution. It ceased to be considered.[5]

Amnesty, on the other hand, makes direct contacts with the governments concerned, whether there is a request or not, whether there is consent or not. The International Secretariat of Amnesty International does not itself contact governments detaining political prisoners. The secretariat has its adoption groups, its members, subscribers and supporters, contact the governments concerned. Contact is not through the professionals. It is through the volunteer membership.

Another point of contrast between Amnesty and the United Nations is impartiality. The Amnesty statute requires impartiality. Amnesty is required, at all times, to maintain an overall impartiality between its activities in relation to countries adhering to the different world ideologies and groupings. Each individual adoption group usually works on behalf of at least two individual prisoner cases in countries which are balanced geographically and politically, to ensure impartiality.

The United Nations is the epitome of politicization. It is grossly unbalanced in its scrutiny of human rights violations. The United Nations has consistently, loudly, and in great detail, in the past condemned Chile and Israel for their human rights violations. Comparable violations in some other countries have met with silence. In recent years there has been a dilution of this selectivity. But it has, by no means, disappeared. United Nations action in the field of human rights is determined, to quote John Humphrey, a former director of the United Nations Human Rights Division, by "political considerations and the hazards of voting patterns."[6]

Even where the United Nations does condemn a human rights violation, the moral force of that condemnation is dissipated by the political atmosphere that generated it. And moral force is the only effective force that these judgments have. Torkel Opsahl has written that the practice of condemning some states too easily and other states not at all "may deprive condemnations of their moral effect, and there is normally no other effect to be expected."[7]

We can compare Amnesty and the United Nations from the point of view of speed. Amnesty runs urgent action appeals on behalf of prisoners in need of medical treatment, individuals under sentences of death, in cases of disappearances, as well as on behalf of victims of torture. Appeals are telexed to national sections of Amnesty who channel the action recommendations to member groups or individuals.

The United Nations procedure, on the other hand, is so slow as to be valueless. Its system is so elaborate it verges on the labyrinthine. According to the International Commission of Jurists, the United Nations delays are so protracted that most cases are either moot or out of date by the time they are considered by the Human Rights Commission.[8]

There are now a number of different thematic rapporteurs or working groups within the United Nations system – such as for torture, for enforced or involuntary disappearances, for summary or arbitrary executions, for religious intolerance. These thematic mechanisms do not work as slowly as the Commission through the 1503 procedure.

The United Nations working group on enforced or involuntary disappearances has, for instance, authorized the chairman, when he receives news of a disappearance, immediately to dispatch a cable seeking information from the government in tracing the individual involved. The chairman has used the authority.

The thematic mechanisms, however, have problems of their own. The choice of themes is scattered. The mechanisms do not cover the whole field of human rights. The choice of themes is politicized. The Commission on Human Rights created the working group on disappearances, for instance, as a political compromise, instead of appointing a special rapporteur for Argentina.

Reporting is inconsistent in quality. Rapporteurs sometimes subordinate their fact-finding practices to mediation attempts. Government replies are not made available to those providing information of violations for response. Ian Martin, then secretary-general of Amnesty International, urged these mechanisms to be such that government responses are made available to those submitting information so that these responses can be tested.[9]

It has been suggested that criticism of the procedural failings of the international human rights system in providing remedies for individual victims is irrelevant. The very attempt to set up a system to provide remedies to individuals at the international level puts the international community on the wrong track.

The argument is that the provision of remedies to individuals is simply not appropriate for the international human rights system. Remedies for individuals at the international level are unrealistic. Where gross and flagrant violations are taking place, the problem is situational. The remedies that are needed have to be themselves general in nature, relating to the situations, rather than to individual violations.

To my mind, this analysis is either resignation to failure or insensitivity to the connection between individual and situational remedies. Situations are changed by helping individuals. The plight of individuals personalizes, humanizes situations. Otherwise, the situations assume an air of unreality. Once torture, imprisonment, or mass killings become divorced from real people being victimized, it becomes easier for the state concerned to dismiss criticism and carry out the practices.

Amnesty is a particularly strong nongovernmental human rights organization. And the United Nations 1503 procedure is a particularly weak implementation mechanism. So the contrast is striking. But the point is a general one. Nongovernmental organizations succeed in the implementation of human rights instruments where governments and intergovernmental organizations fail.

The success of one and the failure of the other is not, I suggest, mere happenstance. It is endemic to the nature of the organizations. Nongovernmental organizations are inherently well equipped to serve as the implementation arm of international human rights instruments. Governments and intergovernmental organizations are inherently ill equipped to create functioning implementation institutions for the standards they articulate.

Every government has a tendency to congratulate its friends and criticize its enemies. Human rights violations of enemy countries loom large. Human rights violations of friendly countries are minimized. Where the violator is an economic partner or a military ally, the temptation is to ignore the violations for fear of harming trade or the military alliance.

For many countries this bias has legislative form. It is not uncommon to find legislation prohibiting arms exports to governments of countries that are gross and flagrant violators of human rights. Less common, but also in existence, are policies of embargoes, boycotts, or sanctions against gross and flagrant violators of human rights.

The problem with this sort of legislation or policy is that it may be the exporting country that wants to sell the arms or the goods as much as the importing country wants to buy them. For instance, in El Salvador and Guatemala, it was not just the governments of these countries that wanted to buy arms to defeat the guerillas. The U.S. government wanted to sell these governments arms so that the guerillas would be defeated. The governments of these countries were viewed as friendly to the U.S. The guerillas were viewed as hostile.

When the exporting government wants the trade to continue for political, military, or economic reasons, there is an inevitable tendency for the violations to be downplayed so that it can continue. What suffers is not the trade, but the intergovernmental implementation of human rights standards. That was certainly true of the U.S., which minimized human rights violations in El

Salvador and Guatemala so that its legislation prohibiting arms trade with human rights violators did not take effect for those countries.

Governments have another reason for downplaying international human rights instruments, the potential boomerang effect. Governments are either violators or potential violators of human rights instruments. Each government will be reluctant to have international human rights instruments triggered quickly, and easily, because the mechanism may one day be triggered against that government.

Because human rights are rights of individuals against governments, it is unrealistic to expect governments to be the best, the most effective source of implementation of human rights instruments.

On occasion, a government will be a strong advocate of a human rights instrument, but it is often for the wrong reason. The reason is all too often political, rather than humanitarian.

It is not impossible for governments and intergovernmental organizations to do things right any more than it is impossible for nongovernment organizations to get things wrong. But, with governments, it is a good deal more difficult to get things right.

Setting out human rights mechanisms that are sometimes little more than mirages does more than disappoint. To the uninitiated, it misleads. It diverts time, energy, and hope away from remedies that may really work. By October 30, 1989, the United Nations had received over 200,000 individual human rights complaints for that year. John Humphrey has called the United Nations Human Rights Division, the predecessor of the Centre, the largest wastepaper basket in the world. Although the 1503 procedure has developed since he made that remark, the nature of the procedure is such that the remark still rings true.

The politicization of the United Nations human rights system is so institutionalized, is so taken for granted, it is hard to see how, in the immediate future, the system will be restructured. At the 1993 World Conference on Human Rights in Vienna, the United Nations created the post of High Commissioner for Human Rights. But how the existence of the Office of the High Commissioner will impact on the human rights work of the United Nations is still unclear.

It is possible to imagine an intergovernmental system functioning effectively in the promotion of respect for human rights. It is, however, unrealistic to expect it in the near future.

The intergovernmental system of remedies is now primitive. But is was once nonexistent. Politicization is rampant. But, whereas, before it had only a handful targets, Israel, Chile, and South Africa, now it has become more diffused.

At the level of remedies, the intergovernmental system has improved over time. However, it would take a quantum leap to get the system to a place where one can say it is functioning effectively or even adequately. But, at least, the trials and errors over the past decade have given us the knowledge of what works, and what does not work, what needs to be done, and what is acceptable at an international level.

Nongovernmental organizations, by providing remedies for the standards the intergovernmental system has set, have created an ideal at which the intergovernmental system can aim. Respect for the Charter principle of independence of the secretariat from governments has, itself, regrettably become only a seemingly unattainable ideal. These ideals, however, do form a program of reforms. Whatever the present state of affairs, the past improvements give hope that the future will bring more improvements still. The target must be the realization of these ideals.

With nongovernmental organizations, we are in a different situation. Impartiality is the norm rather than exception. To be sure, nongovernmental organizations can be political in nature. We see nongovernmental human rights organizations that are nothing more than fronts for particular political options.

In general, however, nongovernmental organizations do not have the same institutional tendency to politicization. Governments are inevitably multifaceted, interested in politics and economics, as well as human rights. Human rights, regrettably, often get lost in a shuffle, in a trade-off with other government interests.

Nongovernmental organizations, on the other hand, can afford to specialize. They can focus on human rights alone, to the exclusion of all other matters. They do not have to trade-off human rights values against other values.

There is a complementary, synergistic relation between intergovernmental institutions and nongovernmental organizations in the promotion of human rights. Governments, operating through intergovernmental institutions, set the standards. Nongovernmental organizations provide remedies.

Standard setting, viewed in isolation from nongovernmental implementation, may seem an idle task. Yet, if the standards are not set, then nongovernmental organizations do not have the instruments they need to go about the work of implementation to which they are suited.

Governments should not hesitate to elaborate standards, even if intergovernmental implementation mechanisms fall short, or do not work at all. For, the nongovernment organizations are ready at hand to take up where governments and intergovernmental institutions leave off.

The hesitancy over instrument proliferation is expressed in a number of different ways. One argument is that proliferation leads to endless and pointless repetition. There is a risk, as existing standards are opened up for discussion, that they will be weakened rather than strengthened.

The answer to that is that new instruments are not repetitions of the old. Some phrases may be repeated. But others are amplified. Even repeating old principles in new instruments serves a purpose. New instruments may have different, additional adherents than the old.

New instruments tend to focus on particular aspects of human rights. Instruments such as the Convention on the Rights of the Child or the Convention against Torture serve as a specific focus for concerns. They serve an educational and consciousness-raising purpose, as well as a legal one.

It is not the opening of debate in human rights issues that puts established principles at risk. It is the existence of violations and the rebarbative attitude of violators. The best response to these violators is to continue to press for the realization of human rights values at every level. One level is the creation of new instruments.

Nongovernmental organizations provide the overall perspective that intergovernmental organizations do not. Nongovernmental organizations make what remedies there are in the system work. For instance, the admissibility requirements for the United Nations 1503 procedures are so strict that only nongovernmental organizations are able to marshall the information so as to conform to the requirements. Individuals simply do not have the expertise. The International Commission of Jurists wrote[10] that up to 1980, all communications which had been referred to the Commission on Human Rights by the sub-commission (one of the steps in a multi-step procedure) had been prepared by nongovernmental organizations, since it was only nongovernmental organizations which had sufficient information to establish a prima facie case of a consistent pattern of gross violations of human rights.

In an ideal world, governments would provide both the right and the remedy. But in an ideal world, we would not have to worry about the domestic implementation of international human rights agreements. In the world as it is, nongovernmental organizations are more than just pressure groups attempting to mobilize governments to provide remedies. Through their own activities, nongovernmental organizations provide the human rights remedies that governments and intergovernmental institutions can not or will not provide.

They not only make intergovernmental remedies work. They provide remedies of their own where there is no functioning intergovernmental remedy available to mobilize at all.

Intergovernmental and nongovernmental organizations each make their own special contribution to the promotion of human rights, the one contributing standards, and the other contributing remedies. That is not to say that governments should stay away from remedies and nongovernmental organizations should stay away from standards. On the contrary, each should be involved in both remedies and standards.

The failure of intergovernmental remedies does not mean a failure of the international human rights system. In advance of the development of a functioning intergovernmental structure for remedying human rights violations, standards serve a purpose, because of what nongovernmental organizations can do with them.

That conclusion, if accepted, has consequences both for the intergovernmental system and for nongovernmental organizations. For the intergovernmental system, it means the articulation of norms, the endless drafting of new instruments should continue. For nongovernmental organizations, it means that the development of new instruments should be encouraged.

Nongovernmental organizations should, in parallel with the articulation of their own internal norms, promote the creations of additional international instruments. Some nongovernmental organizations and some people in all nongovernmental organizations have tended to be bystanders when new instruments are drafted, waiting to grab hold of them once they have been accepted, but doing little to help generate their creation. Indeed, nongovernmental organizations have shared in the general skepticism about instrument proliferation. Yet, this instrument proliferation does serve a purpose. It serves the purposes of nongovernmental organizations and of human rights. Nongovernmental organizations should be a good deal less passive in the process of instrument growth than they have been.

Human rights belong to individuals, not governments. If they are to be respected, it is individuals that must promote them. If promotion of respect for human rights is left to governments, the defence of those rights will wither.

Nongovernmental organizations are the organized force of individuals speaking out on behalf of individual rights against governments. These organizations mobilize individuals to assert their rights. They are essential to the guarantee of those rights.

CONCLUSIONS

Working on human rights requires a commitment to principle and a focus on strategy. At the level of principle, human rights must be universal and indivisible. Universality means a rejection of cultural relativism. Indivisibility means attaching as much importance to economic, social, and cultural rights as to political and civil rights.

The end of the Cold War seems a propitious opportunity for the promotion of human rights. The ideological battles over human rights have disappeared. During the Cold War, the battles over human rights had become battles of delegitimization, each side blaming the other for violations as a means of discrediting it. With world bipolarity and the superpower contest for world domination having disappeared, there is hope that the human rights discussion can now move forward.

However, although the Cold War has ended, repressive regimes remain in power. Perpetrators are as intolerant of criticism as they ever were.

The Cold War served as a convenient shield for human rights violators of both the left and right. Right-wing violators could count on the protection and understanding of the United States government. Left-wing violators could count on the protection and understanding of the government of the Soviet Union. But the disappearance of the Cold War cover does not mean the end of violations nor the end of repressive regimes. It has just meant the scramble for another cover.

One cover now is cultural relativism. Repressive regimes say that promotion of respect for human rights is an attempt to impose Western values. The attempt to use this cover is particularly prevalent in Asia, not so much because the cultural differences between Asia and the West are so great as because Asia today has a regrettably high concentration of repressive regimes in power.

The use of cultural differences to justify human rights violations was evident at a meeting in April 1993 in Bangkok, Thailand, of Asian government representatives preparatory to the World Conference on Human Rights held in Vienna in June 1993. The governments of India, Sri Lanka, and Indonesia claimed the need to waive respect for human rights to hold together multiethnic societies and put down secessionist movements. The Burmese government representative warned far-away governments against judging values they do not understand. The foreign minister of Thailand called Amnesty

International and Human Rights Watch fronts for Western governments. The Singapore representative said: "Some rights are clearly universal. Others – and perhaps the majority – are equally, clearly, essentially contested concepts." He condemned those who "inevitably give priority to the claims of the individual over those of society."

The Malaysian representative contrasted post-Renaissance liberal Western thought with Asian values and culture founded upon the conception of responsibility and obligation of the individual to society. Indonesia complained that concern about human rights at the international level has been expressed without taking into account the tremendous cultural diversity of the world.

For Westerners, the suggestion that human rights values are Western values being imposed on others makes our heads spin. The West has committed the greatest human rights violations of this century. The Holocaust, the murder of six million Jews, and the attempt to exterminate the whole Jewish population, as well as the mass murder of the handicapped, gypsies, and homosexuals by the Nazis was a Western crime. Nazism is Western. Fascism is Western. Communism is Western in origin. Colonialism is Western.

Even today we have only to see how the West treats its refugee or aboriginal populations to see serious disregard for human rights. Refugees in the West are denied access to determination systems, subjected to racist attacks, deterred from making claims, and denied protection. One can as easily talk of a Western culture of human rights violations as a Western culture of respect for human rights.

The point is that there are elements of respect for human rights and violations of human rights that can be drawn from every culture. If human rights violations are disproportionately concentrated in Asia today, that does not mean that the Asian concept of human rights is different from the Western concept of human rights.

Human rights standards are universal standards. They are not culturally based, emanating from any one culture. It is a slur on any culture to say it ignores human rights. It shows an exaggerated appreciation of any culture to say that it is the source of human rights.

Human rights rests on the dignity and inherent worth of the individual. Its foundation is the equality of all humanity. To talk of culturally based human rights is to use a contradiction in terms. Cultures are varied. Human rights are uniform.

Indeed, to talk of culturally based human rights can defeat the realization of human rights. At any given time, human rights violations are more prevalent in one part of the world than another, within one culture more than another. Apologists for those violations will often wrap themselves with the protective cloak of their culture, as Asian governments are doing today, and claim criticism of the violations is relativistic, culturally based. To accept the notion of culturally based human rights is to accept the defence of culturally based violations. We would create a world of first- and second-class cultures. Members of some cultures would be entitled to have their human rights respected. Members of other cultures would not. Accepting the notion of culturally based human rights is a step towards undermining the concept of human rights itself.

The rejection of the indivisibility of human rights takes two forms. One is giving primacy to political and civil rights over economic, social, and cultural rights. Chapter Fourteen of this book confronts and attempts to refute this position. The other is giving primacy to economic, social, and cultural rights over political and civil rights.

We sometimes hear governments of countries that are poor and repressive argue that political and civil rights are a luxury only the wealthy can afford. It is said that the right to vote means little to a person who cannot eat. Securing economic, social, and cultural rights must come first. It costs money to have a functioning democracy, an independent judiciary, a humane prison system. Unless economic, social, and cultural rights are first secured, securing political and civil rights, so this argument goes, is a mirage.

The trouble with this argument is that it assumes an antithesis between economic, social, and cultural rights on the one hand and political and civil rights on the other. Yet the reverse is true. The two sets of rights reinforce each other. A country is more likely to realize economic, social, and cultural rights if it respects political and civil rights. A country is more likely to fail to achieve respect for economic, social, and cultural rights if it violates political and civil rights.

Respect for political and civil rights means respect for freedom of expression. Repression means repression of public debate, including debate about how best to achieve respect for economic, social, and cultural rights. With repression, any position that deviates from the official, governmental position is squelched, including those positions which, if accepted, would lead to an improvement in respect for economic, social, and cultural rights. Finding the best course to pursue in achieving economic, social, and cultural rights can come only from public debate that may be critical of decisions already taken. When public debate is thwarted, so is the possibility of finding the right or the best way to achieve respect for economic, social, and cultural rights.

Repressive regimes are often corrupt regimes. To suggest that repressive regimes are engaged in repression because they cannot afford respect for political and civil rights is, for these regimes, a convenient fiction. What they cannot afford is public scrutiny of their behaviour.

Respect for political and civil rights brings accountability and responsible management of resources. Respect for political and civil rights sets in place the checks and balances that prevent corruption from occurring or stop corruption from continuing once it has occurred.

Corruption is empowered in a system that ignores political and civil rights. Corruption is quickly disempowered in a system that respects political and civil rights.

Respect for political and civil rights is an expense of the state that more than returns its investment. Respect for political and civil rights is a not an extravagance of the wealthy. It is a necessity for any state if it ever hopes to achieve respect for economic, social, and cultural rights.

Human rights activists have tended to focus on principle more than strategy. Human rights are, after all, statements of principle. It is understandable that activists would focus on principle first and foremost. Yet there are broad strategy questions that have to be asked and answered if we are to succeed in promoting respect for human rights.

Should human rights activists combat root causes or just proximate causes? If we are to combat root causes, what can be meaningfully said and done about them?

In times of transition, from a repressive regime to a democratic regime, what are the tactics the old repressive regime uses to remain in power, and how can they be combatted? Should the new democratic regime prosecute perpetrators or grant an amnesty?

When do humanitarian or human rights considerations justify intervention by one state in the affairs of another? What can we learn from the experience of state schemes of compensation for victims of human rights violations?

Should international human rights activists pay any attention to human rights violations in Canada? Should economic, social, and cultural rights be entrenched in the Canadian constitution?

Should activists use the United Nations human rights system, or bypass it? Should the United Nations proliferate human rights instruments and mechanisms or consolidate them?

How should Amnesty International evolve to combat human rights violations? What is the specific contribution that nongovernmental organizations can make to the promotion of respect for human rights?

This book has attempted to address these questions of strategy. Although there are a number of specific answers throughout the book to these questions, its value is not meant to be only in the answers. The book will have served its purpose if it gets human rights advocates thinking more about how to be effective in the promotion of human rights.

A strategy for pursuing human rights has to be distinguished from the strategic use of human rights. There are often debates about trading off human rights against other values. Debates about whether or to what extent human rights violators should be boycotted or embargoed are commonplace. Those sorts of debates bring into play economic considerations as well as human rights considerations. Participants who are deeply committed to trade will argue against boycotts in pursuit of human rights. Both Canada and the United States have gone through this sort of debate recently in deciding whether or and to what extent to trade with China.

In the 1980 United States presidential campaign, the strategic use of human rights was a campaign issue. Presidential candidate Ronald Reagan argued that President Jimmy Carter, by pursuing respect for human rights in Iran and Nicaragua, had destabilized the regimes in place, both of which were friendly to the U.S. The destabilization had led to their replacement by regimes which were unfriendly to the U.S. Again here, the debate was not about what can be done to promote human rights, but rather the trade off between politics and human rights.

These debates about the strategic use of human rights have given the notion of strategy in pursuit of human rights a bad name. The notion of strategy conjures up images of a debate about whether to pursue respect for human rights, about allowing economic or political considerations to trump human rights concerns. However, even if the decision to pursue respect for human rights is unquestioned, strategic questions remain. A person who knows the answer to the question "whether?" still needs an answer to the question "how?"

Gross violations of human rights are situations of such despair that to ask how to succeed at promoting human rights, as this book does, may seem presumptuous. Yet, it is a question activists must ask, as part of an overall commitment to human rights. Promoting respect for human rights need not be quixotic, the forlorn pursuit of a lost cause.

To succeed, activists must not lose sight of principle, which is after all what human rights are all about. But activists must also not forget to think about what can be done to make commitment to principle a reality.

The commitment to human rights must be more than emotional. It must also be intellectual. Human rights activism comes from a sense of moral outrage. There is a tendency to think of human rights work as simply registering that moral outrage. But it should also be a realistic campaign for a positive result.

At the end of the day, pursuit of respect for human rights is neither a religion nor a science, but a bit of both. We must not forget the science in pursuit of the ethic. Making human rights work effective is as much a part of promoting respect for human rights as moral urgings. Science takes patience that may seem out of step with the urgency of human rights. Science takes dispassion that may jar with the passionate response that violations of human rights arouse. Yet unless we devote the time, the energy, and the thought to making promotion of human rights effective, advocacy efforts, though never in vain, will be weakened.

NOTES

Chapter 1
Ideology as a Root Cause of
Human Rights Violations

1 John Maynard Keynes, *The General Theory of Employment Interest and Money* (London: Macmillan, 1961), 383.
2 Hannah Arendt, *Origins of Totalitarianism* (New York: Harcourt Brace and Jovanovich, 1973).
3 UN Doc. A/Res/36/55 (1982).
4 UN Doc. E/CN.4/SUB2/1987/26.
5 UN Doc. E/CN.4/1986/65 Res. 1986/20.
6 Lord Acton, *Essays on Freedom and Power* (1948), 364.
7 Jean-Jacques Rousseau, *The Social Contract* (Everyman's Library, 1966), 114-15.
8 B. Rand, ed., *Modern Classical Philosophers*, 2nd ed. (Cambridge, MA: Houghton Mifflin, 1952), 434, 449.
9 UN Doc. A/40/232 and 232/A. 1, A. 2, A. 3.
10 UN Doc. E/CN.4/1986/SR. 41, p. 10.
11 UN Doc. E/CN.4/1986/65, p. 267, para 536.
12 UN Doc. A/40/232/A. 3, para 16.
13 UN Doc. E/CN.4/1986/65, p. 261, para 529 and p.p. 269-70, para 554.
14 UN Doc. E/CN.4/1986/65, p. 202, para 231, and p. 206, para 259.
15 UN Treaty Series, vol.78, p. 277, Article 3(c).
16 UN Doc. A/6316 (1966), Article 20.
17 UN Treaty Series, vol. 660, p. 195, Article 4 (a).

Chapter 2
Fascism and the National Security State

1 Jeane Kirkpatrick, *Dictatorship and Double Standards* (American Enterprise Institute, 1982), 51.
2 Clyde Kluckholm, *Mirror for Man* (Toronto: McGraw Hill, 1949), 117.
3 Jean-Paul Sartre, *Anti-Semite and Jew* (New York: Schocken, 1974), 19.
4 United Nations Document E/CN.4/1986/SR. 41, p. 7.
5 See Maria H. Alves, *State and Opposition in Military Brazil* (Austin, Texas: University of Texas Press, 1985); Alfred Stepan, *The Military in Politics: Changing Patterns in Brazil* (Princeton, N.J.: Princeton University Press, 1971); John Child, "Geopolitical Thinking in Latin America," *Latin American Research Review*, Vol. XIV, No. 2, 1979.
6 Quoted by Robert Calvo, "The Church and the Doctrine of National Security," *Churches and Politics in Latin America*, ed. D.H. Levine (Beverley Hills: Sage Publications, 1980).
7 Ibid.
8 Ibid.
9 Ibid.
10 Ibid.
11 *Analisis*, September 18 to 24, 1989, p. 19.
12 Quoted by Calvo, "The Church and the Doctrine of National Security."
13 Elio Gaspari, "Os Papeis Secretos de Golbery" ("Golbery's Secret Papers"), *Veja*, No. 994, 23 September 1987, 19 at p. 31.

Chapter 3
Communism as a Root Cause of Human Rights Violations

1 Quoted in V. Chkhikvadze, "The Soviet Constitution: An Inspiring Example," *International Affairs* 26 (1978), 29-30.
2 *New York Times*, January 28, 1990.
3 Charles Taylor, *Hegel* (Cambridge: Cambridge University Press, 1975), 538.
4 Taylor, 427.
5 A.J. Ayer, *Language, Truth and Logic*, 2nd ed. (New York: Victor Gollancz,

1970), 36.

6 G.W.F. Hegel, *Phenomenology of Mind.*
New York: Harper Torchbooks, 1967,
67.

7 George Lichteim, Introduction,
Phenomenology of Mind, XXXII.

8 Bernard Henri-Levy, *Barbarism with a
Human Face.* New York: Harper and
Row 1979, 155, 158.

9 Taylor, 426.

10 See Richard N. Dean, "Beyond
Helsinki: The Soviet View of Human
Rights in International Law" (1980), 21
VA. J.I.L. 55.

11 V. Chkhikvadze, *The State, Democracy
and Legality in the U.S.S.R.: Lenin's Ideas
Today* (1972), 219-20.

12 Quoted in Miklos Haraszti, *The Velvet
Prison: Artists Under State Socialism*
(New York: New Republic, 1987), 3.

13 Haraszti.

14 See Otto Luchterhandt, "The Identical
and Material Significance of Human
Rights in the Constitution of the
Socialist Countries of Eastern, Central-
East, and SouthEast Europe" (unpub-
lished paper).

15 Article 59.

16 Article 39.

17 Article 50.

18 3(1) U.N. GAOR 924, U.N. Doc A/ll9
(1948).

19 Andrei Vyshinsky, *The Law of the Soviet
State* (1954), 497.

20 See Berman, "Human Rights in the
Soviet Union" (1965) 11 *How. L.J.* 333
at 340, 341.

21 Izvestiya, June 10, 1975, p. 1, column 1
as translated in Dean, 64.

22 Haraszti, 120.

23 Zbigniew Brezezinski, *The Grand
Failure: the Birth and Death of
Communism in the Twentieth Century*
(New York: Collier, 1990), 258.

24 Mikhail Gorbachev, *Perestroika: New
Thinking for Our Country and the World*
(New York: Harper and Row, 1988).

Chapter 6
The Soviet Union

1 Article 58.

2 S. Kucherov, *The Organs of the Soviet
Administration of Justice: Their History*
and Operation (Leiden: E.J. Brill, 1970),
707.

3 *Soviet Legal Reform and Human Rights
Under Perestroika* (U.S. Helsinki Watch,
1989), 100.

4 Francis Fukuyama, "The End of
History?" *The National Interest,* Summer
1989.

5 *Canadian Jewish News,* April 13, 1990.

Chapter 7
The Helsinki Process

1 Article 29.

2 Helsinki Document 1992, Chapter III,
paragraphs 12-16.

Chapter 8
Apartheid as a Root Cause of
Human Rights Violations

1 Speech to Parliament, May 19, 1948
quoted in Brian Bunting, *The Rise of the
South African Reich* (London:
International Defence and Aid Fund for
Southern Africa, 1986), 196.

2 Bunting, 254.

3 Ibid.

4 *Sunday Express,* December 1967, quoted
in Bunting, 427.

5 Bunting, 129.

6 Ibid.

7 November 18, 1948, Bunting, 194.

8 Bunting, 125.

9 Bunting, 353.

10 *Star,* Mar. 14, 1912, Bunting, 21.

11 Statement to the Senate, June 1954,
Bunting, 260.

12 Act No. 55 of 1949.

13 Act No. 21 of 1950.

14 Bunting, 129.

15 Bunting, 353.

16 Bunting, 360.

17 Bunting, 260.

18 Bunting, 268.

19 Bunting, 171.

20 Geoffrey Bindman, ed. *South Africa and
the Rule of Law* (London: Pinter, 1988),
16.

21 Bindman, 21.

22 Barbara Roger "D.I.V.I.D.E. and Rule:
South Africa's Bantustans," IDAF,
1980, 17.

23 Bindman, 25.

24 Bindman, 34.
25 Bindman, 57.
26 Quoted in Bunting, 199.
27 Bindman, 67.
28 Bindman, 68.
29 Bunting, 218.
30 Azhar Cachalia and Max Coleman, "Apartheid Under Pressure," unpublished paper, 3.
31 Bunting, 29.
32 Cachalia and Coleman, 4.

Chapter 9
Black-on-Black Violence

1   *Winnipeg Free Press*, August 20, 1990.
2   *Winnipeg Free Press*, August 20, 1990.
3   *Winnipeg Free Press*, August 16, 1990.
4   *Winnipeg Free Press*, September 5, 1990.
5   Milton, "South African Criminal Law and Procedure," Vol. III, 182.
6   C. Plasket, "Sub-Contracting the Dirty Work," 1989 *Acta Juridica*, 165 at 175.
7   Police Act of 1958, Section 27(b).
8   Public Safety Act of 1953, Section 5(b).
9   *SA Barometer*, Vol. 4, No. 18, September 28, 1990.
10 N. Haysom, "Policing the Police," 1989 *Acta Juridica*,139 at 149.
11 "The Natal Violence," IDAF Information Notes and Briefings 90/4 August, 1990.
12 *Toronto Star*, September 16, 1990.
13 IDAF Focus No. 90 September 16, 1990.
14 See note 6.

Chapter 10
Prosecution of Crimes against Humanity

1   *Globe and Mail*, March 3, 1990.
2   Article 7.
3   Paragraph 18, E.C.O.S.O.C. Resolution 1989/65.
4   U.N.G.A. Resolution 3074 (XXVIII), December 3, 1973, para. 1.
5   Article 53.
6   Section 7 (3.7).
7   Section 7 (3.71).
8   *Human Rights Watch*, No. 4, December 1989.
9   AMR 19/05/90.
10 The video tape "The Killing Fields."
11 See David Matas, *Justice Delayed: Nazi War Criminals in Canada*, with Susan Charendoff (Toronto: Summerhill Press, 1987).
12 Article I.
13 Article IV (b).
14 Article I (b).
15 A/CN.4/398 page 85 Article 12(2).
16 Article 4(1); Article 1.
17 Article 86(1).
18 Article 85(4)(c).
19 Article 85(5).
20 Quoted in Christina Murray, "South Africa and the Geneva Protocols," 1984, 33 *I.C.L.Q.* 462.
21 Third Geneva Convention, Article 87.
22 Article 45; Article 1(4).
23 Nelson Mandela, speech to the National Association of Democratic Lawyers conference in Durban, Natal, June 1990.

Chapter 11
Sovereignty and the Rights of the Individual

1   See R. Matthews and C. Pratt, "Human Rights and Foreign Policy," *Human Rights Quarterly* 159; M. Oreja, "Souverainete des etats et droits humains" (1987), 28 *Cahiers de Droit* 511.
2   Article 53.
3   See Heather A. Wilson, *International Law and the Use of Force by National Liberation Movements* (Oxford: Clarendon Press, 1988).
4   See Michael Akehurst, "Humanitarian Intervention," in Hedley Bull, *Intervention in World Politics* (Oxford: Clarendon Press, 1954).

Chapter 12
Compensation

1   See Matas and Susan Charendoff, *Justice Delayed: Nazi War Criminals in Canada* (Toronto: Summerhill Press, 1987); and *Nazi War Criminals in Canada: Five Years After* (Toronto: B'nai B'rith Canada, 1992).
2   See Nahum Goldmann, *The Jewish Paradox* (Fred Jordan Books/Grosset and Dunlap, 1978), chap. 5; Raphael Patai, *Nahum Goldmann; His Mission to Gentiles* (University of Alabama Press, 1987), chap. 7; *The*

Autobiography of Nahum Goldmann (Holt, Rinehart and Winston, 1969), chap. 22; Walter Schwartz, "Redress of Wrongs Suffered by Nationalist Socialist Victims," *Canadian Community Law Journal,* 1985, 151; Leslie Sebba, "The Reparations Agreements: A New Perspective," *ANNALS, AAPSS,* 450, July 1980, 202; Frederick Honig "The Reparations Agreement Between Israel and the F.R.G." (1954) 48 *A.J.I.L.* 564.

3 50 U.S.C. App. s. 1981 et seq. (1982).

4 Section 48, R.S. 1985, C.22 (4th Supp.).

5 H.I. Bird, *Report upon the Investigation into Claims of Persons of the Japanese Race Pursuant to Terms of Order in Council P.C. 1810, July 18, 1947, as amended April 6, 1950.*

6 *Hohri v. U.S.A.* 782 F. 2d 227; 793 F 2d 304; 847 F 2d 779; 586 F. Supp. 769; 107 S. Ct. 2246.

7 Civil Liberties Act, 1988.

8 1988 H. of C. Deb 19499 (Set. 22, 1988, statement of Rt. Hon. Brian Mulroney, Prime Minister).

9 48-49 Victoria, S.C. Chapter 71, Section 4; 63-64 Victoria, S.C. Chapter 32, Section 6; 3 Edward VII S.C. Chapter 8, Section 6; 9-10 Edward VII S.C. Chapter 27, Section 38(a).

10 See annual reports of the United Nations Voluntary Fund for Victims of Torture submitted to the General Assembly.

Chapter 13
Canadian Compliance with International Human Rights Standards

1 Article 2(7).

2 Article 40.

3 A/35/40, p. 86.

4 International Covenant on Civil and Political Rights, Article 8(1).

5 Section ll(b).

6 Article 9(3).

7 Article 1.

8 Section 318.

9 Section l9(1)(a).

10 Section 19(1)(b).

11 July 7, 1989.

12 See Matas and I. Simon, *Closing the Doors: The Failure of Refugee Protection* (Toronto: Summerhill Press, 1989).

13 See Matas and S Charendoff, *Justice Delayed: Nazi War Criminals in Canada* (Toronto: Summerhill Press, 1987).

14 Paragraph 40.1.

15 Saskatchewan Human Rights Code, Chapter S24.1, Sections 14(1)(b).

16 *Re Luscher* (1985) 57 N.R. 386 (F.C.A.).

17 *Re Samisdat Publishers Ltd.* - Report of Board of Review, October 18, 1982.

18 *R. v. Buzzanga and Durocher* (1979) 49 C.C.C. (2d) 369 (Ont. C.A.).

19 *R. v. Zundel* (1987) 58 O.R. (2d) 129 (Ont. C.A.).

20 *R. v. Keegstra* (1991) 61 C.C.C. (3d) 1 (S.C.C.).

21 *R. v. Andrews and Smith* (1991) 61 C.C.C. (3d) 490 (S.C.C.).

22 *R. v. Taylor* (1991) 75 D.L.R. (4th) 577 (S.C.C.).

Chapter 14
Economic, Social, and Cultural Rights and the Canadian Charter of Rights and Freedoms

1 Vierdag, "The Legal Nature of the Rights Granted by the International Covenant on Economic, Social and Cultural Rights," *Netherlands Yearbook of International Law,* 1978, 69-105.

2 See G.J.H. Van Hoof, "The Legal Nature of Economic, Social and Cultural Rights: A Rebuttal of Some Traditional Views," in P. Alston and K. Tomasevski, *The Right to Food* (Martinus Nijhoff, 1984), 99.

3 Article 2(1).

4 Article 2(2) and Article 3.

5 Article 8.

6 Article 13(3).

7 Article 15(3).

8 Article 10(3).

9 Article 10(1).

10 See P. Alston and B. Simmma, "First Session of the U.N. Committee on Economic, Social and Cultural Rights," 1987 (81) *A.J.I.L.* 747; Theodore Van Boven, "Distinguishing Criteria of Human Rights," in Vasak, *The International Dimension of Human Rights,* 52.

11 347 U.S. 483 (1954).

12 14th amendment.

13 See *McKinney v. University of Guelph* (1991) 76 D.L.R. (4th) 545 at 651-52.

14 Article 2(3).

15 Article 4.

16 *Ruparel v. M.E.I.* (1991) 10 Imm.L.R. (2d) 81.

17 *Canadian Council of Churches v. The Queen* (1991), 11 Imm. L.R. (2d) 190.

18 P. Alston and B. Simma, "First Session of the U.N. Committee on Economic, Social and Cultural Rights," 1987 (81) *A.J.I.L.* 747.

19 "Implementation of International Covenant on Economic, Social and Cultural Rights. ECOSOC Working Group," *I.C.J. Review*, December 1981, 26 at 28.

20 See P. Alston and B. Simma, "Second Session of the U.N. Committee on Economic, Social and Cultural Rights" (1988), 82 *A.J.I.L.* 603.

21 See Bossuyt, "La distinction juridique entre des droits civils et politiques at les droits economiques, sociaux et culturels," 8 *H.R.J.* (1975) 783-813.

22 See Van Hoof, 103.

23 Article 7(1).

24 Article 8(1).

25 See D. Matas "The Charter and Racism," 1991 *Constitutional Forum*, Vol. 2, No. 3.

26 (1991) 51 C.C.C. (3d) 1.

27 *RWDSU v. Dolphin Delivery Ltd.* (1987) 33 D.L.R. (4th) 174.

28 At p. 198.

29 See D. Matas "The Working of the Charter" (1986-87), *Man.L.J.*, 111 at 116 following.

30 G.H.L. Fridman, *The Law of Torts in Canada*, Vol. 2, 258.

31 *Re Lavigne and OPSEU* (No. 2) (1988), 41 D.L.R. (4th), 86 at 126 per White J. (Ont.H.Ct.)

32 *C.C.C. v. R.* (1990) 10 Imm. L.R. (2d) 81 (F.C.A.).

33 See Stephen Wexler, "Practicing Law for Poor People" (1969-70) 79 *Yale Law Journal*, 1049 at 1059.

Chapter 15
Human Rights at the United Nations

1 Daniel Patrick Moynihan and Suzanne Weaver, *A Dangerous Place* (New York: Berkely, 1980), 70.

2 *Winnipeg Free Press*, February 17, 1983.

3 See Jeane Kirkpatrick in *Commentary*, November 1981, 44.

4 George Orwell, *Nineteen Eighty-Four* (Harmondsworth: Penguin, 1983), 172.

5 "Amnesty International's concerns at the 49th session of the United Nations Commission on Human Rights," AI Index: IOR 41/10/92, p. 34; "Human Rights; International Instruments; Chart of Ratifications as at 30 June, 1994," UN Document ST/HR/4/Rev.10, for June 30, 1994.

6 Article 41.

7 Jean-Bernard Marie, "International Instruments Relating to Human Rights" (1990) 11 *H.R.L.J.* 175, for 1990.

8 1981 *H.R.L.J.*, p. 22.

9 T.M. Franck, "Of Gnats and Camels: Is There a Double Standard at the U.N.?" (1984) 78 *A.J.I.L.*, 811 at 816.

10 Sheldon Gordon, *Globe and Mail*, October 1, 1982.

11 Article 100(1).

12 *New Yorker Magazine*, October 2, 1989.

13 17/37

14 *I.C.J. Review*, June 1982, 35.

15 82/23.

16 19/33.

17 22/33.

18 *I.C.J. Review*, June 1981, 48.

19 *A.J.I.L.*, Vol. 76, 406.

20 17/37.

Chapter 16
Nongovernmental Organizations at the United Nations

1 "In Depth Evaluation of the Human Rights Programme," E/AC51/1989/2, 21 April 1989.

2 Ian Martin, "Forty years of the Universal Declaration of Human Rights," 1988 *UN Bulletin of Human Rights*.

3 See D. Weissbrodt, "The Three Theme Special Rapporteurs" (1986) 80 *A.J.I.L.*, 697-99.

Chapter 18
Human Rights through Nongovernmental Organizations

1 Lillich, "The UN and Human Rights Complaints," (1970) 64 *A.J.I.L.* 610, reprinted in Lillich and Newman, *International Human Rights*, 335.

2 ECOSOC 1503 (XLVIII), May 27, 1970.

3 Leslie Evans, "Resolution 1503," 1980 *Contemporary Affairs Briefing*, Vol. 1, No. 2, at 6 and 7.

4 A/34/PV 14, p. 6.

5 A/C. 3/35/SR 82, at 2-12.

6 Humphrey, "The International Bill of Rights," (1976) 17 *Wm. and Mary L. Rev.*, 532-533, reprinted in Lillich and Newman, 373.

7 1989 *Human Rights Law Journal.*

8 1976 *I.C.J. Review* 25, reprinted in Lillich and Newman, 366.

9 Ian Martin, "Forty Years of the Universal Declaration of Human Rights," *UN Bulletin of Human Rights*, 1988, 53.

10 *I.C.J. Review*, June 1980.

SUGGESTED READINGS

MAGAZINES/BULLETINS

Amnesty International Bulletin, published by the Amnesty International Canadian Section, Ottawa, Ontario.

Human Rights Tribune, published by Human Rights Internet, Ottawa, Ontario.

Human Rights Quarterly, sponsored by the Urban Morgan Institute for Human Rights, College of Law, University of Cincinnati.

PIOOM Newsletter and Progress Report, published by the University of Leiden Center for the Study of Social Conflicts, The Netherlands.

The Review, published by the International Commission of Jurists, Geneva, Switzerland.

BOOKS

al-Khalil, Samir. *Republic of Fear: The Inside Story of Saddam's Iraq.* New York: Pantheon, 1990.

Arendt, Hannah. *The Origins of Totalitarianism.* New York: Harcourt Brace and Jovanovich, 1973.

Bunting, Brian. *The Rise of the South African Reich.* London: International Defence and Aid Fund for Southern Africa, 1986.

Haraszti, Miklos. *The Velvet Prison: Artists Under State Socialism.* New York: New Republic, 1987.

Moynahan, Daniel Patrick, with Suzanne Weaver. *A Dangerous Place: Defending America at the UN.* New York: Berkley, 1980.

Power, Jonathan. *Amnesty International: The Human Rights Story.* Willowdale, Ont.: Pergamon Press, 1981.